Take This Hammer

Sonics Series
Atau Tanaka, editor

Sonic Agency: Sound and Emergent Forms of Resistance, Brandon LaBelle

Meta Gesture Music: Embodied Interaction, New Instruments and Sonic Experience, Various Artists (CD and online)

Inflamed Invisible: Collected Writings on Art and Sound, 1976-2018, David Toop

Teklife / Ghettoville / Eski: The Sonic Ecologies of Black Music in the Early 21st Century, Dhanveer Singh Brar

Dissonant Waves: Ernst Schoen and Experimental Sound in the 20th Century, Sam Dolbear and Esther Leslie

New for 2024

The England No One Cares About: Lyrics from Suburbia, George Musgrave

Ruins and Resilience: The Longevity of Experimental Film, Karel Doing

Building a Voice: Sound, Surface, Skin, Zeynep Bulut

Goldsmiths Press's Sonics series considers sounds as media and as material – as physical phenomenon, social vector, or source of musical affect. The series maps the diversity of thinking across the sonic landscape, from sound studies to musical performance, from sound art to the sociology of music, from historical soundscapes to digital musicology. Its publications encompass books and extensions to traditional formats that might include audio, digital, online and interactive formats. We seek to publish leading figures as well as emerging voices, by commission or by proposal.

Take This Hammer

Work, Song, Crisis

Paul Rekret

Goldsmiths Press

Copyright © 2024 Goldsmiths Press
First published in 2024 by Goldsmiths Press
Goldsmiths, University of London, New Cross
London SE14 6NW

Printed and bound by Short Run Press Limited, UK
Distribution by the MIT Press
Cambridge, Massachusetts, USA and London, England

Text copyright © 2024 Paul Rekret

The right of Paul Rekret to be identified as the author of this work has been asserted by him in accordance with sections 77 and 78 in the Copyright, Designs and Patents Act 1988.

Every effort has been made to trace copyright holders and to obtain their permission for the use of copyright material. The publisher apologises for any errors or omissions and would be grateful if notified of any corrections that should be incorporated in future reprints or editions of this book.

All Rights Reserved. No part of this publication may be reproduced, distributed or transmitted in any form or by any means whatsoever without prior written permission of the publisher, except in the case of brief quotations in critical articles and review and certain non-commercial uses permitted by copyright law.

A CIP record for this book is available from the British Library

ISBN 978-1-913380-16-8 (hbk)
ISBN 978-1-913380-15-1 (ebk)

www.gold.ac.uk/goldsmiths-press

Contents

Introduction: Work, Song, Crisis		1
1	A Collective and Obligatory Rhythm	19
2	Melodies Wander Around as Ghosts: Playlist as Cultural Form	50
3	This is More Than Rap: Labour, Leisure, and Trap	75
4	So Much Wilder Than Me: The New 'World Music'	103
5	Machine Memory Triumphs in Multiplicity: Nature and Technique	128
	Bibliography	159
	Discography	183
	Acknowledgements	187
	Index	189

Introduction: Work, Song, Crisis

> *This old hammer killed John Henry,*
> *This old hammer killed John Henry,*
> *This old hammer killed John Henry,*
> *But it won't kill me, Oh boys, won't kill me.*
> *Take this hammer, take it to the sergeant* (3x)
> *Tell him I'm gone, Oh boys, tell him I'm gone.*
> *If he ask you, what got the matter,* (3x)
> *Had too long, Oh Lord, had too long.*
> *If he ask you, was I laughin',* (3x)
> *Tell him I was cryin', Oh Lord, tell him I was cryin'.*
> *If he ask you, was I runnin',* (3x)
> *Tell him I was flyin', Oh Lord, tell him I was flyin'.*
> *If he ask you any more questions,* (3x)
> *You don't know, Oh boy, you don't know.*[1]

Song resists transparency and is not reducible to proposition. But the recurrent refrains of 'Take This Hammer', all resigned moans and run-down sighs, deliver a clear-cut missive. It's a message delivered to a chain-gang sargeant or boss by a worker who has fled, a labourer who has downed tools, and it's remarkable for the emotional intensity it condenses to the austere musical economy of a series of rhythmic, plaintive chants.

To begin to understand its affective potency we might look to the song's knotty history and, here, we find ourselves on the circuitous path of a folk culture as it encounters a burgeoning commercial music industry.[2] It was popularised by blues artist Huddie 'Leadbelly' Ledbetter, who first recorded it for RCA Victor in 1940 and on a number of occasions thereafter, though Mississippi John Hurt had already put down a version under the title of 'Spike Driver Blues' for Okeh in 1928.[3] Leadbelly chooses to linger over the moments of elation in the song, his jaunty pace and rising voice propels it downhill while John Hurt's interpretation is steadier and more lyrical, his pensive finger-picking an altogether more matter of fact proclamation. Earlier still, Al Hopkins and His Buckle Busters recorded a variation called 'Nine Pound Hammer' in 1927, whilst another well-known recording was made by country and western singer Merle Travis for Capitol in 1947.[4] Travis's springy rendition adapts the song for Appalachian coal mining while Hopkins's hillbilly construal – all squeaking fiddle and squawking banjo – had already made it palatable for white audiences.

Together, these reflect the racial segregation internal to an emergent popular culture, though the song's origins go back earlier still, to the Black railroad songs of the 1860s and 1870s. There, it accompanied the driving of spikes and the drilling of rock for tunnels by Black workers, often inmates on convict lease compelled to lead America's westward advance. It's a fitting if ugly irony, then, that we know these songs because they were often collected by folklorists working in prisons; inmates served as a rich pool of oral culture otherwise lost in the outside world. In fact, 'Take This Hammer' is merely one iteration of a whole assembly of hammer songs; a complex of overlapping fragments and themes: 'Nine Pound Hammer', 'Ten Pound Hammer', 'Roll on Buddy', 'Asheville Junction', 'Swannanoa Tunnel'; all sung to animate and pace a hammer striking steel, an axe splitting wood, a hoe shaping soil.[5]

The hammer songs often begin with an admonition: 'This old hammer killed John Henry / But it won't kill me, oh boys, it won't kill me', is one rehearsal of a recurring theme.[6] This is a reference to a mythical contest between a steel-driver tasked with boring into mountain rock to make way for train tunnels against the steam-powered drill designed to replace him. John Henry courageously defeats the machine, the story goes, but the exertion is the death of him. It's a tale typically held to encapsulate the dignity of labour; one that, in fusing Christian suffering with industrialization, teaches accommodation with industry and helps consolidate a new class identity.[7] This sort of accounting has generally been the mode by which the dominant society has consumed work song more broadly, too: as a down-home expression of pride in craft and the resilience of labour as it confronts mass industry.

Only 'Take This Hammer' calls for another appraisal, for it offers no such affirmation and instead, it merely assures that the work will come to an end. There's no redeeming the death of John Henry here, only the provision of an imminent escape from his fate. This seems appropriate given recently uncovered historical evidence; John Henry, if such a person really existed, would be the victim of the mass incarceration of mostly landless former slaves in Virginia, arrested under vagrancy laws introduced during reconstruction to capture them, and on convict lease to the Chesapeake & Ohio railroad.[8] Not only does this remind us that to counterpose 'free' and 'unfree' labour is to sanitise a whole spectrum of forms of coercion, it also insinuates that 'Take This Hammer' is no fantasy of renewed dignity but an expression of fugitivity most of all; 'tell him I'm gone, oh boys, tell him I'm gone...'[9] Sure, the song has its social functions; it keeps time, coordinates activity, even diverts the mind from the task at hand.[10] But, above all, it anticipates escape; it awaits the cancellation of the wage relation. In other words, the song is a refusal of work.

Work

Refusal of work: this compact phrase is associated most of all with the founders of the Italian Marxist journal *Quaderni Rossi* founded in 1961; Antonio Negri, Mario Tronti and Raniero Panzieri, its most significant figures.[11] Among the group's most important conceptual innovations is Tronti's so-called 'Copernican revolution'; this is the idea that labour struggle is an originary force which capital can merely capture and subsume. It's a fecund idea for it implies a substantial reframing of history: if capital is always reactive and reactionary then, it follows, technological change appears mainly as an expression of the latter's need to assert control over workers and work. Just as technology is not independent of capitalist accumulation, on this view, neither is labour and so it cannot be the basis of an emancipatory identity: 'workers enter into capital', Tronti writes, 'are reduced to a part of capital, as a working class'.[12] To exchange work for a wage, in other words, amounts to the inevitable reproduction of the conditions of one's own domination; it is to reinforce the structure of a world that premises survival upon the sale of one's time. In this light, demands for the dignity of work can only amount, to quote Tronti again, to 'the organization of alienation'.[13] To adopt such a view is, in short, to take the abolition of wage labour rather than its glorification as one's starting point and, in turn, to anticipate revolution in this institution's manifold workaday contestations: disputes over hours or pay, small acts of sabotage, or even declarations of illness. Refusal, on these expansive terms is, to quote Tronti again, the working class's 'recovery of its autonomy'.[14]

This is a framework, therefore, whose salience extends even further when we also register the embrace by feminist scholarship under Tronti's influence, of struggle over unpaid domestic work gathered under the ideology of the family, too. Here, the activity of refusal is widened still further to encompass drops in the birth rate, declines in marriage, and increases in divorce; being a good wife is hard work to be avoided, all things considered.[15] It's a view that will be instructive for us since it anticipates the abolition of labour in broad terms, even in acts where this is not the stated intention.

But there are some limits to such an accounting of refusal. Above all, it inclines us towards too neat a dichotomy: where struggle takes on an autonomy from capital, this also tends to reassert labour as an independent identity.[16] Not only does this reiterate the very reductions and abstractions of human activity upon which the capitalist subsumption of labour is premised, but we can see how limited such affirmations might appear where we consider, for instance, the extent to which the argument centres on the factional and racialised identity of the industrial labourer or housewife.[17] Refusal all too easily slips into 'self-valorisation', instead of a negation of capital, which is to say, it doesn't quite refuse enough.[18]

In his own variation on this theme, philosopher George Caffentzis situates the transformation of the potential to labour into actual labour – the 'theft of life-time', as he puts it – as the site of refusal.[19] Labour creates value, he argues, *because it can refuse*. It produces value partly, in other words, because it might not. Such an accounting of labour as potentiality has the merit of introducing an 'element of negativity' directly into the wage relation and this is to imply that labour is only constituted through its antagonism to its exploitation.[20] This is very little negativity, for sure, it's almost nothing, but this is the point: it denotes inherent recalcitrance as the feature of a social form rather than the property of an identity; it only affirms, in other words, that which does not yet exist. But we can also uncover an element of negativity, this book will suggest, where we situate song in its relation to work.

Song

The song's transformation of the experience of work, we have already implied in our discussion of John Henry, is premised upon the confrontation it generates with another order of time.[21] To bring labour into contact with an antagonistic world of music is to denote it as alien. But we should nevertheless resist the temptation to posit for it an absolute exteriority; music's pleasures emerge, after all, partly from its very segregation, for it makes available in a sensuous manner that which is not yet in existence. This is to posit refusal as inherent to the song itself, not as a property of its essence but rather as the historical product of its expulsion from labour; the song can refuse *because it is not work*. In this light, negativity appears against an absent horizon of utopian affirmation; the song acts as the residue of that which still might be.

Of course, the performance and production of music involves work in itself too, and this is often organised along capitalist lines as well. Indeed, the recording artist can be a figure of autonomy only if we overlook their subordination to the entertainment conglomerates that tend to govern their activity. Popular music, in other words, tends to invite a highly romanticised picture reflective, as Matt Stahl argues, of a wider neoliberal world where vulnerability and insecurity are inscribed as flexibility and ingenuity.[22] But the point here, just to reiterate it once more, will not be to posit a pure exteriority for music nor an idealised vision of its terms. Instead, it will be to locate refusal as the historical being of the song's unstable and contested relation to the compulsion to labour to survive.[23]

In what follows we'll find the resources to help us to locate this refusal in song through some feminist accounts of work in capitalism and in a Black Studies tradition, above all. The latter has staked its aesthetic principles upon what Sylvia Wynter once described as its 'economic marginality'; exclusion from the full rewards of wage labour and the complete protections of citizenship are reconfigured as a potent liminality.[24] Where social life is lived as unassimilable, marginality can become the site for resistive cultural forms; an 'existential defense', a 'freedom drive' that animates more 'general antagonism'.[25]

This becomes the basis for a view of song as a mediator of oppositions and struggles over the historical form of temporality, and the latter term will bear further scrutiny. It is history, at any rate, that's at stake in the legend of John Henry: after all, the wider setting for his heroic victory is the displacement of water by coal as it becomes the energy source that puts the world in motion. Coal could be moved, whilst water mills could not, and thus a newly mobile and concentrated mechanical power intensified control over production as the nineteenth century went on.[26] So it turns out that John Henry's is a hollow triumph, on the whole; his death spared him from inevitable subjection of his craft to the industrial discipline of the steam-powered machine in any case.

These events, equally, belong to the fading history of work song, too. In this light, John Henry stands at the cusp of a society ever more organised along the lines of a rationalised sphere of labour and its obverse: a 'free', expressive sphere of leisure. Mechanical processes would come to set the tempo of labour, the organising rhythms of the song were no longer required, while the clamor of machine and industry made them inaudible anyhow.[27] Parceled instead as the products of the culture industry, music would be segregated to the evening and the weekend, and this is all usually eulogised as a loss of musical diversity and metrical variety equal to the dehumanising character of industrial work.[28] Such a state of affairs, the claim goes, merely suspends one routine for another: 'the culture industry presents that same everyday world as paradise', and no doubt, 'escape, like elopement, is destined from the first to lead back to its starting point'.[29] But this is only a beginning, not a conclusion. There are still other possibilities. Alienated symptom, certainly, yet also a site of social intervention.[30] Left to hold what's inadmissible in work, the song experiments with chance, sequence, order, juxtaposition, accent, stress, pulse, and phrasing.[31] Sometimes this vocational calling is made explicit: 'workin' for the weekend'; 'take this job and shove it'; 'work this motherfucker'. But there's a more expansive set of historical mediations we should consider as well.

Rock n roll's founding proposition was to revel around the clock rather than submit to the factory timetable.[32] Its later iterations would wallow in intoxication and hallucination in opposition to the oppressive banality of post-war suburban life. Soul would blur sex and politics, eroticising the latter whilst politicising the former. Funk would transmit its audience into other dimensions altogether. Disco and its progeny, house and techno, would take the body itself as an expressive instrument, its movements dictated by the pursuit of pleasure rather than the demands of the machine. Prog and kosmische would ironise post-war attachments to technological development, industrial music would do so too, only with far more cynicism. And so on.

To be sure, the early building blocks of popular music – antiphony, blue notes, and polyrhythms – transmit older, oppositional cultures, but we should, equally, be wary of accounts that relate these to a pre-modern identity. It's true that popular music as we currently know it has its sources mainly in Black Atlantic cultures, but to posit the latter as anchored in a pre-industrial exteriority to the society, as is often done, not only reifies it as a folk-other, it also overlooks how the institutions against whose background they emerged – plantation slavery and other modes of forced labour – have been integral to the history of modernity.[33] In any case, the point – to reiterate it yet again – is that once segregated from work, music can 'measure out doses of pleasure instead of units of labour'.[34] It stands in for refusal by virtue of its isolation, but it only does so against the backdrop of an abstract clock time on whose terms it persists: the weekend will always come to an end, alarms will be set to ring in the morning. The segregation of labour and leisure is an ideological institution for the reproduction of capital, indeed, but this is also a potentially unstable relation.

We have any number of ways to describe this opposition. Stuart Hall, for instance, depicts popular culture as a terrain of 'double movement of containment and resistance' where the terms are not fixed and the cultural object is the site of struggle.[35] For Fredric Jameson, the works of mass culture 'cannot do their work without deflecting [...] the deepest and most fundamental hopes and fantasies of the collectivity' and, in this repression of the unthinkable, they amount to 'strategies of containment'.[36] For both, then, the objects of popular culture can contain a utopian impulse opposed to the present social order. The song can be the bearer of what is unallowed, insurgent, and perverse, and this makes it a rather unstable vessel.

Crisis

Of course, instability is a feature of capitalism too. The pursuit of profit proceeds by keeping wages low and selling the goods produced. But managing these can only ever result in putting off the inevitable collapse of the social order upon which they're premised. So, when around the mid-1960s rising global manufacturing competition compelled capital to economise on labour, mainly through technological innovation, this merely increased the costs of production and so threatened revenues only more so.[37] Since the late 1970s, capital has managed this episodic crisis of profitability mainly through the fragmentation of industrial production on a global scale and the transformation of the wage contract to hold down costs.

This is variously known as the 'post-Fordist' or 'neoliberal' response to capitalist crisis and it is especially significant for us since it represents a decline in the status of the white male industrial worker and his displacement, as Melinda Cooper and Angela Mitropoulos have it, by the emblematic figure of an independent contractor roving from firm to firm.[38] Employment becomes increasingly contingent, on-call, fixed-term, or zero hours and here, the conceptual and practical boundaries between the time of work and non-work are in a state of decay. The social wage transforms into socialised credit; education, health, old age all become tradeable securities, and the home is converted into an asset. The 'household frontier' which once partitioned periods of work from intervals of rest and play is, as Cooper and Mitropoulos argue, in a state of seemingly protracted decline and here we observe the monotony of 'time extracted from any material or identifiable demarcations', to borrow from Jonathan Crary; 'a time without sequences or recurrence.'[39]

The point is that the organising boundaries through which song was segregated from, and through which it confronted labour, are changing once again. There have been, in this regard, any number of formulations for relating economic crisis to cultural form. Of course, the present is often registered as the loss of the final vestiges of aesthetic autonomy and modernism, a moment of the full integration of the cultural object with the pursuit of profit. But if the collapse of the critical distance afforded to culture is among the features of our postmodern epoch, even so, this is a schema for the exhausted sovereignty of high art which popular music, a thoroughly commercial enterprise from the start, had less purchase on to begin with. Still, we can recognise these processes only in more diminished terms in, for instance, the erosion of rock music as a liminal space of enjoyment which, in musicologist Lawrence Grossberg's terms, once inscribed a difference upon the surface of social reality.[40] Rock n roll's particular combination of the blues with rugged individualism lost its affective charge decades ago and has been gradually displaced by other styles. RnB, hip-hop, house, and techno, to name a few, substituted the guitar hero's performance of authenticity with other dynamics of pleasure and forms of community; less anchored in the singer as a vessel of emotion and more premised upon the body as a zone of desire.[41] This transformation serves to confirm a central contention developed throughout this book: 'the cultural form of our crisis is a crisis of cultural form.'[42]

I've just been describing cultural transformations that occurred throughout the 1980s and 1990s and these have already been well documented. But the focus of this book lies in tracking some of the threads of this ongoing crisis as expressed in music since the 'Great Recession' of 2008. Sure, this interval is an expedient framing device, serving to mark out our present more or less plainly. Yet it's also a periodisation bearing theoretical pretensions. The global downturn in economic activity that, in fact, began in the U.S. in 2007 before spreading to much of the world, went hand in hand with a significant escalation of longer trends for growing precarity and low wage jobs, along with public programmes of austerity leaving the remaining threads of a social safety net in tatters. To acknowledge this is to be confronted with the abject obverse of the ethos of entrepreneurialism that has dominated the past four decades. Which is to say, the coercive character of the wage becomes palpable when it comes to be an altogether erratic and contingent means of survival.[43] These are the terms in which the segregation of music from work confronts us today: by way of the rising contingency and abject character of the latter.

That Same Everyday World as Paradise

In this light, the aims of this book are theoretical: to suggest how moving between music and labour supports an account centred upon the mediations between economy and song. Yet while it seeks to propose one way of uncovering wider social conditions within the cultural object, it has no pretension to an exhaustive history or theory of music and operates primarily by way of particular cases. It presents an episodic account which necessarily leaves a good deal out of frame since its objectives are reserved to gesturing at themes all too often overlooked, and which will help to locate the society within the song and place the latter within a wider history.

Any number of metaphorical associations between music and its social context have been put forward by critics and theorists, and all too often these are lacking in an examination of their mediations or offer too truncated an accounting of the conditions of their object. To start from labour, then, is to seek the society immanent to music, for it offers a means of relating the work of its composition, technical reproduction, and circulation to the wider world in which it appears. This involves, moreover, a rejection of the dominant modes of theorising popular music today. For starters, we should eschew those accounts which mourn the present-day decline of authenticity of popular music or the sovereignty of the artist. We'll unpack the limitations of assertions of the terminal condition of authentic popular culture throughout, but suffice it to say these are altogether too attached to a martial grasp of aesthetic development and so insufficiently attuned to the overlapping yet disparate temporalities of the present. We ought also beware theories centred upon the materiality or ontology of sound, for in their pursuit of speculations regarding the nature of sound in itself, scarce heed is paid to the historical conditions by which their object is constituted in the first place. To claim unmediated access to pre-subjective phenomena, to a sound anterior to its human perception, in other words, tends to amount to withdrawal from reflection upon the epistemic conditions of such an account altogether. Studies of popular culture today, in short, all too quickly take up the 'fallacious concreteness' of the given as their frame of reference, to echo an argument of Herbert Marcuse.[44] This, in turn, is to abjure a critical position upon the music and its social conditions, more broadly.

But a bit more precision is called for here. What we call 'music' encompasses a whole series of distinct but related processes: performing, arranging, composing, or listening, to name a few; not to mention the panoply of other practices upon which these depend: instrument-making, engineering, manufacturing, or education, to name some more. These activities might be oriented exclusively for exchange in the market or they might be performed beyond the logics of economic value. But to determine whether a particular music's production or performance has been organised along capitalist lines, or subsumed by the latter, demands an analytic of how it's produced and circulated in each instance, and this would demand a methodical sociological inquiry beyond the bounds of this book.[45]

Nor will we seek a systematic examination of working conditions within the music industry, even if the activities of artists and labels will come up on occasion.[46] For instance, we'll consider how changes to music's commodification via streaming platforms have conditioned changes to its form; we'll encounter sub-genres of hip-hop which, excluded from major markets and distribution networks, generated some rather outrageous experimentation and independent means of funding; and we'll also take in new trends in the repackaging of global popular musics for Western audiences and the changing dimensions of the exotic this involves.

But our central concern will be to try to locate contemporary music's inner temporality as a shifting site of struggle; to recover a desire to abolish the wage relation as well as to dissect aesthetic strategies for the containment of that struggle. To foreground antagonism at the level of both economy and culture in this way is to affirm the latter is itself not external to the economic. But it is also to avoid the monotony of accounts of ideology which endlessly locate in cultural objects the same message, as if a single content inheres to all cultural forms. To pursue our line of inquiry is rather to attend, where possible, to a residue that remains unallowable, a refusal through which music does its work, and which the dominant society will always seek to cancel or constrain.

Outline of Chapters

We have already gestured at a changing temporal experience inaugurated by the collapse of the segregation of labour from leisure and the monotonous experience of time this engenders. This is an idea we'll unpack in the course of a discussion of online music streaming and the integration of listening within the proprietary enclosure of the platform. We'll encounter it again through the ennui expressed in the out-of-time iconography of obsolete consumer products – from computers to shopping malls – that both sonically and visually ornament some contemporary electronic musics and again, albeit in a very different register, in contemporary hip-hop's expressions of the interminable work of the drug dealer or sex worker. We'll understand the art of environmental field recording and to modular deployments of genre and rhythm in electronic musics as in pursuit of the recovery of a sonic contingency, an extra-human time in light of capital's intensifying control of the soundscape. Along similar lines, we'll examine the changing logics of the internment to a distant time and place of exoticised and racialised contemporary 'world music'.

But these transformations of the experience of time invite reflection upon the spatial logics of crisis as well. Here, we should register a process of uneven social and economic development conditioned by the fragmentation of production on a global scale characteristic of the epochal markers of 'post-Fordism' or postmodernism. The society might 'advance' technologically, but might also move 'backwards' where cheap, antiquated techniques of production are leveraged across dispersed markets via global communications and transport infrastructure. In this way the twentieth century 'standard' of secure, permanent, unionised employment becomes an exception where anachronistic forms of wage contract – more contingent and erratic – become the means of survival. As we proceed, we'll connect these geographical changes to representations of the soundscape in a digital society by both the field recordist and the electronic music artist as well as changing strategies in the presentation of global popular musics for Western markets. We'll consider the diffusion of the U.S. sub-prime housing market as it intersects Southern rap music as well as the changing impulses of the contemporary tourist as these overlap with the shifting desires of the consumer of 'world music'.

Earlier, we established that social crisis intersects a crisis in cultural form. Accordingly, changing experiences of time and space will serve to index stylistic changes in popular music since the 'Great Recession' of 2008 began, and these are often expressed in terms of negotiations with the logics of artistic authenticity. For if the latter is premised upon a *metaphysics of presence*, conceived by way of an artist's proximity to a musical community or tradition through unvarnished emotional expression, then we can observe modulations to these sensibilities given social, economic, and technological change in, for instance, the increasingly desperate and grievous claims to realness by the rapper; the preference for archival recordings of global musics using out-dated or unconventional genre stylings, instruments, and studio techniques; or in the ways the natural environment is framed by contemporary field recordists. We will further relate these shifting coordinates to contemporary figures of labour: the indefinite extension of the working day in view of the streaming platform; the racialised experience of wagelessness in contemporary hip-hop; the affective imperative for creativity and flexibility discernible in the 'new world music'; or the idealised techno-utopianism that permeates so much contemporary electronic music, to name a few examples.

The theoretical principles of these arguments will occupy chapter 1 as it seeks to understand how capitalist time-discipline has affected the experience of popular music, both for the male body once anchored to the Fordist factory but also for the growing ranks of those marginal to the rewards of wage labour. Here, the chapter reads histories of popular music against the backdrop of the modern emergence and extension of an experience of abstract time. In the course of doing so, it looks especially to critical theoretical receptions of popular culture, Theodor Adorno's above all, as well as accounts of Black music, from Amiri Baraka and Sylvia Wynter to Paul Gilroy and Fred Moten, among others, to help locate the expression of refusal in the song. These thinkers will also help us to examine the historicity of the crisis which we're after as well. For one thing, they point us towards a notion of aesthetic development that rejects the vanward logics of a forward, linear movement through time. For another thing, to relate the exclusion of the sonic from political aesthetics to the exclusion of Blackness from political space, to use an argument deployed by Moten, is to situate us elsewhere than the organising boundaries of a Fordist industrial regime which prioritised the productive white male body and regimented the experience of space and time, too. Such a perspective becomes all the more salient where secure employment is increasingly eradicated in any event.

Readers less inclined to theoretical elucidation might move ahead to the remaining chapters, each of them studies in specific intersections of work, song, and crisis. Chapter 2 looks to transformations wrought upon song-form as it is made to circulate through online streaming platforms; modes of automated indexing, organising, and curation of music. The chapter considers how the distinct technical and economic logics of streaming mean that music comes to be deployed in support of the sale of a service (to sell subscriptions or generate data for advertisers) rather than the sale of tangible commodity (a single album). Where the circulation of music becomes premised, in other words, upon the frictionless ubiquity of its consumption, this is a process which recoils back onto musical form as well. Chronology and context are evacuated, narrative is displaced, and texture and atmosphere come to the fore where new principles of searching and selection of information come to predominate music's production, distribution, and consumption.

Chapter 3 sets off from the absorption of trap, a sub-genre of Southern hip-hop, into pop. This is a process that begins in earnest with a series of hits in the early 2010s produced by the virtuoso producers Mike-Will-Made-It and Lex Luger, proceeds past the use of trap's sonic palette by pop megastars including Lana Del Ray, Lorde, Arianna Grande, and others in the mid-2010s, to culminate in *Billboard* number one albums for Atlanta rapper 2 Chainz and the group Migos in 2017. The ascent of trap parallels the rise of streaming as a dominant music format and this is partly given the decentralisation of artist discovery to platform users, but herein lie other prospects too. As a music whose setting is initially the drug trade, trap can be considered a type of work song, continuous with earlier iterations of 'crack rap', but going back to much older Black American oral cultures as well. This a theme the chapter takes in by way of two of trap's founding documents, Gucci Mane's *Trap House* and Young Jeezy's *Thug Motivation 101*, as these condense the aestheticisation of work and criminality, the spatial logics of the U.S. economy, and a truncated desire of which Gucci and Jeezy are the bearers.

Chapters 4 and 5 deal with less well-known cultural material that rests at the peripheries of the popular. This makes their subjects no less significant for they each present expressions of crisis that reverberate more widely too. Chapter 4 takes recent reissues of music originally made by the remarkable Cameroonian-French artist and writer Francis Bebey in the 1970s and 1980s as an opportunity to interrogate the vicissitudes of musical exoticism. Alongside reissue labels such as Sublime Frequencies, Sahel Sounds, and Awesome Tapes From Africa, the rediscovery of Bebey represents the work of preserving otherness for 'world music' in an era where the expansion of the global economy has intensified and sameness comes to prevail over difference in important ways. The coordinates of the exotic have shifted, in other words, and increasingly involve packaging artists from the global South evacuated of context and with little meaningful information besides. Audio tends to be lo-fi, graphics are construed as slapdash and Do-It-Yourself, the recording techniques used are all but obsolete. All of this acts to signal the absence of commercial intents by projecting an analog milieu upon a digital surface and in doing so, conjures a demand for creativity in labour and for rituals of consumption in excess of the everyday. What I prefer to call the 'new world music' works a lot like contemporary tourism, simply put, and this calls for further analysis of its motivating desire.

Chapter 5 comes in two parts. First, it looks at contemporary field recording in light of ecological crisis, and to the work of artists Chris Watson, Peter Cusack, and Franciso López, in particular. Next, it takes in electronic musics associated with ideas of accelerationism, Holly Herndon, James Ferraro, and Daniel Lopatin, above all. Seemingly disparate, all these artists share a concern over the relation of technique to the agency of musical composition. For the field recordist, these issues revolve around the use of microphone and editing technologies to represent the soundscape in an epoch where human activity has irrevocably transformed the planetary ecosystem to the point of its annihilation. Frequently conceived in terms of a capacity to invoke 'entanglement' with nature, soundscape recording nonetheless implies a rather unstable position for the techniques through which this effect is generated. Conversely, what we'll consider as accelerationist music betrays anxiety over creativity given the saturation of a mediatised consumerism. How can the artist respond to a world, it seems to ask, where every eventuality has already been priced in and all possibilities are destined to be subsumed by the market? Herndon will take up a didactic pose, in this regard, adopting automation as an opportunity for public experimentation. Conversely, Ferraro and Lopatin assume a cynicism for which all that remains is to comb over the detritus of a terminal culture. What unites these artists is the way in which they seek to preserve and defend the sovereignty of the artist; either through a fantasy of technical control or a snickering cynicism committed to mourning the collapse of its own exceptionality.

All in all, these chapters encompass recent episodes in a much more expansive story of the relation of work and song, the rest will have to be told elsewhere. But where to begin? With the ends of a modernist impulse in popular music.

Notes

1 These lyrics are taken from Joseph 'Chinaman' Johnson and Group, 'This Old Hammer Killed John Henry' in: Bruce Jackson (Ed.) *Wake Up Dead Man: Afro-American Prison Worksongs From Texas Prisons*. Cambridge: Harvard University Press, 1972, pp.238–39.

2 The history of 'Take This Hammer' is addressed in Norm Cohen, *Long Steel Rail: The Railroad in American Folksong*. Urbana: University of Illinois Press, 2000; Scott Reynolds

Nelson, *Steel Drivin' Man: John Henry, the Untold Story of an American Legend*. Oxford: Oxford University Press, 2006; Ted Gioia, *Work Songs*. Durham & London: Duke University Press, 2006; Archie Green, *Only a Miner: Studies in Recorded Coal-Mining Songs*. Urbana: University of Illinois Press, 1972.

3 Leadbelly's version is included on *Take This Hammer*. RCA Victor Group, 2003. John Hurt's 'Spike Driver Blues' is found on *The Greatest Songsters 1927-1929*. Document Records, 1990.

4 Al Hopkins and His Buckle Busters, *The Nine Pound Hammer/C. & O. No.558*. Brunswick, 1927; Merle Travis, 'Nine Pound Hammer', *Folk Songs of the Hills*. Capitol Records, 1947.

5 A comprehensive overview of the hammer songs is provided by Cohen in *Long Steel Rail*, pp.571-77.

6 Johnson and Group, 'This Old Hammer Killed John Henry'.

7 See Gioia, *Work Songs*, pp.150-69; George Lipsitz, *Time Passages: Collective Memory and American Popular Culture*. Minneapolis: University of Minnesota Press, 1997, p.115; Shana L. Redmond, *Anthem: Social Movements and the Sound of Solidarity in the African Diaspora*. New York: New York University Press, 2014, pp.115-16; Ralph Ellison, *Shadow and Act*. New York: Vintage, 1995, p.270; Joel Dinerstein, *Swinging the Machine*. Boston: University of Massachusetts Press, 2003, p.130.

8 See Nelson, *Steel Drivin' Man*.

9 On free labour see Jairus Banaji, 'The Fictions of Free Labour: Contract, Coercion, and So-Called Unfree-Labour', in *Theory as History: Essays on Modes of Production and Exploitation*. Leiden: Brill, 2010, pp.131-54.

10 On this point see Archie Green (Ed.), *Songs about Work: Essays in Occupational Culture for Richard A. Reuss*. Bloomington: Indiana University Press, 1993; and Marek Korczynski, Michael Pickering & Emma Robertson, *Rhythms of Labour: Music at Work in Britain*. Cambridge: Cambridge University Press, 2013.

11 A historical overview is provided in Steve Wright, 'Quaderni Rossi and the Workers' Enquiry' in: *Storming Heaven: Class Composition and Struggle in Italian Autonomist Marxism*. London: Pluto Press, 2002, pp.29-57.

12 Mario Tronti, *Workers and Capital* (David Broder, Trans.). London: Verso, 2019, p.138.

13 Tronti, *Workers and Capital*, p.274.

14 Tronti, *Workers and Capital*, p.221.

15 Leopoldina Fortunati, *The Arcane of Reproduction: Housework, Prostitution, Labor and Capital*. New York: Autonomedia, 1996, p.146 and passim.

16 Nicholas Thoburn, *Deleuze, Marx and Politics*. London: Routledge, 2003, p.15.

17 See Angela Y. Davis, 'The Approaching Obsolescence of Housework: A Working Class Perspective' in: *Women, Race & Class*, New York: Vintage Books, 1983, chapter 13 and Kathi Weeks, 'Marxism, Productivisim, and the Refusal of Work' in: *The Problem with Work*. Durham & London: Duke University Press, 2011, pp.79-112.

18 On this point see Marina Vishmidt, *Speculation as a Mode of Production: Forms of Value Subjectivity in Art and Capital*. Leiden: Brill, 2018, p.83.

19 George Caffentzis, *No Blood For Oil: Essays on Energy, Class Struggle, and War 1998-2016*. New York: Autonomedia, 2017, p.161.

20 Caffentzis, *No Blood For Oil*, p.161.

21 Korczynski, Pickering, & Robertson, *Rhythms of Labour*, pp.62-86.

22 Matt Stahl, *Unfree Masters: Popular Music and the Politics of Work*. Durham & London: Duke University Press, 2012.

23 On this point see Sarah Brouillette 'On Art and Real Subsumption', *Mediations* 29, no.2, 2016, p.171.
24 Sylvia Wynter, *We Must Learn to Sit Down Together and Talk About a Little Culture: Decolonising Essays, 1967-1984*. Leeds: Peepal Tree Press, 2022, p.465.
25 Fred Moten, *In the Break: The Aesthetics of the Black Radical Tradition*. Minneapolis: University of Minnesota Press, 2003, p.12; Louis Moreno, 'The Sound of Detroit: Notes, Tones and Rhythms from Underground' in: Matthew Gandy & B.J. Wilson (Eds.) *The Acoustic City*. Berlin: Jovis, 2014, pp.98-109, p.102; Dhanveer Singh Brar, *Teklife/Ghettoville/Eski: The Sonic Ecologies of Black Music in the Early 21st Century*. London: Goldsmiths Press, 2020.
26 On this point see Andreas Malm, *Fossil Capital: The Rise of Steam Power and the Roots of Global Warming*. London: Verso, 2016.
27 See Korczynski, Pickering, & Robertson, *Rhythms of Labour*, pp.62-86.
28 See for instance, Gioia, *Work Songs*, p.37; Marek Korczynski, *Songs of the Factory: Pop Music, Culture, and Resistance*. Ithaca: Cornell University Press, 2015.
29 Max Horkheimer & Theodor Adorno, *Dialectic of Enlightenment* (G. Noeri, Trans.). Stanford: Stanford University Press, 2002, p.113.
30 I paraphrase here from John Roberts, *Philosophizing the Everyday: Revolutionary Praxis and the Fate of Cultural Theory*. London: Pluto Press, 2006, p.62.
31 This point is drawn from Simon Frith, *Performing Rites: On the Value of Popular Music*. Cambridge: Harvard University Press, 1996, p.156.
32 See Lipsitz, *Time Passages*, pp.109-16.
33 On the first point, see Alexander Weheliye, *Phonographies: Grooves in Sonic Afro-Modernity*. Durham & London: Duke University Press, 2005. On the second, see Louis Moreno, 'The Urban Regeneration of the Plantation Age' in: K. Vermeir & R. Heiremans (Eds.) *A Modest Proposal*. London: Jubilee, 2018, pp.2-10; and Stefano Harney, 'Logistics Genealogies: A Dialogue with Stefano Harney', *Social Text* 36, 2018, pp.95-110.
34 George Lipsitz, *Time Passages*, p.113.
35 Stuart Hall, 'Notes on Deconstructing the Popular' in: David Morley (Ed.) *Essential Essays, Volume 1*. Durham & London: Duke University Press, 2018, pp.347-61. Quoted on p.348.
36 Fredric Jameson, *The Political Unconscious: Narrative as a Socially Symbolic Act*. London: Routledge, 2013, p.X and passim.
37 Robert Brenner, *The Economics of Global Turbulence: The Advanced Capitalist Economies from Long Boom to Long Downturn, 1945-2005*. London: Verso, 2006.
38 Melinda Cooper & Angela Mitropoulos, 'The Household Frontier', *Ephemera: Theory and Politics in Organization* 9, no.4, 2009, pp.363-68.
39 Jonathan Crary, *24/7: Late Capitalism and the End of Sleep*. London: Verso, 2013, pp.19, 29.
40 This point is drawn from Lawrence Grossberg, 'Another Boring Day in Paradise: Rock and Roll and the Empowerment of Everyday Life', *Popular Music* 4, 1984, pp.225-58.
41 Susan McClary, 'Living to Tell: Madonna's Resurrection of the Fleshly' in: *Feminine Endings: Music, Gender and Sexuality*. Minneapolis & London: University of Minnesota Press, 1991, pp.148-68.
42 Here, I paraphrase Peter Osborne, *Crisis as Form*. London: Verso, 2022. Of course, Osborne's reference is to the ways the fine arts increasingly lose medium-specificity in the current epoch. But his account of form can productively encompass changes to

popular song-form too, especially as it is affected by streaming platforms, for instance, as we'll see in chapter 2.

43 Melanie Gilligan & Marina Vishmidt. ' "The Property-Less Sensorium": Following the Subject in Crisis Times', *South Atlantic Quarterly* 114, no.3, 2015, pp.611–30.

44 Herbert Marcuse, *One-Dimensional Man: Studies in the Ideology of Advanced Industrial Society*. Boston: Beacon Press, 1991, p.110.

45 On the relationship of music-making to capitalism see Timothy D. Taylor, *Music and Capitalism: A History of the Present*. Chicago: Chicago University Press, 2015. We can extend the excellent analysis of the relation of performance to value to music provided by Michael Shane Boyle, 'Performance and Value: The Work of Theatre in Karl Marx's Critique of Political Economy', *Theatre Survey* 58(1), 2017, pp.3–23; and a concise account of the relation of commercial art to value in Sarah Brouillette 'On Art and Real Subsumption'.

46 On working in the contemporary music industry see Stahl, *Unfree Masters*; David Arditi, *Getting Signed: Record Contracts, Musicians, and Power in Society*. Cham: Palgrave MacMillan, 2020.

1

A Collective and Obligatory Rhythm

Mind over Matter

Among the founding gestures of the study of popular music is the rejection of the distribution of cultural objects into high and low forms, an opposition one can define along any number of lines: edifying or commercial intentions; struggle against convention or immanence to social function; contemplative consumption or mere sensual abandon. Whilst this is by no means an exhaustive list, it should suffice nevertheless to make apparent what's at stake: the value of popular music as an aesthetic object hinges upon the dismissal of a modern hierarchy in which it sits as a commercially vulgar conformism looking up at truly expressive and authentic art.

But what's repressed returns. It does so in the form of a consonant opposition of high and low art that, like a nesting doll, is internal to popular music itself: punk versus pop, alt rock versus hair metal, backpack versus commercial rap, and so on. The terms will vary yet the struggle over what constitutes authentic expression will persist, even if this is all rather unstable as far as aesthetic economies go. Ever threatened by audio or video that's too glossy, poses too studied, genre-borrowings too calculated, authenticity is infamously difficult to maintain, so much so that, especially over the past decade or so, critics have increasingly come to reject these martial logics altogether – as if a war were fought with convention. This is the argument of what's come to be known as 'poptimism', a nebulous idea best defined by its displacement of rock's heroic pretences by a more democratic sensibility oriented towards the sensual pleasures of pop.[1] Sure, interlocutors will scorn what they see as the poptimist's wholesale abandonment of critical distinction, but this won't concern us for the time being, and besides, neither view is much interested in the wider heteronomy that makes the experience of music possible, so the terms of critical distinction are altogether truncated, in any case.[2]

High or low, contemplative or sensual, authentic or democratic: the oppositions recur again and again. They emerge at the level of aesthetic form, persist at the level of popular genre, and they structure the theoretical reception of pop, too. In the latter case, its commonplace to characterise the present by the foreclosure of the possibility of authentic or autonomous popular culture. Needless to say, the operative logic dividing dominant and marginal cultures has always been nebulous, and it's equally indisputable that where aesthetic value is premised upon authenticity and autonomy, the fear of absorption by the popular remains an existential one. But only with the emergence of intensifying neoliberal processes of commodification, the argument goes, does popular music's autonomy from capital collapse altogether.[3] At issue is a dystopian view of a more or less total identification of culture with capital and, in turn, this induces the theorist towards rather byzantine theoretical strategies for the preservation of authenticity for pop.

Take as an example an essay on music and neoliberalism by philosopher Robin James. On her analysis, where an individualising neoliberal power has come to redirect all creativity for the purpose of profit, only a final aesthetic strategy for the preservation of music's independence remains; this is the valorisation of 'uncool'.[4] The logic here is rather perverse: an escape from co-optation by capital is effected by rejecting ideals of autonomy and authenticity altogether. These are swapped for a cynical embrace of the regular, the average, or, to echo James's Foucaultian inflection, the 'norm'. As an approach, we might call this 'blander is better' and, in this regard, James's references index what's implied: English group The Human League's abandonment of post-punk for synth-pop on their 1981 album *Dare*, or the tawdry soft rock romanticism of Spandau Ballet. To relinquish any transgressive impulse as these groups do, the logic runs, is to withdraw aesthetic raw material from capitalist commodification. For if transgression has become a new normal, it follows that only what's featureless and banal, what generates no creative material for capital to consume, might offer a site from which to resist its encroachments.

For James then, we might say, cynical embrace of convention – of cultural repetition, broadly conceived – represents the final recourse against colonisation by capital. For others, surrender to convention is instead only symptomatic of a terminal culture. This is a notion encapsulated in Mark Fisher's widely circulated diagnosis of the present as haunted by 'lost futures'.[5] For Fisher our predicament is to have been suffocated of utopian desire by the forces of reaction, personified initially by Margaret Thatcher and Ronald Reagan, and condemned to mining utopian impulses from epochs where these were still operative. Fisher detects this 'nostalgia mode' operating widely, but especially in the collapse of mass cultural experimentation, of which dance music is his privileged example. The extraordinary stylistic innovations that characterise electronic music from Chicago house and Detroit techno in the mid-to-late-1980s up to jungle in the UK in the early 1990s are, for Fisher, exhausted by the 2000s; capital's conquest of the present grows so all-encompassing that the future can no longer be secured. More recent electronic music sub-genres, Footwork or Dubstep for instance, are no longer capable of soliciting 'signifiers of the future' and so are, at best, limited to drawing attention to their own exhaustion. The rapidly repeating beats, samples, and melodies of Footwork express 'temporal desiccation', while the low resonances and slowed pace of dubstep evoke post-party melancholia.[6] These, in turn, stand for a pathological social imaginary, caught in a state of timelessness, 'haunted' by pasts for which political and cultural revolution was still conceivable. Here, repetition in popular music becomes symptomatic of historical closure, it is stuck in time and confined to an expression of its own failure of imagination. So, Fisher mourns what he calls a 'popular modernism'; an inventive and counter-hegemonic culture running roughly from the 1960s to the 1990s, now discernible only in its withdrawal, whilst James seeks to save authenticity through an embrace of its absence. Between tragedy and cynicism then, we confront the impasse of the theorisation of the popular today.

Another set of theorists, however, seek to evade altogether the aporias thrown up by attachments to modernism, and they do so by a dispersal of music into the wider ontological arena of sonic matter, material, or simply, to 'sound'. This sort of move is exemplified in Anahid Kassabian's influential study of *Ubiquitous Listening*.[7] As technologies extend it ever further into everyday life, Kassabian argues, music grows ever more 'sourceless'. That is to say, music dissolves ever further into omnipresent atmosphere, away from intentional listening and, in doing so, will reveal that our sovereignty over our senses was always illusory. In turn, this will destabilise once clear divisions between the listening subject and the musical object. This is one means of arriving at 'sound', an ontological realm irreducible to any aesthetic register or even cochlear reception.[8] Here, questions of authenticity or aesthetic autonomy, conceived as altogether anthropocentric, are put aside in favour of speculation regarding sonic matter independent of human aurality.

This is also an idea that rehearses a wider taste for ontological speculation still fashionable across the humanities and social sciences.[9] At its core, it's premised upon displacing what it takes as the dominant view of the mind as rational, abstract, and disembodied, by foregrounding what Brian Massumi has called the 'bodily and autonomic nature of affect'.[10] Doing so lays the ground for attending to the non-conscious, pre-subjective forces and 'intensities of feeling', and, to return to the question of sound, to understand how decisively they shape sonic experience.[11] A politics follows from this ethical avowal too, since to look to the affective, embodied experience of sound is, the claim goes, an emancipatory gesture: where sound is understood as independent of its capture by consciousness, it persists as excess over the society in which it appears.

Such a view, however, merely reproduces the very dualism of mind and body it seeks to destabilise. To presuppose a rationalist conception of meaning which one then contrasts to bodily affect amounts to adoption of the very categories one seeks to oppose.[12] Whilst the theorist of 'sound' gives priority to embodiment over mind, such a claim hinges upon a sleight of hand that generates its contrary. That is, to claim unmediated access to pre-subjective phenomena tends to amount to withdrawal from reflection upon the epistemic conditions of such an account. How can thought be granted immediacy except by denying it is thinking altogether, after all? To posit direct access to the being of sound in-itself then, is merely to preserve the very innocence and independence of mind the theorist had claimed to overcome. Arguing along similar lines, Marie Thompson and Annie Goh have each stressed the racialising and gendering logics of such a move: to fail to interrogate the listening subject is to idealise the (Cis white, masculine) one that already dominates.[13] Instead of an excess over the subject then, the central gesture of the ontology of sound amounts to the pose of a pre-reflective listener beyond the bounds of critique.

Given the privilege it extends to a savage, sensuous, pre-critical experience, we might refer to this ontology of sound as 'theory poptimism', only its opposition to the popular modernist's nostalgia for aesthetic authenticity and autonomy is only apparent. Both are ultimately attached to a rather occidental modernity. In this regard, the popular modernist's commitment to a conception of time as sequential, progressive, and secular is explicit in the account of historical closure that they present, and this is so whether we consider Fisher's view of a present haunted by its own limited desire or James's detachment from aesthetic innovation altogether. In either case, an intensification of capitalist processes engenders the demise of linear development. It might be apparent that popular modernism thus amounts to a thesis about the end of history and, in this regard, is inextricable from a teleological project.[14] But an attachment to progress through time extends equally to the theorist of sound. For here the generic embodied subject of sonic matter merely persists outside of history altogether, hence leaving the latter unaffected, not unlike those feminised and racialised subjects long situated at the margins of modern history and whose very exclusion and exoticisation was the basis of their attraction for occidental patriarchy.

Mind over body, body over mind, to mourn the end of history or shirk it altogether, these binaries continue to dominate as the aesthetic strategies adopted by a telenomic Western culture; a society still premised, as Richard Middleton has argued, upon the individuality of each successive work as it seeks to guarantee the means of modelling wider cultural development: of the person, the society, and technology.[15] For where repetition implies consensus and convention, to echo Middleton once more, rhythm is rarely a goal and repetition seldom an object of pleasure or of beauty in itself. Or, to borrow James Snead's formulation: '[w]hat recent Western or European culture repeats continuously is precisely the belief that there is *no* repetition in culture but only a difference defined as progress and growth.'[16] To oppose a concrete, progressive experience of history against the lifeless repetitions of capitalist time is to overlook that the former is reified too.

Multiplied Time

So, a further unpacking of the relation to time is called for to help us to grasp music's vocation as a site of refusal. We should start with our most expansive claim developed through a well-known essay of E.P. Thompson's: as capitalism expanded across the world from the seventeenth to the nineteenth centuries, an experience of time oriented to daily, seasonal, and generational rhythms of agricultural production gradually gave way to the discipline of quantitative and abstract time detached from natural rhythms and specific tasks.[17] For a society where survival is premised upon selling one's time for a wage and so compelled by the demand to dominate, rationalise, and standardise labour, 'time becomes necessity', to quote Moishe Postone.[18] That is, where labour is made commensurable through its measure by quanta of time, abstraction comes to dominate the concrete so that 'a collective and obligatory rhythm', to borrow from Foucault this time, appears as independent of human action, it becomes second nature.[19] 'Temporality as a measure of activity', to return to Postone once more, is therefore 'different from temporality as measured by events.'[20] So clock time becomes hegemonic where an abstract social power pervades over processes of subsistence, and comes to penetrate all elements of life.[21]

But if our analysis were to stop here it would be restricted to a still too truncated perspective that valorises the concrete over the abstract. Further assessment of the changing experience of work and, more broadly, of historicity itself is called for if we're to arrive at the historic conditions of rhythm today.[22] As capitals compete, in part, by driving down the time it takes to produce particular goods, the worker's experience of time intensifies; workshops are transformed into assembly lines, craft is converted to industry. Industrialisation, from this perspective, amounts to capital's direct seizure of the labour-process.[23] Or, to recite Harry Braverman's influential formulation: the execution of work is increasingly detached from its conception.[24] Where the head is separated from the hand in this way, to paraphrase Alfred Sohn-Rethel, labour confronts its own past in the objectified form of the technologies to which it must submit.[25] Together, these accounts describe the practice by which capital abstracts from skill and craft to produce an organised system of machines, of 'dead labour'. This is the process that Marx calls the 'real subsumption' of labour, and it reaches something of an apex in the era of Fordism, the period running roughly from the 1910s to the 1970s; and whose contours are defined in part by labour's abdication of control over production and submission to intensifying discipline in exchange for higher wages and welfare. In any case, the point here is that what might look like technological progress from one perspective is experienced as intensifying alienation from another. This implies a 'multiplied time', in Daniel Bensaïd's words, one where 'plural rhythms and cycles' suggest 'time is no longer the motor of history, its secret energetic principle, but the conflictual social relation of production and exchange.'[26]

Our argument, thus far, revolves around the alienating effects of an increasingly intensive rationalisation of industrial society and our central point hangs on a dialectic between abstract time-discipline and its concrete experience. In other words, it hinges on the relation between the *measure* by which capital exploits labour and the *rate* by which it does so. That is, to generate profit capitalists must decrease the costs of inputs relative to the market price for outputs. If they fail to do so, they risk becoming unprofitable. Extending the working day has its limits in this regard, but increases in productivity, in principle, do not. Abstract clock-time might not change, in other words, but it is experienced increasingly intensely where productivity rises and so the pace of work tends to rise too. Not only does this orient us towards a politics of time, it situates the domain of historical consciousness itself as a product of social relations.[27] That is, the experience of progressing through time, of the present as ahead of the past and bearing towards the future, is irreducible from innovations and developments that signal historical change and these, in turn, are ultimately induced by competitive pressures from other producers to rationalise production, which is to say, to produce more and more quickly, conditioned by the market. Capitalist time, in sum, is defined by both eternal repetition and by perpetual forward movement.

This dialectic between the experience of abstract and concrete time, this 'abstraction of social time', to echo Bensaïd again, provides us with a fuller sense of popular music's conditions and, in particular, helps us to theorise a model of musical repetition not premised upon historical closure and the melancholia that attends it.[28] This is a line of argument put down by musicologist Mark Abel, who develops it through a lengthy negotiation with Theodor Adorno's philosophy of mimesis.[29] In its classic formulation, of course, aesthetic presentation is said to be driven by an expressive mimetic impulse, a primitive sympathy by which the subject discovers itself in objects, assimilating them to experience in the process.[30] On Adorno's view, however, art is not merely mimetic, since the imposition of form also calls upon reason. So, the production of the artwork involves, in fact, a dialectic between mimesis and rationality; one which swings increasingly towards the latter as art and society develop in tandem across history. Just as an alienated modern reason gains a growing mastery over the world, so too is subjective expression increasingly subsumed by reason. For instance, modern compositional procedures come to displace an ideal of spontaneous inspiration, yet in doing so, make greater control over musical material possible. The development of scale, tuning, and notation, for instance, condition increasingly intricate forms of collective performance.[31] Such rationalisations are progressive, Adorno argues, provided they're restrained by expressive dynamic elements; art is either autonomous in its deployment of rationality as an expression of human suffering or it is 'standardised'; embraces the predictability and rhythmic inflexibility of the market.[32] The latter, he avers, lacks any individuality; what sounds unique is merely an 'opulent surface' cloaking the mundane.[33]

All in all, such an accounting of mimesis offers a powerful frame to understand aesthetic autonomy. But it's premised, as Abel notes, upon the restriction of its logics away from the relation of rhythm to meter.[34] That is, Adorno's philosophy of music still favours the thematic development of motif as an expression of autonomy. For Adorno, musics anchored in repetition, therefore, are ultimately symptoms of social degeneration; rhythmic accent or stress is merely insincere embellishment. But to view syncopation as a merely superficial distraction from music's enslavement to the repetition of static pulse, as Adorno does in his accounts of popular music, is to fail to appreciate metrical discipline as the condition for twentieth and twenty-first century popular music. For meter underpins rhythmic sophistication and the dialectic between them is the condition for the audibility of its beauty. Repetition is not, as Abel suggests, the sign of reification but the basis of collective creativity.

We return, then, to the wider question of the conception of time and of history. Modernist aesthetic commitment to musical development, thematic unfolding, authenticity, or reflexive play with their limits are opposed – whether by Adorno, Fisher, or James – to the lifeless repetition wrought by capitalist time, the colonisation of expression by logics of exchange. But this seems, to echo Abel again, a rather myopic perspective. Sure, the exhaustion of development this perspective detects in popular music is inseparable from the instrumentalisation of time to the demands of a capitalist society. But so too, we have seen, is the very conception of development and progression itself. In this context, neither rhythm nor repetition are signs of capitulation to the forces that oppress us but a suspension of the imperative to sell something to survive; they are even, perhaps, figures of a different experience of time.

Week's End

The claim being pursued here, just to be clear, rests with a view of musical time as opposed to capitalist time-discipline, as a site where popular music might uncover its emancipatory dimension. Historically, art's hostility to capital derived, in part, from its aristocratic origins beyond the world of labour, but popular music, as it's understood here, makes no such claim to exteriority. At stake are commodities, for sure. And yet, popular music can also press against the limits out of which it emerges; it is, in other words, the sensuous intimation of an abolition of the wage, even if its denotative meanings might not be. Such a view proposes, therefore, a fecund terrain upon which we might situate music as a social relation, where its rhythms would be experienced, in other words, as an expression of the struggle against work *insofar as it is not work*.

But this formulation demands some provisos. As we have seen, Fordism is characterised by the subsumption of labour by capital, but it involves the subsumption of music too. This is illustrated in the extension of a rationalised discipline and division of labour to musical performance itself: from the nineteenth century market for written scores to a growing specialisation of roles and wider industrialisation of performance.[35] It's apparent at the level of music's tools as well. The growing presence of pianos in bourgeois households in that era, for instance, reflects a new capacity for their mass production. Indeed, the piano itself might stand as a metonym for an increasingly rationalised social order: organised into 88 regular pitches, its use is premised upon the player's execution of a preconceived score and, in this sense, it's exemplary of a process of alienation from the means of cultural production.[36] This is a process all the more apparent in the invention of the phonograph, for this is a machine which takes control of the skill of music-making more or less completely.[37] All in all, in question is a historical process, both material and ideological, that displaces making music with its purchase.

We might take an even wider view, to grasp industrialisation itself as effecting a new control over music. Whilst in pre-capitalist societies song is widely integrated into everyday life, the presence of the factory evicts it to become a stand-alone practice.[38] This has its *de jure* and *de facto* causes. On one hand, the noise of machines made singing all but impossible whilst the pace of machines made its rhythmic qualities redundant. On the other hand, prohibitions on singing were common amongst restrictions imposed by bosses in pursuit of efficiency and control.[39] Thus restricted by the opposition between labour and leisure, production and consumption, popular song comes to stand here for 'free time'. Of course, this is a freedom restricted by its 'appendage to work'.[40] 'There is no escape', as Henri Lefebvre once noted; leisure is conditional upon one's return to the factory the following morning.[41] This is a 'vicious circle' indeed, to cite Lefebvre again.[42] To experience time as music is inseparable from routine then, yet it can also exceed these terms; it involves an encounter with change, sequence, and order, and this means it stands for the possibility of an intervention into the course of time; of a temporality that might be measured by pleasure instead of the abstractions conditioned by capital accumulation.[43]

Still, up to now, we have restricted our analysis to music as it takes its place in relation to the Fordist social contract. This offers a picture still confined to the control imposed by capital in the factory, whilst the aesthetic forces which might be opposed to it are confined to labouring subjectivity on its time off. We should register, for instance, that in the very period assembly lines were rattling into motion to spew out Model Ts or phonographs, the imperial economies of which they were a part meant their objects circulated from port to port, continent to continent, at the peripheries of capital's purview.

It's through this colonial economy that what Michael Denning deems a new 'vernacularisation' of music emerged in the 1920s.[44] Away from the surveillance of metropolitan elites, beyond imperial music halls, samba, tango, son, tarab, and jazz circulated amongst the sailors, longshoremen, and sharecroppers of New Orleans, Rio de Janeiro, Cairo, or Jakarta. This is a soundscape, Denning avers, that upset the conventional hierarchies of form and function, sacred and secular, urban and rural, polite and popular. It also lay the foundations of popular music for a century: multi-timbral textures and multi-vocal timbres, repeating rhythms and improvisations, vocal modulations, blue notes, unresolved dissonances. These are expressions of a 'peripheral modernity' beyond the machine of colonial wealth extraction, but for us, they also denote a wider point: the Fordist labour contract was never a universal experience in any event. The latter gestures at an asynchronous experience outside the hegemonic experience of time: to hold the Fordist factory alone as the context for understanding the conditions of emergence for popular music would, therefore, be altogether parochial.

Docility and Domesticity

We should expand our frame of reference if we want a fuller grasp of the temporal coordinates at stake. In this respect, we have already seen that Fordism reinforced the boundaries between labour and leisure. These then also served a 'compensatory distinction', in Angela Mitropoulos's words, between those granted the authority to contract and those who worked under conditions of slavery or 'unproductive' labour.[45] Conceived as a distributive mechanism for the white male wage as well as a psychological safeguard, the standard family wage actively policed the boundaries between men's paid and women's unpaid domestic work, between white people and people of colour. Indeed, if ever there's been an institution to which the hackneyed label of 'identity politics' truly does apply, Melinda Cooper suggests, it's the Fordist politics of class which established the white male husband and father as the point of access to full economic and social protection, and whose racialisation acts as compensation for his own exploitation.[46] The point, in part, is that the coordinates of race and gender are inseparable from the experience of labour, and thus, also of music, for capital accumulation produces 'differentiated and devalued forms of humanity.'[47] Populations are sorted and valued with shifting structural needs.

It bears remarking too that the exclusion of white women and children from waged work preceded Fordism by several decades. Industrial society consolidates the family as an economic unit mediating production and the reproduction of labour early on. There are nevertheless disagreements here over causal variables: the threat women represented to men's wages, to bourgeois morals, or the need to develop a more disciplined workforce that pushed women and children out of the factory and into the home.[48] In any event, what matters for us here is that in the very period in which the factory separated music from work, it expelled women and children too. Restrictions on their employment thus institutionalised the home as a private sphere whilst it divided family responsibilities between productive and reproductive work. The Fordist family wage – indexed by the costs of maintaining a wife and children – intensifies an already existent division of labour.

We have thus encountered industrial capital as a force that relegates women to the quasi-sacred space of kinship and the precarious employment or unpaid housework this implies.[49] It would nonetheless be an error to conclude that those subjected to capitalist time-discipline were uniquely men; it's more precise to say that we're dealing with a mode of domination organised partly along heteronormative lines of gender. To grasp this, however, requires moving beyond an orthodoxy whose tendency is to disregard work except that which is exploited to generate a surplus. Certainly, women's unpaid domestic labour – childbearing and rearing, cooking, and cleaning – is not *directly* governed by a wage. But it's nonetheless compelled to succumb to the latter and, therefore, to yield to the discipline of a hegemonic abstract time. To hold otherwise is to contribute to a mystification that presents domestic work as natural simply because it's not paid.

Here, we arrive at a debate over the precise form taken by capital's power over unpaid domestic labour. For Leopoldina Fortunati, women enter a relation with capital to the extent that they produce the commodity it requires most of all: that is to say, labour-power. Her point is that 'women's work' is both structurally necessary for the capitalist accumulation of value to proceed and yet, is made invisible since it's only ever paid indirectly in the form of a husband's wage.[50] But to Fortunati's critics this is to collapse labour that is productive – which is to say performed at competitive levels indexed by some socially average time – with labour which is not.[51] In any event, this is a rather technical argument that hinges primarily over how domestic activities participate in capitalism, and so also how they might be organised against it. Its significance for us, however, rests mainly with the shared assumptions from which it proceeds: that the working week still dictates the rhythms of domestic labour, even if it does so indirectly. Productive and unproductive, public and private, masculine and feminine; the point is that a series of oppositions come to define the gendered character of a Fordist experience organised around the time of work and the time of non-work.

These categories are certainly operative in the music industry too. For instance, a hierarchy that mostly restricted composition and performance to men and relegated women to the role of backing singer or as the member of a group was a general rule up to the 1960s at least.[52] The divisions of labour among genders were equally prevalent in consumption. This is apparent if we note that just as the listening housewife supplanted the image of the Victorian expressing herself at the piano, early recordings were frequently sold to women in department stores as they performed the family's shopping.[53] It's equally manifest in the fact that music echoed through those commercial spaces to generate a domestic atmosphere.[54] Women's perceived docility and the lower wages they could be paid also meant they were often vastly over-represented in the factories that produced LPs as well.[55] More widely, women in the music industry were typically restricted to secretarial and public relations roles; it was the very conviviality and compassion of the good wife and mother for which they were sought.

As we've implied, the restriction of white women to the home entailed the constitution of the latter as a quasi-sacred space; an ideological project whose outline is discernible in the extent to which loyalty, domesticity, and sexual inhibition prevail as musical themes in post-war pop. 'Let's Play House', Elvis Presley suggested, 'Will You Love Me Tomorrow', asked the Shirelles, and 'Stand By Your Man', Tammy Wynette pleaded. But this is still more evident in the way the whole history of post-war popular music is defined by its own hierarchy of high and low cultures. That rock's claim to authenticity was mainly a masculinist gesture is apparent in the way its terms are defined mainly through an opposition to the feminine superficiality of pop.[56] Where rock tended to be a performance of male sexuality, pop instead gravitated around an ideology of romance. Suffice it to say popular music was for a long time anchored in a naturalised white heterosexuality. Of course, these hierarchies have been contested and unravelled endlessly, and the history of popular music is inconceivable without them, but there are also other oppositions to which we need to attend.[57]

General Antagonism

In a number of essays Theodor Adorno asserts that the sort of playful quotation of folk music for which the central European composers Béla Bartók and Leoš Janáček are known was no longer legitimate in his own era. Pre-industrial cultures might've once offered a raw aesthetic material for the self's confrontation with society, but no longer. Today, it can only represent a false reconciliation; 'there is no longer any "folk",' Adorno writes, 'whose songs and games could be taken up and sublimated by art; the opening up of markets and the bourgeois process of rationalisation have subordinated all society to bourgeois categories.'[58] He was writing in 1932, yet his diagnosis that a music outside the forces of capital no longer exists has been reiterated by critics in each era since. Where no more site for its autonomy is found, as we have seen, music and art are condemned by the critic to replay their own powerlessness and failure. Where a will for the new announces the end of history, perhaps it merely projects its own exhaustion.

One wonders whether Amiri Baraka had Adorno in mind when he too referred to Bartok's deployment of folk music in *Blues People*, his history of African American music. But where Adorno discerns only alienation from pre-capitalist forms, Baraka insists instead that the exclusion of African Americans from legal status and the paltry rewards of waged work effects its own freedom from the dominant culture and, in turn, preserves the authenticity of Black musics: 'jazz could do with the shout, the work song, the blues, what Bartok did with Hungarian Gypsy music, but with the added advantage of a constant natural reference.'[59] Contra Adorno, then, Baraka maintains that 'extra-territoriality', a certain autonomy from capital, persists for Black expressive culture on the condition of its political and economic exclusion.[60]

This is a significant claim, for it reiterates our premise that the experience of capitalist modernity is internally differentiated and that time-discipline is not imposed on an invariable plane. To relate the sources of authentic expression to Black life lived at the limits of capitalism is thus to engage a wider tradition of thought, one which implies a still more variegated, uneven experience of time and of history. A mode of survival at the fringes of the wage relation, in other words, poses a liminality conditional of a still living tradition of modernism.

This is a view neatly expressed in Sylvia Wynter's contention that the conditions of plantation life formed the basis for a culture autonomous from capital.[61] Her central premise resides with the plots given to slaves to produce their own food. For while these were intended to save the plantation owner from feeding his forced labour, they also functioned as a site through which African structures of value could be preserved. In this way, the plot acts, Wynter argues, as a vessel which connects the community to its pre-capitalist folk culture and so preserves the authenticity of its products, even in the face of their commodification. The plot, in other words, stands for a capacity for social reproduction partly outside the wage relation and is asynchronous to its rhythms.

A related argument also emerges in the examination of criminality in Stuart Hall and colleagues' monumental *Policing the Crisis* where, in the course of a discussion of the Black British working class in the 1980s, they reject the Marxist orthodoxy that holds so-called 'lumpens' (criminals, vagabonds, etc.) as parasitic upon the ruling class, and so an altogether reactionary force. They hold instead that the 'criminal' activities colloquially known as 'hustling' – racketeering and informal dealing – amount to a mode of survival that happens to be crucial to the sustenance of the infrastructure of the ghetto.[62] Wagelessness, on their account, only appears as marginal and parasitic when viewed from the truncated framing of the British imperial core. Conversely, once seen as continuous with the experience of unemployment in the Caribbean colony, it comes to be understood as a majoritarian act of refusal.[63] *Policing the Crisis* thus brings us to an expansive iteration of Wynter's concept of the plot, one where the separateness of the ghetto comes to be conceived as the 'material base for cultural revival', and hustling is ascribed its revolutionary potential.[64] This is especially given that in question is mainly a cultural activity; its primary sites are the street, the pub, and the record shop, and its main medium is the production and distribution of reggae, calypso, and soca.[65] Social life, in short, is understood as inherently resistive here.

For Hall as for Wynter, then, reproduction beyond the wage preserves a mode of cultural expression not alien to vernacular form and so, in a position outside and critical of the society. But Hall's accounts of popular culture have too often registered the latter in functional terms as an object of class struggle; determined by the interest of the subject who consumes it. Conversely, Baraka has registered that struggle at the level of musical form itself. More exactly, he locates it in an impulse that for him originates in African cultures which operated without distinctions between art and life and are redeployed to the conditions of the plantation. There, song structures once intrinsic to the everyday are stripped of their ritual functions to accompany forced labour, yet preserve their original expressive power. This is what Baraka famously calls the 'blues impulse' that inflects the history of Black music and whose elements can be more or less itemised: a rejection of the diatonic scale system, emphasis on rhythmic over harmonic or melodic qualities, vocal expression through changing pitch and timbre, antiphonal singing, and an emphasis on improvisation.[66]

In the course of a narrative of a music growing ever more alien from its immanence to everyday life and more autonomous from social function, Baraka traces a continuum passing from reconstruction era blues to the urban forms that follow the Great Migration; from New Orleans jazz to ragtime to swing. As it develops the music struggles to retain an emotional directness lost to the combined forces of commercialism, white cultural appropriation, and middle class moralism as it's consumed by swing, Dixieland, or white rock. A renewal occurs nonetheless with free jazz in the late 1950s and 1960s, and it's generally associated with a series of proper names: John Coltrane, Sonny Rollins, Thelonious Monk, and especially Cecil Taylor and Ornette Coleman; and indexed by a series of innovations: orientation around polyrhythms, melodies derived from rhythm, and an expansive improvisational aesthetic extending to all instruments and encompassing the chords on which melodies are based. This is by no means an exhaustive accounting of free jazz, but what's significant for our argument is that, on Baraka's reading, its emergence is irreducible from its artists' singularly liminal position: partly incorporated into the dominant society, yet cynical of the limited compensations of American liberalism; compelled to assert their music's autonomy from that culture whilst being irredeemably stamped by it. The condition of a truly modern artform is found here for Baraka; at the society's periphery yet not reducible to revivalist romanticism; anchored in the expressive power of folk culture but autonomous from social function.[67]

To pose a music whose liminality is a condition of its opposition to social domination returns us once again to the question of time. As we have seen, contemporary theorisations of pop as an exhausted modernism tend to relate to the present in terms of its own failure. In doing so they betray their own biases and, above all, underemphasise the extent to which the promises of modernity were always impoverished in the first place. It's in this latter sense that Paul Gilroy has insisted upon a continuity of Black diaspora experience from the start of modernity to our own present.[68] This is to reject an ontological gap between the modern and postmodern as well. It is equally to refuse a break with the pre-modern too. No such ruptures with the past exist, Gilroy insists, for a mode of being committed to the validation of a culture erased by slavery and propelled by the recovery of a lost unity of art and life.[69]

To characterise music in these terms is to ascribe to it an altogether 'distinctive and disjunctive temporality of the subordinated', to return to Gilroy.[70] It's thus also to oppose it to capitalist time-discipline. Indeed, an antagonism to work is discernible in the prominence Black music gives to performance, an aesthetic priority that leaves the artwork in a permanently incomplete state. It's equally audible in the music's syncretic dynamics: frequent deployment of non-linear techniques, such as montage in hip hop, stresses both the cultural unity and difference among its elements. Anchored in syncopation, it revolves around unexpected temporalities and these, Gilroy says, express its basic desire for liberation. Accents, rests, and breaks posit the primacy of sensuality, a zone where the music can make 'unsayable claims to truth.'[71]

But Black popular music's challenge to the capitalist compulsion to labour for a wage is also evident where lyrics revel in hedonism without remorse or decry economic irrationality.[72] There's also a powerful inversion of the values of grift and pleasure in the polysemy by which 'work' and 'working it' can signify both dance and sex. But this is a theme also discernible at the level of its institutions: the unsociable hours devoted to the dancehall divert, for instance, the period for rest and reproduction to the pursuit of pleasure.[73] The contours of a Black popular modernism become more or less clear here: for one thing, it involves divesting the modern of its progressive assumptions and, as such, it rebuffs those who would mourn its demise as well.[74]

Such an aesthetic strategy, to speak in schematic terms, also bears risks. Most of all, to solicit autonomy on the basis of social exclusion hazards summoning a folk-other whose claim to authenticity imperils it to perpetual marginality. This is the warning expressed by Richard Iton in the course of his own study of Black diaspora aesthetics.[75] His imperative is to register Black music's political aesthetics against any tendency to auto-estrangement in the widest possible terms; which is to say, against the very separation of politics and aesthetics itself.[76] Nothing short of substantive emancipation – sexual, ethical, political – is in question.

Richard Iton thus alerts us to the risk of reifying authenticity as the marker of aesthetic value. Nahum Chandler warns of another hazard:

It may be that the status of a putative subject of whiteness can be reauthorized with even more hegemonic force by the narrative of its heterogeneous reference if that narrative is recast simply or primarily as its capacity – whether realized or 'ostensibly' failed (and hence potentially recuperable by way of the arrival of a certain liberal dispensation) – to become other, as simply describing the plurality of the ideals that it can encompass.[77]

To inscribe alterity or difference within whiteness, in other words, risks an extension rather than disruption of its terms. A further theoretical move is thus called for: we must demonstrate that hegemony is conditional upon that which it subordinates. At stake is not merely modernity's periphery but its very nucleus. It's in this regard that Chandler's own analysis of Black experience is premised upon a 'generalized question of identification' rather than a limit case of Western subjectivity.[78]

Chandler's argument is complex and takes any number of turns. But it hinges upon the claim that the experience of sovereignty or self-possession of the modern subject is inconceivable without the institution of chattel slavery. This is evident if we consider that the slave must preserve some level of autonomy for his owner to profit from his work. Equally, the law which strips them of rights must nevertheless implicitly recognise the subject's capacity to transgress its prohibition in the first place. The very desire for total control only testifies to the incompleteness of the hegemon who pursues it.

To say this is thus to affirm a universal, revolutionary politics that begins from the premise of Blackness as an irreducible excess; one that confounds Iton's apprehension of the essentialising logics of authenticity. This is a theoretical project for which we have any number of names: Cedric Robinson used the phrase 'ontological totality' to refer to the Black mode of being which precedes and responds to European oppression; Fred Moten sometimes says 'appositionality'; Fumi Okiji calls it 'nonrelationality'.[79] Together, they describe a force that both precedes the law and which the law fails to suppress and which is not the property of an essentialised subject but, to quote Moten, '(racial) difference mobilised against the racist determinations it calls into being'; 'a gift that moves us towards this anarchic, resistive sociality we have in common.'[80]

Such claims concern us here insofar as they articulate an originary refusal which extends to the systems of oppression that compel us to sell our labour to another in order to live; a 'motive force', an 'anoroginal criminality' which precedes the law.[81] This is an account of refusal that bears no attachment to the rewards of wage labour, from which it was mostly excluded in any case. And it is on this basis, to return to Okiji again, that Black expression reflects 'a facet of life that cannot help but be a critical reflection on the integrity of the world.'[82] Music functions, Dhanveer Singh Brar says, as a 'holding space' for generalised social antagonism.[83] Or, to return to Moten: 'the universalisation or socialisation of the surplus, the generative force of a venerable phonic propulsion, the ontological and historical priority of resistance to power and objection to subjection, the old-new thing, the freedom drive that animates black performances.'[84]

This brings us back to the question of repetition. For we encounter here, at the level of the song, an ontology of sociality attuned to a generalised sonic discontinuity, a suspension of time where, Adorno says, we would hear only sameness. This is a knowledge of rhythm, to return to an earlier theme, where syncopation withholds easy resolution between meter and pulse. Hence, we find ourselves in the presence of an avant-gardism, indeed, one that observes no separation between art and life but honours instead the historical continuities out of which the music is constituted. This is, further, a conception of aesthetic development that rejects the modernist's martial logic and it posits instead a 'changing same' in place of an incessant forward movement through time and the ceaseless sacrifice of tradition to experiment that this demands.

Finally Got the News

The aesthetics of the Black Radical Tradition are especially significant for us insofar as they gesture at a resistive conception of music and situate us outside the hegemonic experience of modern time. But they place us in a different conception of space too. This is a feature that emerges in the course of Fred Moten's reading of Fredric Jameson's well-known appeal, first elicited in the mid-1980s, for a political aesthetic of 'cognitive mapping'. With this neat phrase Jameson intended a representational practice able to connect the postmodern capitalist world-system to the existentialia of everyday experience.[85] This is especially important in an epoch where, according to Jameson, the forces that govern social life grow increasingly distant, diffuse, and oblique.

As an example of the failure to deal with the representational challenge of the postmodern, Jameson cites the League of Revolutionary Black Workers, the militant group organising in Detroit auto factories in the late 1960s and early 1970s, and, in particular, *Finally Got the News*, the film the group produced in 1970.[86] If the film is archetypal of political failure, for Jameson, this is insofar as, on his view, its truncated focus upon struggle in Detroit is reflective of an incapacity to adopt a wider, dialectical perspective suitable to global capital. But in a *tour de force* argument, Moten has shown that this call for an expansive political aesthetic is especially impaired by its own blinkered view of what this might mean. Not only does extra-diegetic narrative in the film – voiced by activist lawyer and politician Ken Cockrel – evince a rather sophisticated conception of the League's tactical position vis-à-vis global capital. More importantly, its tonality, its sequences of rhythms and chants, Moten argues, is something other than a mere monument to defeat: 'If the film is image and spectacle it is also sound and music ... something that will have been encountered as a product of a Black aesthetic ongoingly stages the piercing insistence of the excluded. Such insistence is not only of excluded identity but also of excluded sense.'[87]

The correspondence between the exclusion of the sonic from political aesthetics and of Blackness from the political space of labour deciphered by Moten is apposite here, for it is through its sonic elements that the utopian drive for the representation of totality is most discernible. And, in turn, it's the all too occidental perspective betrayed in Jameson's cognitive map – poised as it is at the core of the world-system – that leaves it so imperceptive to this sonic rejoinder against the compulsions of capitalism. This is an especially significant idea where we confront arguments for the exhaustion of modernity itself.

We have seen, in this regard, that reports of a crisis of popular modernism hinge upon a view of capital's subsumption of social life since this creates conditions in which the new no longer emerges as new. As such, popular music is condemned to play out its own terminal condition. This is an argument, we saw, most commonly associated with the work of Mark Fisher. But its underlying themes were earlier developed by Jameson, in whose terms Fisher affirms his own work originates.[88]

At stake is Jameson's assessment of the present as an epoch where no outside to capital exists, in which 'the survival, the residue, the holdover, the archaic has finally been swept away without a trace.'[89] Such a claim is premised on the notion that postmodernity is defined by the disappearance of pre-modern social forms, whether wilderness, aristocracy, or handicraft. Their eradication, Jameson argues, signals that capital's subsumption of that which had exceeded it is complete. As a periodisation, it is among the most sophisticated iterations of the argument for the exhaustion of modernity that we have and, on this basis, demands further examination.

Jameson has often designated capital's postmodern subsumption of all that exceeds it as a spatialisation of temporality; an argument that charts the 'spatial fix' that capital has sought in response to its crisis of profitability. As post-war manufacturing came under pressure from competition, capital increasingly sought to restore profits by seeking out cheaper labour markets and faster speeds in turnover time.[90] Beginning in the 1970s, developments in information technology and container shipping enabled a global regime of 'flexibility' premised on outsourcing and subcontracting as strategies to lower the costs of supply chains. Certainly, 'the annihilation of time by space' is a widely disseminated description of globalisation, but the sophistication of Jameson's version of this narrative rests with the facility by which it relates historical change to existential experience, and connects economy to cultural form.[91] The modern epistemic separation of the colony from the metropole, for instance, generates a sense of profound spatial disjuncture of past and present. Conversely, a postmodern era characterised by the instantaneity of information and the globalisation of culture marks a breach of this temporal chasm.[92] A flat surface prevails where synchronicity supplants the unevenness of the modern world; past and future dissolve into the perpetual 'now' of a wholly transparent world system.

We have arrived at a picture of globalisation as the accomplishment of capital's spatial extension. But as an account of the exhaustion of linear history this offers still too monotonous a view, one whose impression of the completion of capital's colonisation of life is exceedingly clear-cut. To begin with, Jameson's argument is premised, in part, on the notion that the end of history is signalled by the demise of nature as 'ultimate content or referent'.[93] There are grounds to question such a claim. Where we're confronted with global warming as the possibility of planetary exhaustion as such, Andreas Malm suggests, we face not the culmination of an experience of moving from past to future but a confrontation of the future as the looming nihilation of the present.[94] We arrive at an endpoint, in other words, whose calendar is in disarray, for under consideration is an ecological catastrophe that culminates out of several centuries of the consumption of fossil fuels and these, in turn, are themselves the result of processes that are millions of years old. To look to ecological crisis is not merely to sense that linear time has expired, it's to see that it's come unhinged from its coordinates altogether.

Jameson's account, as we have seen, centres on a view of postmodernity as the resolution of the modern unevenness of development; everything becomes a flat surface equally transformed by the dictates of the laws of capital accumulation. But we should also question whether a uniformity of experience follows capital's spatial expansion. This is the central point in Peter Osborne's own periodising analysis, itself developed in dialogue with Jameson. For Osborne, the present is better characterised by a dialectical play between the abstract, unifying power of exchange value and the concrete planetary sites at which it operates.[95] Rather than the completion of history theorised by Jameson, such a view implies the self-differentiating temporalities of a multiplicity of territorially discrete modernities of which, it bears remarking, the Black Radical Tradition is exemplary. Osborne's point is, ultimately, that concepts of postmodernity or globalisation are necessarily *speculative* unities, projections upon a totalising yet fractured constellation of distinct but overlapping temporal experiences. Such fractures are, moreover, effected in the process of capital's subsumption of variant experiences of time and this generates still further tensions and struggles.

Part of what's at stake here are the spatial dynamics of the management and organisation of capitalist crisis and these are particularly palpable in the history of the circulation of hip-hop. Not only is this a music often taken to emerge out of and express the conditions of capital's post-industrial withdrawal from U.S. inner cities, but despite its subjects' routine confinement to the ghetto, their cultural practices are permitted to circulate freely provided they're submitted to the abstractions of the commodity-form.[96] Racialised criminalisation generates new value where Black vernacular traditions and styles are consumed by an imaginary for which the ghetto is fantasised as a site of indulgence and excess.[97] But hip-hop's themes, as well as the terms of its consumption by the dominant society, also reflect a wider, horrifyingly cruel and brutal carceral response to the people at the edges, or completely outside of, labour markets and situated in communities characterised by, in Ruth Wilson Gilmore's words, 'utter abandonment by capital.'[98]

But the chapters that follow will locate the spatialisations of crisis in other ways too. For instance, the migration of music to online streaming platforms was devised to rescue flagging industry profits, only it has also served music's transcendence of the barriers which once gave it meaning. No longer segregated to the evening or weekend or to the home stereo or music hall, music becomes ubiquitous. Equally, changes to the aesthetics of 'world music' are occasioned by a growing proximity between global North and South so that the exoticisation of cultural objects demands new strategies and greater effort.

Expendables

We should also register here that, as a support to capital's spatial expansion, credit has long been deployed to support new investment or to mitigate risks. Yet where investing in production or new labour markets has failed to restore profitability, a 'temporal fix' displaces a spatial one in significance.[99] At least, this is one way to conceive of the rising importance of financial markets to global capitalism. For where stocks once funded investment, contemporary financial activity is increasingly an end in itself given that, in an era of stalled growth, treating anticipated profits as if they've already occurred appears to be among scarce ways of generating rising rates of return.[100] On these terms, time itself comes to be reified, for the future only counts for financial capital insofar as it appears in the form of an abstract quantity. This is to relate to history as a repository of risks that can be hedged and where meaningful change is literally off the charts; an apparent necessity where no new source of economic dynamism appears, and capital's cyclical expansion emerges exhausted.[101]

Osborne suggests that the logics of capital accumulation are such that a spatial unevenness of development necessarily prevails; an argument evidenced by the gross disparity between, say, life in a shantytown and a nearby middle class suburb. For others, rather than the completion of modernity identified by Jameson or the disaggregation diagnosed by Osborne, the contemporary era exhibits an even deeper continuity among capital's structural contradictions. That is, as Nathan Brown has suggested, capital's response to the crisis of its profitability since the 1970s has increasingly taken the form of a renewal of *older* mechanisms of value production.[102] This is exemplified in its outsourcing and offshoring of production to zones where regulations don't prohibit lower wages or do much to govern working conditions. Where profit is generated by compelling labour to work longer for less, we're in the ambit of pre-industrial iterations of capitalism. Time, it seems here, proceeds backwards as well as forwards.

Earlier, we saw that labour experiences the dynamism of history as the process of its disciplining by increasingly efficient machines or, indeed, its displacement of cheaper workers living elsewhere. Yet where growth has begun to falter on a global scale, workers find fewer new sites to absorb them, and this places downward pressure on their wages and the conditions of their reproduction. And yet here we encounter something of an anomaly: notwithstanding some upticks in 2008, unemployment rates have remained low across the global North in recent decades despite an absence of dynamism in the global economy.[103] For where states have used austerity as an approach to social welfare, labour has had few options but to seek out paid work, no matter how meagre its rewards.[104] Marx famously used the term 'surplus population' to describe that portion of the workforce expelled from production by technological development. But to be surplus to the economy is still to remain integral to it. It is to be 'a human material always ready for exploitation', to use Marx's phrase, or 'expendables', to quote James Boggs, lacking any means of subsistence besides working for a wage.[105] Only the work this material is compelled to accept is overwhelmingly badly paid, precarious, and accomplished in bleak conditions.

From this perspective, we can register a wider and altogether pathetic incongruity in the fact that the majority of the world's workers today find themselves absorbed into so-called 'non-standard' jobs if they can be absorbed at all.[106] This is a reference to roles that are neither full-time nor permanent and it's an increasingly anachronistic holdover from a twentieth century Fordist system of statutory labour protections reserved for white male industrial workers. This has mostly been displaced by a contemporary regime of 'flexibility' for whom workers are more often, at best, expendable private contractors.

Accordingly, the argument underlying this book, to put it plainly, is that the Fordist regime was premised on the protection of the white male body and the sorting of populations organised primarily around gender and race. This implied a whole set of hierarchies and these, in turn, set the terms for the organising boundaries and stratifications of much of twentieth century life: labour and leisure, public and private, free time and time dedicated to work. These then governed the hegemonic conditions by which popular music was produced and consumed and so also, the terms in which it could express an experience of time outside the wage.

But in the contemporary era where the 'standard' job has become the exception and not the rule, things grow more and more messy and indistinct. For one thing, the growing market for care work tends to blunt once sharp divisions between productive and reproductive labour. This is the case given that a great deal of this activity is premised upon the sale of capacities historically developed within the confines of the family. This involved the compulsory hospitality and dispositions associated with women and the stigma of this affective labour with housework keeps its wages low. For another thing, the boundaries between work and non-work grow porous where labour contracts may not actually guarantee any work.

For another still, the lines between the worker and entrepreneur grow fuzzy where outsourcing constitutes the former as a private contractor. This is where capital frees itself of the burden of social insurance; in other words, risk is outsourced to the service provider now responsible for hedging contingencies once insured by the state. Indeed, the demarcation between worker and investor is complicated where families become increasingly dependent upon the value of assets and on debt for their reproduction. On-call, fixed-term, 'zero hours', the wage itself increasingly becomes, to borrow Melinda Cooper's phrase, a 'speculative proposition'.[107]

If a particular experience of time governed the experience of popular music, if a 'standard' relation to abstract time organised the dominant tempos and rhythms of leisure and play, then today, in the context of an ongoing crisis of capitalism especially intensified since 2008, those coordinates are increasingly all messed up. And so, to return to where we began this chapter, an assessment of contemporary music is called for that is not limited to accounts of the exhaustion of 'popular modernism'; the historical time underlying song-form are far more complex and variegated than is usually admitted. Equally, it calls for an account not beholden to the 'pseudo-concreteness' of discourses of the ontology of sound either where these tend to be premised upon the erasure of history altogether.[108] Instead, our accounting of the present insists on the salience of the aesthetics of the Black Radical Tradition as all the more evident, for this is a theoretical position, as we have seen, through which we can locate the expressive power of song, in part, by way of its subject's exclusion from easy access to employment and the benefits of capitalism, more broadly. In this light, we are directed to a residue that remains unallowable, a gesture of refusal through which music does its work and whose gestures as well as whose containment we will seek to trace in the remaining chapters.

Notes

1 The classic articulation of the poptimist position is in Kelefa Sanneh, 'The Rap Against Rockism', *The New York Times*, 31 October 2004. See also Chris Richards, 'Do You Want Poptimism? Or Do You Want the Truth?', *The Washington Post*, 16 April 2015 for a good overview of the debate.
2 Some of this was already parsed in Grossberg, 'Another Boring Day in Paradise'. See also Michael Hann, 'Is Poptimism Now as Blinkered as the Rockism it Replaced?', *The Quietus*,

11 May 2017, https://thequietus.com/articles/22389-rockism-poptimism [accessed 6 October 2020]; Rob Horning, 'Poptimism: The Death of Pop Criticism', PopMatters, 11 May 2006, www.popmatters.com/2413-poptimism_the_death_of_pop_criticism-2495679181.html [accessed 6 October 2020].
3 See for instance, Javier F. Léon, 'Music, Music Making and Neoliberalism', *Culture Theory and Critique* 55, no.2, April 2014, pp.129-37.
4 Robin James, 'Neoliberal Noise: Attali, Foucault & the Biopolitics of Uncool', *Culture, Theory & Critique* 55, no.2, 2014, pp.138-58. In other work, James seeks to show how dissonance is incorporated into neoliberal capitalism.
5 Mark Fisher, *Ghosts of My Life: Writings on Depression, Hauntology, and Lost Futures*. Alresford: Zero Books, 2014.
6 Mark Fisher, *K-Punk: The Collected and Unpublished Writings of Mark Fisher (2004-2016)*, Darren Ambrose (Ed.). London: Repeater Books, 2018, p.322.
7 Anahid Kassabian, *Ubiquitous Listening: Affect, Attention, and Distributed Subjectivities*. Berkeley/Los Angeles: University of California Press, 2013.
8 See for instance, Christoph Cox, 'Beyond Representation and Signification: Toward a Sonic Materialism', *Journal of Visual Culture* 10, no.2, 2011, pp.145-61; Steve Goodman, *Sonic Warfare: Sound, Affect, and the Ecology of Fear*. Cambridge: MIT Press, 2009; Nina Sun Eidsheim, *Sensing Sound: Singing and Listening as Vibrational Practice*. Durham & London: Duke University Press, 2019; Marcus Boon, *The Politics of Vibration: Music as a Cosmopolitical Practice*. Durham & London: Duke University Press, 2022.
9 For an overview see Paul Rekret, 'The Head, the Hand and Matter: New Materialism and the Politics of Knowledge', *Theory, Culture & Society* 35, no.7-8, 2018/2019, pp.49-72.
10 Brian Massumi, 'The Autonomy of Affect', *Cultural Critique* 31, 1995, pp.83-109.
11 The quotation is from Nigel Thrift, 'Intensities of Feeling: Towards a Spatial Politics of Affect', *Geografiska Annaler: Series B, Human Geography* 86, no.1, 2004, pp.57-78.
12 On this point see Ruth Leys, 'The Turn to Affect: A Critique', *Critical Inquiry* 37, no.3, Spring 2011, pp.434-72.
13 See Annie Goh, 'Sounding Situated Knowledges – Echo in Archaeoacoustics', *Parallax* 23, no.3, 2018; Marie Thompson, 'Whiteness and the Ontological Turn in Sound Studies', *Parallax* 23, no.3, 2018, pp.266-82. See also Brian Kane, 'Sound Studies Without Auditory Culture: A Critique of the Ontological Turn', *Sound Studies* 1, no.1, 2015, pp.2-21.
14 I draw here on James Snead, 'On Repetition in Black Culture', *Black American Literature Forum* 15, no.4, 1981, pp.146-54.
15 I draw here on Richard Middleton's discussion of repetition in *Voicing the Popular: On the Subjects of Popular Music*. London and New York: Routledge, 2006, and in '"Play It Again Sam": Some Notes on the Productivity of Repetition in Popular Music', *Popular Music* 3, 1983, pp.235-70.
16 Snead, 'On Repetition in Black Culture', p.147.
17 E.P. Thompson, 'Time, Work-Discipline and Industrial Capitalism', *Past and Present* 38, 1967, pp.56-97.
18 Moishe Postone, *Time, Labor and Social Domination: A Reinterpretation of Marx's Critical Theory*. Cambridge: Cambridge University Press, 1993, p.191.
19 Michel Foucault, *Discipline and Punish: The Birth of the Prison* (Alan Sheridan, Trans.). New York: Vintage Books 1995, p.151.

20 Postone, *Time, Labor and Social Domination*, p.211.
21 See Jonathan Martineau, *Time, Capitalism and Alienation: A Socio-Historical Critique into the Making of Time*. Leiden: Brill 2015, p.130. The becoming hegemonic of abstraction, through the subsumption of the labour process to capitalist valorisation, is argued by Christopher J. Arthur, 'The Practical Truth of Abstract Labour' in: R. Bellofiore, G. Starosta, & P. Thomas (Eds.) *Marx's Laboratory: Critical Interpretations of the Grundrisse*. Leiden: Brill, 2013, pp.101–20.
22 As I make plain further on, my analysis here follows the suggestion of Mark Abel in *Groove: An Aesthetic of Measured Time*. Leiden: Brill, 2016.
23 On this point see Alfred Sohn-Rethel, *Intellectual and Manual Labour: A Critique of Epistemology*. New Jersey: Humanities Press, 1978. The canonical articulation of this argument is found in Karl Marx, *Capital: A Critique of Political Economy, Volume I* (Ben Fowkes, Trans.). London: Penguin, 1976.
24 Harry Braverman, *Labour and Monopoly Capital: The Degradation of Work in the Twentieth Century*. New York: Monthly Review Press, 1998.
25 This formulation is drawn from Sohn-Rethel, *Intellectual and Manual Labour*.
26 Daniel Bensaïd, *Marx for Our Times: Adventures and Misadventures of Critique* (Gregory Elliott, Trans.). London: Verso, 2010, p.71.
27 On this point see Peter Osborne, *The Politics of Time: Modernity and Avant-Garde*. London: Verso, 1995.
28 Bensaïd, *Marx for Our Times*, p.75.
29 This is parsed in Abel, *Groove*, pp.171–75.
30 See for instance Max Horkheimer & Theodor Adorno, *Dialectic of Enlightenment*.
31 Theodor Adorno, *Introduction to the Sociology of Music* (E.B. Ashton, Trans.). New York: Seabury Press, 1976.
32 Theodor Adorno, 'On the Social Situation of Music' in *Essays on Music*, Richard Leppert (Ed.), Susan H. Gillespie (Trans.). Berkeley & Los Angeles: University of California Press, 2002, pp.288–317.
33 Adorno, 'On the Social Situation of Music', p.430.
34 On this point see Abel, *Groove* and Fumi Okiji, *Jazz as Critique: Adorno and Black Expression Revisited*. Stanford: Stanford University Press, 2018.
35 Korczynski, Pickering, & Robertson, *Rhythms of Labour*, pp.142–44.
36 David Suisman, 'Sound, Knowledge and the "Immanence of Human Failure": Rethinking Musical Mechanization Through the Phonograph, Player-Piano, and the Piano', *Social Text* 28, no.1, 2010, pp.13–34. Of course, improvisatory traditions have used the piano against the grain of this discipline, especially beginning with early blues and jazz.
37 Suisman, 'Sound, Knowledge and the "Immanence of Human Failure"'. We might add that control would come to be seized back from the phonograph when it is made an instrument once again beginning in the late 1970s in the Bronx and elsewhere.
38 Gioia, *Work Songs*; Korczynski, Pickering, & Robertson, *Rhythms of Labour*.
39 Korczynski, Pickering, & Robertson, *Rhythms of Labour*. We should also include here the restrictions on song on American and Caribbean plantations. See, for instance, Thomas P. Barker, 'Spatial Dialectics: Intimations of Freedom in Antebellum Slave Song', *Journal of Black Studies* 46, no.4, 2015, pp.363–83.
40 Theodor Adorno, 'Free Time' in: *The Culture Industry*. London: Routledge, 1991.
41 Henri Lefebvre, *Critique of Everyday Life*. London: Verso, 2014, p.62.

42 Ibid.
43 I paraphrase here from Frith, *Performing Rites*, p.156 and Lipsitz, *Time Passages*, p.113.
44 Michael Denning, *Noise Uprising: The Audiopolitics of a World Musical Revolution*. London: Verso, 2015.
45 Angela Mitropoulos, *Contract and Contagion: From Biopolitics to Oikonomia*. Wivenhoe, New York, Port Watson: Minor Composition, 2012, p.166.
46 Melinda Cooper, *Family Values: Between Neoliberalism and the New Social Conservatism*. New York: Zone Books, 2017. See also David Roedinger, *The Wages of Whiteness: Race and the Making of the American Working Class*. London: Verso, 1991.
47 Samuel Fisher, 'Race and Real Abstraction'. Unpublished paper shared by the author.
48 Maria Mies, *Patriarchy and Accumulation on a World Scale: Women in the International Division of Labor*. London: Zed, 1999; Michele Barrett & Mary McIntosh, *The Anti-Social Family*. London: Verso, 2015; Viviana Zelizer, *Pricing the Priceless Child: The Changing Social Value of Children*. Princeton: Princeton University Press, 1994; Wally Seccombe, *Weathering the Storm: Working-Class Families from the Industrial Revolution to the Fertility Decline*. London: Verso, 1995.
49 Cooper, *Family Values*; Mitropoulos, *Contract and Contagion*.
50 Fortunati, *The Arcane of Reproduction*.
51 Endnotes, 'The Logic of Gender: On the Separation of Spheres and the Process of Abjection', *Endnotes*, 3 September 2013. https://endnotes.org.uk/issues/3/en/endnotes-the-logic-of-gender.
52 Sheila Whiteley (Ed.), *Sexing the Groove: Popular Music and Gender*. Abingdon & New York: Routledge, 1997.
53 Roshanak Kheshti, *Modernity's Ear: Listening to Race and Gender in World Music*. New York: New York University Press, 2015.
54 David Suisman, *Selling Sounds: The Commercial Revolution in American Music*. Cambridge: Harvard University Press, 2012.
55 Kyle Devine, *Decomposed: The Political Ecology of Music*. Cambridge & London: MIT Press, 2019, pp.64–66.
56 Simon Frith & Angela McRobbie, 'Rock and Sexuality', in: Simon Frith & Andrew Goodwin (Eds.) *On Record*. London: Routledge, 1990, pp.317–32.
57 This is a line of thought I develop to examine the changing divisions of public and private and labour and leisure through the figure of the child in popular music in Paul Rekret, *Down With Childhood: Pop Music and the Crisis of Innocence*. London: Repeater, 2018.
58 Theodor Adorno, 'On the Social Situation of Music', p.427. See also, Theodor Adorno, *Philosophy of New Music* (Robert Hullot-Kentor, Ed. & Trans.). Minneapolis: University of Minnesota Press, 2006, p.176, n.4.
59 Amiri Baraka, *Blues People: Negro Music in White America*. New York: Harper Perennial, 1999, p.221.
60 'Extra-territoriality' is the phrase used by Adorno, in *Philosophy of New Music*, p.176, n.4.
61 Sylvia Wynter, 'Novel and History, Plot and Plantation', *Savacou* 5, June 1971, pp.95–102. The same argument is made in *Black Metamorphosis*, unpublished manuscript. I owe this reference to Dhanveer Singh Brar and Louis Moreno, 'Plot and Plantation/Algorithm and Urbanisation' paper presented to Goldsmiths University, 4 October 2018. The argument in this section has been developed in dialogue with Brar and Moreno.

62 Stuart Hall et al., *Policing the Crisis, Mugging, the State and Law and Order*. London: Bloomsbury, 2017, pp.350–52.
63 Hall et al., *Policing the Crisis*, pp.363–79.
64 Hall et al., *Policing the Crisis*, p.351. This is a point I owe to discussion with Dhanveer Singh Brar.
65 Hall et al., *Policing the Crisis*, pp.373–75.
66 Baraka, *Blues People*, pp.25–27.
67 Baraka, *Blues People*, p.200.
68 Paul Gilroy, *The Black Atlantic: Modernity and Double Consciousness*. Cambridge: Harvard University Press, 1993, p.42.
69 Paul Gilroy, *There Ain't No Black in the Union Jack*. London: Routledge, 2013, p.217.
70 Gilroy, *The Black Atlantic*, p.212.
71 Gilroy, *The Black Atlantic*, p.37.
72 Gilroy, *Ain't No Black*, pp.270–72.
73 Gilroy, *Ain't No Black*, pp.270–80, 284.
74 Gilroy's own later laments for a lost immediacy or authenticity in Black popular music thus appear apposite to his own theoretical position.
75 This is also an argument made by Weheliye in *Phonographies*. Weheliye seeks to theorise Black cultural production as not external to technological development and thus, as irreducible to vernacular authenticity.
76 Richard Iton, *In Search of the Black Fantastic: Politics and Popular Culture in the Post-Civil Rights Era*. Oxford: Oxford University Press, 2010.
77 Nahum Dimitri Chandler, *X: The Problem of the Negro as a Problem for Thought*. New York: Fordham University Press, 2014, p.137.
78 Chandler, *X*, p.133.
79 Cedric Robinson, *Black Marxism: The Making of the Black Radical Tradition*. Chapel Hill & London: University of North Carolina Press, 2000, p.73; Okiji, *Jazz as Critique*, p.52; Moten, *In the Break*, p.34.
80 Fred Moten, *Stolen Life, Consent Not to Be a Single Being, Vol.2*, Durham & London: Duke University Press, 2018, p.21; Fred Moten, 'The Subprime and the Beautiful', *African Identities* 11, no.2, 2013, pp.237–45; and as Okiji explains, 'a state that can be taken on by anyone willing to relinquish claims on the world', Okiji, *Jazz as Critique*, p.53.
81 See Stefano Harney & Fred Moten, *Undercommons: Fugitive Planning and Black Study*. Wivenhoe: Minor Compositions, 2013, pp.47, 57; Moten, *Stolen Life*, p.19.
82 Okiji, *Jazz as Critique*, p.13.
83 Brar, Teklife/Ghettoville/Eski, p.41.
84 Moten, *In the Break*, p.12.
85 Fredric Jameson, 'Cognitive Mapping' in: C. Nelson, & L. Grossberg (Eds.) *Marxism and the Interpretation of Culture*. Chicago: University of Illinois Press, 1990, pp.347–58.
86 League of Revolutionary Black Workers (dir. Stewart Bird, Rene Lichtmann, & Peter Gessner), *Finally Got the News*, Icarus Films, 1970.
87 Moten, *In the Break*, p.223.
88 Cf. Mark Fisher, *Capitalist Realism: Is There No Alternative?* Hampshire, UK: John Hunt Publishing, 2009, p.7.
89 Fredric Jameson, *Postmodernism, Or, the Cultural Logic of Late Capitalism*. Durham & London: Duke University Press, 1991, p.309.

90 This argument is made in Brenner, *The Economics of Global Turbulence*.
91 Cf. David Harvey, *The Condition of Postmodernity: An Enquiry into the Origins of Cultural Change*. London: Wiley-Blackwell, 1991.
92 Fredric Jameson, 'The End of Temporality', *Critical Inquiry* 29, no.4, Summer 2003, pp.695–718.
93 Jameson, *Postmodernism*, p.ix.
94 This point is made by Andreas Malm, *The Progress of this Storm: On the Dialectics of Society and Nature in a Warming World*. London: Verso, 2018.
95 Peter Osborne, *Anywhere or Not At All: Philosophy of Contemporary Art*. London: Verso, 2013.
96 On this point see Tricia Rose, *Black Noise: Rap Music and Black Culture in Contemporary America*. Middletown: Wesleyan University Press, 1994.
97 Robin D.G. Kelley, *Race Rebels: Culture, Politics, and the Black Working Class*. New York: Simon and Schuster, 1996, p.191.
98 Ruth Wilson Gilmore, *Golden Gulag: Prisons, Surplus, Crisis, and Opposition in Globalizing California*. Berkeley: University of California Press, 2007, p.74.
99 Annie McClanahan, *Dead Pledges: Debt, Crisis, and Twenty-First Century Culture*. Stanford: Stanford University Press, 2018, p.12.
100 David McNally, 'From Financial Crisis to World-Slump: Accumulation, Financialisation and the Global Slowdown', *Historical Materialism* 17, no.2, 2009, pp.35–83.
101 McNally, 'From Financial Crisis to World-Slump', p.59; Gopal Balakrishnan, 'Speculations on the Stationary State', *New Left Review* 59, September/October 2009.
102 Cf. Nathan Brown, 'Postmodernity, Not Yet: Toward a New Periodisation', *Radical Philosophy* 2, no.1, February 2018. www.radicalphilosophy.com/article/postmodernity-not-yet.
103 Kim Moody, *On New Terrain: How Capital is Reshaping the Battleground of Class War*. Chicago: Haymarket Books 2017.
104 Jason Smith, *Smart Machines and Service Work: Automation in an Age of Stagnation*. New York: Reaktion Books, 2020.
105 Marx, *Capital, Volume I*, p.784; James Boggs, *Pages From a Black Radical's Notebook: A James Boggs Reader* (Stephen M. Ward, Ed.) Detroit: Wayne State University Press, 2011, p.103.
106 Aaron Benanav, *Automation and the Future of Work*. London: Verso, 2020, p.15.
107 Melinda Cooper, 'Workfare, Familyfare, Godfare: Transforming Contingency into Necessity', *South Atlantic Quarterly* 111, no.4, 2012, pp.643–61.
108 Quoted from Marina Vishmidt, 'Bodies in Space: On the Ends of Vulnerability', *Radical Philosophy* 2, no.8, Autumn 2020, p.34.

2

Melodies Wander Around as Ghosts: Playlist as Cultural Form

Studied Ambivalence

In interviews Midori Takada has said that she made her 1983 ambient music masterpiece, *Through the Looking Glass*, in response to the swelling urbanisation and hurried pace that characterised that decade's economic boom in her native Japan.[1] Rapid historical change is also implied by the album's title, not, as one might imagine, a reference to Lewis Carroll's pastoral depiction of childhood. Takada has said it gestures more narrowly towards the sensual experience of time pervading Carroll's work.[2] It's a fitting allusion; the album weaves together dense layers of percussive, polyrhythmic patterns, spiraling together marimba, tam-tam, piano, harmonium, at one point even a Coca-Cola bottle. It moves through melodic changes in gradual, measured terms; the effect is of simultaneous stasis and motion not unlike the best of Steve Reich's work, with the exception of the album's closing track, 'Catastrophe Σ', which eschews tranquility for ascending intensity by a harmonium and rising hand drumming to gradually, over 15 minutes, build towards an explosive crescendo.

There's a further circularity of time at issue though, given *Through the Looking Glass* only attracted anything beyond a miniscule audience three decades after its release, when around 2013, it began to be recommended by YouTube's 'Autoplay' software to listeners of new age and ambient recordings.[3] It's neither clear how nor why the website's algorithms happened upon this obscure album, but doing so led to a rapid growth in its notoriety, going from a few hundred plays – a miniscule figure by YouTube standards – to millions in a couple years, with originals of the LP selling for a thousand US dollars by the time it was reissued by Palto Flats and

WRWTFWW Records in 2017. It was a huge hit by independent music standards; coming second in sales only to Radiohead's *OK Computer* on the *Discogs* site in 2017. A suddenly in-demand Takada began playing sold out concert halls across Europe and North America in 2018.

Through the Looking Glass, it turned out, marked the beginning of an explosion, by the standards of reissue label turnover, in sales of Japanese ambient music from the 1980s and early 1990s. By 2017 editors at trendsetting music presses were commissioning features and guides to overlooked Japanese ambient composers – we've been spared the portmanteau of 'Japambient' thus far.[4] Scores of further reissues followed, of which Hiroshi Yoshimura's *Green* and *Music For Nine Postcards*, and Satoshi Ashikawa's *Still Way*, are standouts, but they reflect a wider taste for vintage minimalist, rhythmic song constitution; a preference for musical texture over narrative; and a melodic style that's less temporal development and more a spatial, atmospheric experience.[5] This is especially underscored by those instances where the music in question was made with the functional in mind: Yoshimura's 1986 album *Surround* was designed to be played in Misawa Home Corporation's model homes, *Music For Nine Postcards* was composed in 1982 especially for listening in the Hara Museum of Contemporary Art, while *Sound Process*, the label that originally released them, doubled as a sound design consulting firm.[6]

Of course, as an aesthetic strategy, ambient music has always had an explicit relation to social function, a fact underscored by its best known iteration, Brian Eno's 1978 album, *Music for Airports*.[7] And even if we take 2017 as something of a high point, it's undeniable that interest in the sort of understated, minimalist composition at issue here echoed a wider nascent fascination among underground music circles in new age and other styles of sonic atmospheric subtlety throughout the 2010s. In this regard, a 2013 decades-spinning survey of DIY new age scenes, *I Am the Center*, was significant in drawing attention to the post-hippy world it surveyed.[8] Despite the banal spiritualism and naïve romanticism that excessive sonic and visual references to crystals, waterfalls, or rainbows tend to stand in for, new age was also the site of early synth adoption and a wider inclination to electronic and studio experimentation.

A year after the release of *I Am the Center*, Brian Eno and John Hassell's 1980 collaboration, *Fourth World Vol. 1: Possible Musics*, was reissued while the second volume, Hassell's *Dream Theory in Malaya*, followed soon thereafter.[9] Their combination of the sort of layered, pattern-oriented repetitions of minimalism and ambient music also audible in Takada's work, with looser improvisational flourishes and primitivist tropes such as slapping hand drumming and other 'tribal' effects, was widely lauded by critics. A 'fourth world' imaginary, at 'the nexus of electronic and ethnographic' sound, as Andy Beta put it for *Resident Advisor*, has since reverberated rather widely, a state of affairs reflected not only in a critically extolled compilation of 'fourth world' music by tastemaking Glasgow DJ duo Optimo or the first new album from Hassell in a decade, but also a wider stylistic register discernible amongst a whole ecology of reissue labels, of which RVNG, Music From Memory, and Light in the Attic, are the best known amongst an expanding market for reissues of the sort of restrained mood music in question here.[10] There's no doubt one could look still further back, to the posthumous releases and reissues of Arthur Russell's solo cello and voice compositions from around 2005 or even further, to David Axelrod's orchestral work, famously sampled to great effect by DJ Shadow on his now classic album *Endtroducing*, to find the origins of the sort of atmospheric music pervading middlebrow tastes today.[11]

In any event, at stake is an aesthetic premised upon the evacuation of any cutting notes and the layering of arrangements so that anything potentially jarring – a too assertive saxophone or a jangly guitar, for instance – is carefully modulated or removed altogether. There's a further tendency to delicate progression through textural changes that avoids sudden fluctuations in emotion, the repetition of chord progressions without any set key, sustained melodic lines, reiterated waves of sound and liberally employed reverb and echo.[12] Collectively, the effect is that of emotional ambivalence.[13] Indeed, to borrow a visual metaphor, this is music akin to the picturesque; devoid of discernible figures in the foreground. Where the hierarchy among sonic elements is undone, we're presented with the musical illusion of harmony one obtains from a distant gaze: tensions and social strife are lost to the blurring beauty of broad brushstrokes.

While the release of *Through the Looking Glass* marks a high point for contemporary atmospheric music, when looked at from the broader perspective of a global music industry, it's a comparatively trivial phenomenon. But it serves here to figure a wider shift in popular music, discerned by critics in recent years, and especially pronounced around 2017. Scores of journalists that year observed the artistic bankruptcy of overblown 'diva triumphalism' as well as the actual bankruptcy of what was an escalating electronic dance music arms race of brickwall limiting, ever-expanding nightclubs, VIP rooms, and pyrotechnics budgets.[14] This was the demise of what critic Simon Reynolds had called 'digital maximalism', a reference to what he'd diagnosed as the spasmodic intensity definitive of the previous decade or so of popular music, now displaced by a flatter, more hushed sound, its peaks and valleys ironed out.[15]

In an especially astute 2017 year-end review, critic Craig Jenkins discerned this newly 'downbeat affect' in a pervasive deployment of discrete genre elements.[16] Indie flourishes, especially horns and guitar licks, EDM synth staccato or stabs, trap snare rolls, Cali rap finger snaps and hand claps, and tropical house bass lines are all detected swapping across more than a dozen or so singles taken by Jenkins seemingly at random from that year's top 40. The point is not to condemn a current homogeneity, a defining feature of pop in any case, but to illustrate the music's dispassion, an affect of apathy discernible in the way hand claps appear in the same places or synths swell in a similar way. Where genre elements are used in a modular fashion like building blocks, the music seems smoother, more equivocal. Along similar lines, others have shown pop songs employ key changes far less than they ever did along with a growing dependence on hooks and builds.[17] All in all, if we define music as an intensified experience of time, then what seems to sell today is sound that neither takes its audience too high nor too low.[18]

Equivocation is also at stake where curation, as much as composition, is concerned. Indeed, it's an often-remarked characteristic of music streaming platforms that they're mobilised for the purpose of composure and self-possession. Spotify is littered with playlists called things like 'Happy Relaxing', 'Mellow Beats', or 'Decompression'. A YouTube playlist titled 'Lofi hip hop mix – Beats to Relax/Study to' currently has more than 13 million plays; another, 'Weekend Relaxation', is nearing 10 million. Not unlike the pop songs catalogued by Jenkins, here too genre boundaries become fluid. Rappers convene easily alongside indie bands, pop stars, or EDM producers, provided they fulfill their decisive function, of which 'chill' is an especially omnipresent descriptor. The platform user is invited to 'Chill Down' by one playlist, to 'Chillax' by another, or even have an

'Evening Chill'. For a number of years, Spotify's most popular playlist was called 'Chillwave'.

The Condition of Perfume

So why might popular music seem oriented to quietude? Critics have tended to invoke one periodisation or another where music's placid state is made to stand in for a wider set of responses to social and economic crisis. This has been articulated at a series of metaphoric equivalences operating at the level of the music industry itself, in terms of an overstretched dance music economy driving listeners to its opposite or more widely, in terms of the end of Obama-era optimism, rising youth unemployment, an opiate addiction crisis, or the exhaustion of a hurried, punishing neoliberal entrepreneurialism.[19] Music is assigned a primarily functional role here: a 'chill' aesthetic responds to financial crisis and its effects with a stylistic approach that soothes by amplifying an emotional vacancy serving as coping mechanism for the traumas associated with it.

It bears remarking that as a trope 'chill', along with its precursor 'cool', was first put to use by Black Americans striving for composure in the face of a society that sought to ravage them. To appear aloof and detached, as bell hooks has suggested, preserves dignity in the face of one's exclusion from full membership in 'humanity' along with the forms of violence and humiliation this entails.[20] Of course, as a set of aesthetic resources 'chill' has a long history of being put to use by the dominant culture. Beatniks, for instance, converted it from a mode of survival to encompass a wider, a bohemian expression of disinterest in the products of post-war mass society.[21] This situates 'chill' within a broader history of the wider circulation and ultimate commodification of Black survival strategies, whether the art of dissimulation known as 'hustling' or modes of performance and play associated with the abandoned inner city.[22] These are issues we will come to unpack in the following chapter.

But a more immediate history of 'chill' as a sonic trope begins with the name given to those rooms where dancers sought temporary respite from the combined intensity of music and drugs at raves in the late 1980s and early 1990s. By most accounts the VIP room at Paul Oakenfold's legendary Land of Oz parties at London's Heaven nightclub – The KLF's Jimmy Cauty, The Orb's Alex Patterson, along with Mixmaster Morris all had residencies at one time – is the first proper 'chillout' room. Free from the task of entertaining dancers, instead providing a backdrop to their repose, these DJs were free to experiment rather wildly. The result was an erratic mix of dub, minimalism, steel guitar, field recordings, early electronic, and synth music organised around protracted textural changes. It's as distracted and effortless as one might expect music explicitly existing to soothe the over-stimulated to be.

The so-called 'ambient house' genre invented at Heaven bestowed a template for the private, contemplative post-rave music fashionable throughout the 1990s and beyond. Aphex Twin's *Selected Ambient Works 1985–1992* (1992) and Autechre's *Incumabula* (1993) are high points, as are Warp's *Artificial Intelligence* compilations (1992–94).[23] Countless further iterations appeared on the Ninja Tune, Mo'Wax, and Warp labels in the years that followed, along with scores of more commercially oriented, often Ibiza-branded, chillout imitators. The latter implies an antagonism between ambient house experimentation and mercantile mediocrity and this is an argument that reverberates amongst the genre's most influential commentators. In Simon Reynolds's rockist view, 'chillout' amounted to the imposition of a restrained bourgeois disposition upon the wild proletarian abandon he'd discerned in the early rave scene.[24] Conversely, on David Toop's reading, it seems that it was only once freed from the function of serving dancers, that electronic music fashioned a space for meditative experimentalism.[25] Toop's outlook mostly echoes Brian Eno's accounting of 'ambient' in the liner notes to *Music for Airports*, widely considered the genre's founding text. There, Eno rejects the idea of ambient as background music, positing instead that it be 'able to accommodate many levels of listening attention,' and in doing so, he foregrounded the listener as agent rather than passive consumer.[26] In any case, the distinction between background and foreground music has little purchase in the current epoch where music has become 'ubiquitous'; where it is potentially everywhere it becomes divorced from either context or concerted attention.[27] Here, music itself takes on ambient qualities, it has 'the condition of perfume,' as Toop once wrote, or, as Eric Satie imagined when composing his 'Musique d'ameublement,' usually considered ambient composition *avant la lettre*, music becomes merely a piece of the furniture.[28]

In fact, an affinity to music's ever-present availability on Internet platforms is frequently cited in reference to the current prevalence of 'chill' tropes in pop. For instance, the playlist's withdrawal of emphasis from the album is said to increase the song's mood-enhancing function; a non-linear textuality of genres prevails.[29] But there's also a wider analogy to be gleaned here. For philosopher Robin James, music streaming offers a boundless 'stream of sound' that soothingly washes over the listener.[30] Journalist Liz Pelly is more emphatically dismissive, viewing the playlist as a mode of mood manipulation that turns music into 'emotional wallpaper'.[31] In this context it makes little sense to arbitrate between detractors such as Reynolds and devotees like Toop. At stake is not merely the music's aesthetic merit, but also the wider role it assumes in the listener's auditory ecology where 'music that aspires to the condition of perfume', to return to Toop's formulation, has become generalised.[32] That is, 'chill' is no longer restricted to the marginal spaces of nightclubs nor to easing ravers back into everyday life and so its assessment is not reducible to those terms.

Such an intensification of music's functionality is not limited to 'chilling' either. In fact, this is only one of seven 'key audio moments' among which Spotify categorises music for advertisers, and implicitly, for its audience, along with 'working', 'chores', 'gaming', 'workout', 'partying', and 'driving'.[33] Likewise, the identification of music with mood becomes even more intimate where users interface with 'smart speakers'; vocal interfaces abolish the activity of scrolling through collections altogether and so assimilate the playlist ever further.[34] 'Ambient' makes less sense as a genre category here, as it comes instead to describe the experience of music itself. Where the music streaming platform 'want[s] to soundtrack every moment of your life', as Spotify's founder has said, at issue is a style premised upon unobtrusive and smooth instrumentation, contextual flexibility, and the triumph of atmosphere and mood over narrative.[35] Here, music begins to take on the qualities usually ascribed more narrowly to ambient as genre, and this is evident whether we register the resurgence of once overlooked ambient artists, the transgression of genre boundaries at the level of the pop song, or as 'every song blends smoothly with the next', at the level of the streaming platform playlist.[36]

Mobile Privatisation

Given their associations with mood manipulation, music streaming platforms are frequently deemed a twenty-first century form of Muzak.[37] This is a reference to the Cleveland-based corporation active between the

1940s and 1990s in the production of music designed for use in commercial settings. By taming the rough edges of popular music, especially rock and RnB, reducing rhythmic shocks, and carefully moderating tempo, Muzak sought to generate a domestic atmosphere for consumers; a sort of sonic thermostat to generate warmth in alien spaces.[38] It was, in fact, initially intended for industrial contexts, as a means to capture and manage the wandering thoughts of workers – the company claimed to reduce absenteeism by over 80%. Early iterations were organised around the time of day in the form of a 15 minute 'Stimulus Progression Curve' indexed by tempo, genre, instrumentation, cycling from relaxation to moderate stimulation, and back again, as a means of moderating inertia and boredom.[39] As a sonic palette, neither too distracting nor too soporific, Muzak was widely imitated throughout the post-war era and this situates it as a distinctly Fordist incorporation of song into industry.[40]

But if music streaming can be said to effect an analogous 'harmonization of productive capacities with the living body', if it also is a form of work song, it does so on terms less uniform, more individualised, and thus reflective of a wider post-Fordist tendency to de-standardisation and personalisation.[41] Admittedly, this is a claim in need of qualification. In the first place, music has long played the role of what Tia DeNora calls 'emotional self-regulation'; a sort of sonic technology of the self (to echo DeNora's Foucaultian reference).[42] Different sonic grammars are mobilised to accentuate or embellish particular activities, whether workouts or cocktail parties. Moreover, programmed music had already come to be deployed across retail and service sector spaces by the 1970s, if not much earlier.[43] But never before has this sonic accompaniment been so mobile and so ubiquitous. Where Muzak functioned as a sonic embellishment of the specific spaces where it was deployed, once personal stereos became mobile, responsibility for managing the sonic environment could be delegated to the individual subject whose music could now potentially accompany them across time and space. The ubiquity of music at issue here gestures towards the blurring of labour and leisure itself taken as characteristic of a post-Fordist epoch.

This requires still further provisos: after all, the capacity to record music likewise entailed the ability to transport it.[44] But while the phonograph had freed music listening from its restriction to particular times and spaces, scholars usually identify an equally severe historical rupture with the emergence of the personal stereo, often framed by Raymond Williams's view of the automobile as a form of 'mobile privatisation'.[45] Where for Williams the car implies a mobile commodification of space, a 'secession' to the private *within* the public, so too mobile music is said to entail an analogous 'isolationist strategy' where the listener's chosen soundtrack eliminates an existing acoustic ecology.[46] In this vein, the scholar Michael Bull has discerned in the personal stereo a colonising impulse, one expressed in the desire for isolation from the polyrhythmic urban landscape and for control over the sonic environment through a continually regulated and micro-managed listening. Where the street becomes a function of sonically mediated mood, it comes to reflect an unparalleled dominance over, but also responsibility for, the management of daily life.

Yet if the personal stereo entails a new individualisation of the sonic environment and a new responsibility for mood management, the streaming platform involves the extension of that power, but also signals a more acute rupture. For while the portable cassette, CD, or MP3 player required the subject to carry or curate playlists of items they 'own', the online stream automates personalised curation and selection. Unlike preceding media forms premised upon inducing audiences to buy some album or another, this is a model that incites passivity in the user. Where the platform is concerned, the era's largest retailers of music – Spotify, Google, Amazon, Apple – are not so much the merchants of any particular catalogue as they are the peddlers of an 'experience'.[47] That is, they sell a mode of indexing and organising music whereby curation is automated through its correlations to social function. Where profit margins rest partly with the rollover of subscriptions and use and sale of user data, ambitions hinge around the production of uninterrupted consumption; a state of dependency among users generated through a recursive process of user surveillance and intervention. The point, in other words, is not to influence what users listen to, but to ensure they persist in listening.

In light of these contemporary transformations to music curation as a technology of the self, to return to DeNora's formulation, we should consider the terms by which a listening subject is mobilised by the streaming platform in more detail. Here, we can take into account the argument of musicologist Eric Drott, who identifies a decisive split internal to the agent of mood manipulation; one that lies between the reflexive power of the curator and the passivity of the listener. As Drott has it, 'music at once empowers and disempowers, in that the agency thus provided is one that *allows them to act upon themselves as objects*'; for where activity is mediated by music, this involves a necessary (auto)subjection of the listening self whose mood or action is to be transformed.[48] This, in turn, troubles accounts of music streaming which, following DeNora, insist on listener agency above all. That is, some scholars have suggested that analyses of music streaming tend to betray an unduly pessimistic view of user passivity that has not been substantiated by analyses of listener behaviour, and insist further empirical study of platform use is required.[49] But this appears a rather tenuous argument in view of Drott's claim. Where musical mediation of activity has been automated and, moreover, where individual taste is disaggregated into the multitude of data points deployed by the platform, user reflexivity necessarily remains a rather hazy and opaque proposition to begin with.

Indeed, we have no shortage of evidence for structural transformations wrought to song-form in the current epoch. Songs have generally grown shorter since 2013 (no doubt the result of a system which pays rights holders per listen), key changes are almost non-existent and the presentation of hooks and drops of heavy bass occur much sooner (certainly driven by the need for the song to play for 30 seconds in order to generate revenue).[50] To take these changes into account is to register the stream's abstraction of the song from its context and its ensuing re-inscription as metadata as a *formal condition* of music listening today, but we should also note that this does not exhaust its meaning or import. This is a point to which we'll return later in this chapter, for among the central convictions running throughout this book is the notion that cultural form might not be reducible to value, yet nor is it extricable from it either. But we should first attend further to the historical changes to listening effected by the streaming platform.

Against Ambience

The year 2013 was a significant milestone for the mass adoption of ambient computing, for this was the year in which over half the U.S. population came to own a smartphone.[51] This also happened to be the year that Spotify introduced its 'Browse' functionality, a feature that suggests playlists to users.[52] As an event, the launch of 'Browse' reflected a growing significance for playlists on streaming platform hierarchies. More widely, it was an important moment in the rising automation of music consumption. However, it bears noting a continuity here with radio and TV as vehicles of media, characterised as they are by an experience of 'flow', to borrow a term from Raymond Williams once more.[53] Williams was referring to the sequential nature of broadcasting: for while TV or radio might comprise temporally distinct units, whether programmes or songs, the audience experience is centred upon the activity itself, watching or listening, rather than its discrete events. This holds for streaming too, with the stipulation that the stream effects a movement away from music's embedded social meaning towards its identification with social function. Given that the stream explicitly presumes one is doing something besides listening – chilling, working out, and so on – the activity of listening itself recedes in significance; music disperses into the atmosphere, like perfume.

There are further valences of continuity and change in the commodification of music, all too often overlooked, that bear noting here. As we've already seen, audiences have long appropriated music to serve diverse social registers and activities. However, given its mobility and automation, music streaming reflects a colossal extension of the power to do so. Moreover, while the album persists as a mode of organising music for sale, it grows increasingly anachronistic, not unlike the lingering tendency to refer to mobile computers as phones.[54] It's worth mentioning that the tendency to mourn the streaming platform's displacement of the album by the playlist, as the mark of lost meaning, neglects the more or less recent invention of the album itself as a space for developing creative ideas and of music as an intimate and personal experience.[55] Indeed, the long player (LP) was introduced as a means of selling excess music to postwar audiences, only over time did it come to serve a wider aesthetic principle of the development of a set of musical ideas over sixty or seventy minutes.[56]

If we adopt a narrower view however, the contemporary decline in the cultural and economic significance of the album can be dated to the turn of the millennium, as peer-to-peer file sharing networks became a major source of music acquisition. Once music could circulate and be shared as individual song files, the album declined in importance as a format in which music was consumed.[57] While retailers and distributors faced heavy losses in this period, other sectors of capital, especially telecoms, profited immensely from the increasing demand for Internet bandwidth that downloading required. In other words, music came to be de-commodified both for consumers, increasingly likely to 'pirate' material, as well as for capital, for whom music's relevance as a direct source of value declined.[58] While a number of companies in this period, most notably Apple's iTunes, combined playback and retail functions as a means of continuing to secure retail profits, despite a short-lived boost to sales from audiences converting catalogues to digital formats, the unbundling of the album implied a decrease in physical sales revenues that has never recovered.[59]

So while the automated playlist emerged around 2013, that year was also widely viewed as marking the crash in catalogue sales, and in the year or two that followed, revenues from music streaming surpassed all others for major labels. The year 2013 might also be chill degree zero. It happened to be the release date of *I Am The Center*, the still definitive archive of independently released new age music; an album that might stand in here for a wider interest in electronic, non-linear, and distracted listening marked by an emergent interest in new age, ambient, and vintage electronic composition. After all, this was the year that Oneohtrix Point Never released *R Plus Seven*, a mesmerising inventory of post-digital tonalities.[60] *Pitchfork* characterised the album, in a reference to Jon Hassell, 'fifth world', noting that where Hassell intersects the primitive and the electronic, Oneohtrix Point Never's Daniel Lopatin supplemented these with the sort of granular manipulation associated with the Internet era.[61] The Haxan Cloak's *Excavation*, perhaps best described as 'doom ambient', also came out that year.[62] So did Laurel Halo's *Chance of Rain*, an album characterised by its 'industrial rhythms and corrosive synth textures.'[63] And along with artists Tim Hecker, Fuck Buttons, Stellar Om Source, and James Holden, all peppering 2013 best of the year lists, these stand in for a wider interest in fragmented and viscous electronic music often anchored in the sonics associated with vintage synthesisers definitive of the 'underground' music of the period.

More widely, 2013 was also the year cited by theorist Seth Kim-Cohen in *Against Ambience* as marking the rise of the contemporary prominence of 'immersive' and, in his view, asinine, sound, and light art installations. For Kim-Cohen, these reflected a wider desire for a pre-cognitive, affective immersion into artworks as a means of responding to, but also escaping, the information overload of contemporary society. On this account, immersive or ambient art lacking in unambiguous content or human investment offered the sort of emotional blankness demanded by an over-stimulated society.[64]

Broader still, 2013 can be considered the high point of a range of speculative ontologies seeking to displace the human subject altogether. Jane Bennett published *Vibrant Matter* in 2010, while a collection on *New Materialisms* and another on the *Speculative Turn* appeared in the years that followed; and further widely cited books by Rosi Braidotti, William Connolly, and Timothy Morton were published in 2013.[65] The ideas they advocated became widespread across the humanities and social sciences in the years that followed. Despite important differences among them, these theorists all share a conviction in the priority of affective sensation over cognitive reflection as a means of affirming the power of all material objects to act while decentring the prominence of the human agent from its theoretical frameworks. In fact, the ontological primacy of the human is taken to signal an epistemic violence wrought by an anthropocentric worldview. An all too human-centred perspective, the claim goes, not only overlooks the increasing imbrications of the human and the technological in the current epoch, it is also an echo of the hubristic disposition in relation to the natural world that underlies ecological destruction.

While these theories posit 'new materialist', 'speculative realist', or 'posthuman' ontologies anchored in an ethos of 'humility', or sense of 'entanglement' in relation to the non-human world, at best, such ontological formulations merely reflect the conditions of Web 2.0 value production where, on the basis of data gleaned from user surveillance, sentiment analysis, or neuromarketing, online platforms seek to influence behaviour at a pre-conscious, affective level.[66] That is, the affective, pre-rational realm, valorised by both the social theorist and Internet platforms seeking to influence consumer behaviour alike, serves the former's deflection of their own imbrications in new forms of capitalist control. Moreover, where the desire for explanation is displaced by deliberation upon affect and mood, critique is relegated to the status of anthropocentric narcissism.[67]

Ambient Computing

At issue here is an era of ambient music, ambient aesthetics, and ambient theorising. It also happens to be an era characterised by ambient computing. This refers to the current demand for 'real time' transmission of copyrighted content, and the wider turn from 'desktop' to 'cloud' they reflect, as modes of conceiving the storage of digital material. Premised upon easy access to powerful, highly portable devices, it's noteworthy that migration to cloud computing was explicitly motivated by a desire to transform consumer behaviour; an expediency driven by the vulnerability of single file download models such as iTunes to piracy, and the limited profits gleaned from the conversion of catalogues to digital formats.[68] It turned out that music rental, restricting access to an online interface and, thus, absorbing it by legal requirements, was far more profitable than music collection.[69] In other words, rather than persist in the losing battle against the file sharer's piracy of music, sectors of the media industry instead transferred music sharing back into spaces in which they could extract value. In this context, Spotify's dominance of the music streaming sector can be put down to having quickly adapted to the industry's new strategy; a detail underscored by the fact that Daniel Ek, the company's co-founder, had previously been the CEO of torrenting software company μTorrent and thus, long a student of piracy.[70] Major label buy-in was quickly signaled by an agreement to trade equity in the company for the right to access catalogues. In this respect, we should understand streaming as a response to the music industry's declining profits and, as an aside, it's worth noting that the expansion of digital communications itself arose in support of the spatial reorganisation of capitalism on a global scale as it sought bulwarks against declining profitability in the 1970s and 1980s.[71]

Spotify is often condemned for its destructive effects on the music industry, but taking such a view hinges upon one's understanding of what exactly this industry entails and whether it deserves saving. While heavy losses have been incurred by many artists, distributors, and retailers, as a result, the emergence of music streaming has also generated a range of new sources of income.[72] This is especially so given the way in which the turn to cloud computing has 'lifestyled' music, extending consumption to an ever greater array of moments of existence, and in doing so, has entailed a substantial increase in average annual consumer spend.[73] In addition, the guaranteed income from subscriptions to streaming services, the use and sale of user data, advertising, and the sale of devices and concordant increases in e-commerce traffic has come to far outstrip those ever gleaned from album sales.[74] Moreover, music streaming platforms operate upon a market share system of royalty payments based upon revenues; such a model merely reflects a 'consumption-based' model upon which record companies have long operated.[75] This is a logic whereby a miniscule fraction of releases are expected to generate meaningful profits and for which music itself is only ever truly relevant where it's viewed through the frame of the bottom line. So, to return to an earlier point, where Spotify's critics have derided the nefarious effects the company has had on music, one is led to wonder just what elements of that industry they're proposing to save: the deferral to market laws for music distribution and income, the arbitrary hierarchies between performer, studio engineer, studio cleaner, coltan miner, and audience, or simply the commodification of recorded music upon which these are premised?

This is not to say that streaming hasn't transformed the music industry, it's just that grasping these transformations entails abjuring moral attachments to commercial forms and instead looking to where profits are generated and how they accrue. For one thing, while income from music has been steadily rising in recent years, largely due to streaming, it's nonetheless proportionately low for the huge conglomerates that control major labels and for whom money generated from other businesses – device or bandwidth sales for instance – are far more important.

In any case, the sale of recorded music has always operated in terms of what critical theorists call a 'real abstraction'; this refers to the way commodity exchange practically abstracts from the qualitative properties of the object: in our minds we think of the practical, sensual object – in this case music – while in practice the action – access to music – is premised upon the exchange of money.[76] In other words, the relation to music in the era of its mechanical reproduction has always been premised upon an idealisation, one which neglects the reality of the market as its condition. But this changes where the streaming service does not sell any particular piece of recorded music as a commodity, as a traditional label or retailer might, but instead flogs an 'experience'.[77] On offer is access to recorded music itself, in exchange for user data, ad viewing, and possibly a subscription fee. This further implies that where record labels and distributors had an interest in selling albums to which they held the rights, and their profits depended on audiences continually buying new music, the platform has no interest in the consumption of any particular record, only that the consumer continues to listen. That is, music consumption becomes a mode of mediating the activity of attracting, defining, and micro-targeting audiences.

A different form of abstraction occurs where the song is reduced to its quantitative characteristics in the form of the metadata that is its organising device. For here it is subsumed by computation – abstracted from its sensual qualities – in order to extend the production of value into ever wider domains.[78] The quantification of listening, in other words, entails the enclosure of the sociality of music itself.

As scholars of digital capitalism have long argued, the production of data in the course of time spent on Internet interfaces, insofar as it's a major source of value, might be considered a form of unpaid labour, even if this isn't strictly accurate.[79] It's not actually the audience who produces value, but rather the designers of algorithms or the assemblers of the listening device, among others.[80] It's nonetheless a useful image where endless decisions of taste, preference, not to mention content construction, are outsourced to users themselves. Where the user deploys mood-based playlists to accommodate and enhance particular activities (such as chilling, studying, chores, and so on), mood, or, more exactly, particular patterns of behaviour associated with it, are deployed by the platform for the production of future recommendations.[81] Music acts as a means of surveilling and modulating user cognition and, equally, works to keep the user within proprietary space so value production can continue uninterrupted. Where older distributional models had an interest in selling as much music as possible, the platform's imperative is to incite users to continue to listen, and thus 'labour', since its profits are premised upon the rollover of subscriptions, the maximal production of user data to be sold or used to forecast, predict, and intervene in consumer behaviour.

Where music content providers act like 'data brockerage houses' then, this implies a further perspective on music's social function today, beyond its associations with mood or social activities.[82] Music 'able to accommodate many levels of listening attention', to return to Eno's formulation for ambient music, suits an era where music is deployed with the objective of continual production of listener data with minimal friction.[83] Whether we consider the layered textures of ambient as a genre, the modular de- and re-constructions of the pop song, or the flattened effect of the post-genre playlist, along with the emotional blankness these entail, collectively they reflect the stream's abstraction of the song from its context and its ensuing re-inscription as metadata. Ambient music for ambient computing, one might say, for where music is deployed as a means of organising data production, its functionality rests with its ubiquity, its becoming a part of the furniture.

Database Experience

Music that functions to support data production has its visual referent in the platform interface. Where the platform defuses tensions among elements and textures at the level of the song or playlist, the interface ensures a frictionless continuity across spaces and devices. But it also operates at the intersection of a whole series of imaginary relations.[84] For one thing, even if curation is delegated to data mining algorithms or corporate sponsored playlists, in framing the user as an active agent of discovery, it gives the illusion of control. In one marketing campaign, Spotify depicted its personalised 'Discover Weekly' playlist as 'like having your best friend make you a personalized mixtape every week'.[85] This seems at the very least to imply a dubious definition of friendship – one study of Spotify established an exaggerated ability to recommend music by its playlists.[86] In any event, the explorer subject fantasised here projects an equally imagined relation to hardware; the iconography of 'folder', 'desktop', and 'library' divorces the visual from the mechanic, and serves a broader mystification of all its forms of labour: from mining and assembly, to coding and installation.[87]

But if the interface thrusts an increasingly obsolete pre-digital world onto the screen, we can also discern a projection of the ontology of the computer back onto the music. This is what Lev Manovich, in an influential study of post-digital cultural form, has called the 'database'; a reference to the representation of the world as a list of items.[88] Where chronology and context are evacuated, narrative is displaced by the searching and selection of information. It might be apparent that these happen also to be qualities of both the ambient song and the playlist: the priority of texture over narrative, the modular redistribution of genre and subgenre elements. Mediated by the platform, music comes to be framed by newly derived principles of organisation and indexing. In this way, the abstraction of music, mediated by the playlist, comes to rebound back onto cultural form.

Thus parcellised, the song is left to float freely, quasi-autonomous from its context. David Clarke has called this the playlist's 'double semantic action'; where the song or its elements are atomised as discrete units, they're given new meaning through the statistical or functional logic by which they're assembled.[89] A 'chill' playlist on Spotify or YouTube, for instance, is likely to mingle American hip-hop artists, early British folk singers, Swedish dance music producers, and blues guitar legends. These sorts of consolidations of divergent subject positions constitute, as Clarke asserts, an ideological act: the playlist creates an imaginary unity, governed only by the abstract principle of general equivalence of its own making that unites the individual songs, in most cases under the umbrella of a particular mood. Music becomes homologous with capitalism where every song is potentially exchangeable with every other on the basis of its metadata.

While Clarke helps us theorise the playlist as a mode of ideological interpellation, a means of making the subject complicit with the false unity it inhabits, his account is still too oriented around radio's consolidation of classes and cultures. There are further coordinates at issue where the platform is concerned. For instance, the platform is premised upon a distracted mode of perception, and it follows that where listening need not be conscious, music may bypass perception to act directly upon the body. Such is the claim made by Lawrence Kramer, though he was writing of a sonic registration of bodily docility in the context of 'soothing' music played over public address systems.[90] Yet if we extend the terms of his analysis to music streaming, then we can construe the terms of a wider argument: chill isn't about escape or respite. Instead, it reflects the broad features taken by music where consumption and production become interminable and where the ultimate point is to tether the body to the machine. Here, the social function of the song as an index of mood does not amount to the projection of a particular social position exactly; instead, this is an ideological interpellation acting on slightly different terms. That is, it seeks to integrate the subject into seriality itself, to fuse the self with digitally mediated activity.[91]

This implies that the song does not only serve mechanisms designed to extract user data and therefore its quantification and attendant colonisation by the digital; it also involves a new and changing experience of time. If the radio, by marking the timetable of household chores and so on, making them advertising opportunities, had already redefined the domestic as an aural space, by comparison, the playlist enters the song into a real time churn of content removed from any historicity and adjustable to any given daily task. This is an experience where literally everything is marked temporally – the ever-receding chronology of Twitter or Facebook (emblematised in those ubiquitous notices: 'posted 5 minutes ago') is indicative here.[92] Once migrated to the proprietary enclosure of the platform, the song or media object metamorphoses into a temporal unfolding, of code, stream, or data, its existence mediated by a real time flow modulated by the activity of users. This further entails the loss of futurity: the ceaseless intervention into statistical patterns marks an endlessly modified and narrow temporal horizon.[93] If music is a specific experience of time, then in the era of the platform, it's one premised upon what Jonathan Beller has called the 'splicing of machines and brains into the same circuit.'[94]

Force of Memory

In the previous chapter we established a disagreement between Theodor Adorno and Amiri Baraka over the persistence of music outside the forces of capital; an argument about the endurance of an 'extra-territorial' identity, to use Adorno's phrase, and it's worth returning to this here in light of the platform's extension of logics of commodification ever further into musical activity.[95] To frame the problem in terms of 'territoriality', however, is to pose the question in terms that are perhaps too topographical, exceedingly spatially determined, such that a vision of capitalism's colonisation of life that is all too linear and clear-cut persists. This is, we have seen, to posit a uniformity of experience insufficiently attendant to the ongoing unevenness of capitalist development and which compels us to a futile pursuit for absolute exteriority in a world where nothing is not already potentially economic value, or worse, sinks us into the melancholia of permanent defeat. But we have also seen that there are other theoretical strategies we should take into account – we looked to the Black Radical Tradition, above all – if we're to attend to the refusal which even the most intensely commodified musics continue to bear. These arguments revolve around, we have seen, Blackness as a 'critical, disjunctive living', at once irreducible to the modern world yet situated at its very core.[96]

But there are other prospects to be gleaned from Adorno's work too, and these can be especially significant for the epoch of the streaming platform. Writing in 1934 on the then emergent use of recorded background music in bars and cafes, Adorno registers the perverse irony that the more pervasive music becomes, the less it is heard. As background or mere accompaniment, music is exiled and in such a state, 'the melodies wander around as ghosts.'[97] His point was that, reduced almost wholly to social function, no longer heard, a mere part of the furniture, songs are released from their administration as goods for the culture industries or the self-consciousness of art. But it's here also that we glean a sense of the song's power, when we sense the emptiness prompted by its absence. Put to use, music stands, albeit in desecrated form, as a kind of undead immediacy; it summons a time beyond its alienation from everyday social life and against its segregation to isolated spaces and times of day. That is, it goes beyond the loss of the song as a collective object, beyond its becoming the property of a sovereign artist or a commodity broadcast back to us. In this, the song continues to stand in for a world not determined by necessity. Ignored, no longer listened to, songs stand for what might have been and may still be.

This is to deem music as the bearer of a ghostly experience of lost immediacy, and it's in contemplating in these temporal terms rather than only the spatial completion of capitalism's expansion that we might be better placed to attend to the claim that cultural form might not be reducible to value nor extricable from it either. This is also an argument we can discern, albeit posed in a different register, in an essay of Baraka's. 'If you play James Brown (say, "Money Won't Change you… but time will take you out") in a bank', Baraka says, 'the total environment is changed.'[98] Like Adorno, then, Baraka is not in search of a site wholly external to capital, but rather a liminal experience that the music delivers from within. Except for Baraka, the 'force of memory' by which the musical impulse persists, even in the most alienating sites, is not interred deep in the primal depths of the psyche as it is for Adorno, but in the trace of Black diasporic experience.[99] It's given its socially liminal position, in other words, that Black music's expressive force endures, repels its dilution, and appropriation; 'conditioned and unconditioned', as Nathaniel Mackey puts it, by the dominant culture in whose territories it struggles.[100] But this begs the question of how we can detect the operations of this impulse today. Or, put otherwise, what would it sound like if we played James Brown in a bank? This is a question from which the next chapter departs.

Notes

1. Andy Beta, 'How a Digital Rabbit Hole Gave Midori Takada's 1983 Album a Second Life', *The New York Times*, 24 May 2018, www.nytimes.com/2018/05/21/arts/music/midori-takada-through-the-looking-glass.html [accessed 22 January 2019]; Midori Takada, *Through the Looking Glass*. RCA Red Seal, 1983.
2. Beta, 'How a Digital Rabbit Hole Gave Midori Takada's 1983 Album a Second Life'.
3. Geeta Dayal, 'Ambient Pioneer Midori Takada: "Everything on Earth Has a Sound"', *The Guardian*, 24 March 2017, www.theguardian.com/music/2017/mar/24/midori-takada-interview-through-the-looking-glass-reissue [accessed 27 October 2023].
4. Lewis Gordon, 'Another Green World: How Japanese Ambient Music Found a New Audience', *Factmag*, 14 January 2017, www.factmag.com/2018/01/14/japanese-ambient-hiroshi-yoshimora-midori-takada/ [accessed 22 January 2019]; 'Listen to 10 Recently Uncovered Japanese Ambient Masterpieces', Electronic Beats, 31 May 2017, www.electronicbeats.net/the-feed/listen-to-a-10-record-primer-of-japanese-minimal-master pieces/ [accessed 22 January 2019]; Jack Needham, 'How Japan's Landscape Inspired a New Kind of Electronic Music', Bandcamp Daily, 23 June 2017, https://daily.bandcamp.com/2017/06/23/japanese-landscape-inspired-electronic/ [accessed 22 January 2019].
5. Horishi Yoshimura, *Green*. Sona Gaia Productions, 1986; *Music for Nine Postcards*. Sound Process, 1982; Satoshi Ashikawa, *Still Way*. Sound Process, 1982.
6. Gordon, 'Another Green World'.
7. Brian Eno, *Ambient 1: Music for Airports*. Polydor, 1981.
8. *I Am the Center: Private Issue New Age Music in America 1950–1990*. Light in the Attic, 2013.
9. Jon Hassell & Brian Eno, *Fourth World: Possible Musics*. Polydor, 1980; Jon Hassell, *Dream Theory in Malaya*. Editions EG, 1981.
10. Andy Beta, 'Fourth World in the 21st Century', *Resident Advisor*, 12 June 2017, www.residentadvisor.net/features/2984 [accessed 19 January 2019].
11. DJ Shadow, *Entroducing*, Mo Wax, 1996.
12. These are all, incidentally, qualities that Joseph Lanza associates with 'elevator music' in *Elevator Music: A Surreal History of Muzak, Easy Listening and Other Moodsong*. Ann Arbor: University of Michigan Press, 2004.
13. Some critics argue that in its most accomplished iterations ambient music retains a sense of uncertainty generated by very careful and localised sonic inconsistencies. See Victor Szabo, 'Unsettling Brian Eno's *Music for Airports*', *Twentieth-Century Music* 14, no.2, 2017, pp.305–33.

14 Carl Wilson, '2017 Saw Empowering Pop Replaced By Mumbling Men', Slate.com, 25 December 2017, https://slate.com/culture/2017/12/2017-saw-empowering-pop-replaced-by-mumbling-men.html?via=gdpr-consent [accessed 22 January 2019]; Robin James, 'Toned Down for What? How "Chill" Turned Toxic', *The Guardian*, 2 July 2018, www.theguardian.com/music/2018/jul/02/toned-down-for-what-how-chill-turned-toxic [accessed 22 January 2019]; Chris Richards, 'Soft, Smooth and Steady: How Xanax Turned American Music Pill-Pop', *The Washington Post*, 20 April 2017, www.washingtonpost.com/lifestyle/style/soft-smooth-and-steady-how-xanax-turned-american-music-into-pill-pop/2017/04/19/535a44de-1955-11e7-bcc2-7d1a0973e7b2_story.html?noredirect=on&utm_term=.2750ab1c27fb [accessed 22 January 2019].

15 Simon Reynolds, 'Maximal Nation', *Pitchfork*, 6 December 2011, https://pitchfork.com/features/article/8721-maximal-nation/ [accessed 19 January 2019].

16 Craig Jenkins, 'The Sound of Modern Pop Peaked This Year – and Now It Needs To Change', Vulture, 11 December 2017, www.vulture.com/2017/12/defining-the-decade-in-pop-music.html [accessed 19 January 2019].

17 Chris Dalla Riva, 'The Death of the Key Change', Tedium, 9 November 2022, https://tedium.co/2022/11/09/the-death-of-the-key-change/ [accessed 29 October 2023].

18 This definition of music is Phillip Tagg's, see 'Understanding Musical Time Sense: Concepts, Sketches, Consequences', 1997, http://tagg.org/articles/xpdfs/timesens.pdf [accessed 27 April 2019].

19 James, 'Toned Down for What?'; Richards, 'Soft, Smooth and Steady'.

20 bell hooks, *We Real Cool: Black Men and Masculinity*. New York & London: Routledge, 2004.

21 Joel Dinerstein, *The Origins of Cool in Postwar America*. Chicago: University of Chicago Press, 2017.

22 Robin D.G. Kelley, *Yo Mama's Disfunktional: Fighting the Culture Wars in Urban America*. Boston: Beacon Press, 1998.

23 Aphex Twin *Selected Ambient Works 1985–1992*, Apollo, 1992; Autechre, *Incunabula*, Warp Records, 1993; *Artificial Intelligence*, Warp Records, 1992.

24 Simon Reynolds, *Energy Flash: A Journey Through Rave Music and Dance Culture*. London: Picador, 1998.

25 David Toop, *Ocean of Sound: Ambient Sound and Radical Listening In the Age of Communication*. London: Serpent's Tail, 2018, p.54.

26 Eno, *Music for Airports*; Toop, *Ocean of Sound*, p.21.

27 Kassabian, *Ubiquitous Listening*.

28 Toop, *Ocean of Sound*, p.21.

29 Wilson, '2017 Saw Empowering Pop Replaced By Mumbling Men'.

30 James, 'Toned Down for What?'

31 Liz Pelly, 'The Problem With Muzak', The Baffler, December 2017, https://thebaffler.com/salvos/the-problem-with-muzak-pelly [accessed 19 January 2019].

32 Toop, *Ocean of Sound*, p.21.

33 Spotify for Brands, *Understanding People Through Music: Millenium Edition*, https://spotifyforbrands.com/en-GB/insights/millennial-guide [accessed 26 April 2019].

34 Eric Harvey, 'How Smart Speakers Are Changing the Way We Listen To Music', Pitchfork, 29 June 2018, https://pitchfork.com/features/article/how-smart-speakers-are-changing-the-way-we-listen-to-music/ [accessed 26 January 2019].

35 David Pearce, 'The Secret Hit-Making Power of the Spotify Playlist', Wired, 5 March 2017, www.wired.com/2017/05/secret-hit-making-power-spotify-playlist/ [accessed 23 January 2019] cited in Mike Glennon, 'Mixtapes v. Playlists: Medium, Message, Materiality', Sound Out!, 25 June 2018. https://soundstudiesblog.com/2018/06/25/mixtapes-v-playlists-medium-message-materiality/ [accessed 26 January 2019]. See also Spotify for Brands, *Understanding People Through Music*.
36 Aisha Hassan & Dan Kopf, 'The Reason Why Your Favorite Pop Songs are Getting Shorter', QZ, 27 October 2018. https://qz.com/quartzy/1438412/the-reason-why-your-favorite-pop-songs-are-getting-shorter [accessed 29 October 2023].
37 Pelly, 'The Problem With Muzak', Paul Allen Anderson, 'Neo-Muzak and the Business of Mood', *Critical Inquiry* 41, no.4, 2015, 811–40.
38 Anderson, 'Neo-Muzak and the Business of Mood'.
39 Ibid.; Lanza, *Elevator Music*.
40 Nick Groom, 'The Condition of Muzak', *Popular Music and Society* 20, no.3, 1996, 1–17.
41 Groom, 'The Condition of Muzak'; Simon C. Jones & Thomas G. Schumacher, 'Muzak: On Functional Music and Power', *Cultural Studies in Mass Communication* 9, 1992, 156–69.
42 Tia DeNora, *Music and Everyday Life*. Cambridge: Cambridge University Press, 2003.
43 Jones & Schumacher, 'Muzak: On Functional Music and Power'.
44 Mark Katz, *Capturing Sound: How Technology Has Changed Music, Revised Edition*. Berkeley: University of California Press, 2010.
45 Raymond Williams, *Television: Technology and Cultural Form*. London: Routledge, 2003, p.26; Michael Bull, *Sound Moves: Ipod Culture and Urban Experience*. London: Routledge, 2007; David Hesmondhalgh & Leslie M. Meier, 'What the Digitalisation of Music Tells Us About Capitalism, Culture and the Power of the Information Technology Sector', *Information, Communication & Society* 21, no.11, 2018, pp.1555–70.
46 Bull, *Sound Moves*.
47 Rasmus Fleischer, 'If the Song Has No Price, is it Still a Commodity? Rethinking the Commodification of Digital Music', *Culture Unbound* 9, no.2, pp.146–62.
48 Quoted from Eric Drott, 'Music in the Work of Social Reproduction', *Cultural Politics* 15, no.2, 2019, pp.162–83 [emphasis added]. See also, Eric Drott, 'Music as a Technology of Surveillance', *Journal for the Society of American Music* 12, no.3, 2018, pp.233–67. I'm grateful to an anonymous reviewer for pointing me to this argument.
49 For instance, see George Burdon, 'Immunological Atmospheres: Ambient Music and the Design of Self-Experience', *Cultural Geographies* 30, no.4, April 2023; David Hesmondhalgh, 'Streaming's Effects On Music Culture: Old Anxieties and New Simplifications', *Cultural Sociology* 16, no.1, 2022, pp.3–24.
50 Hassan & Kopf, 'The Reason Why Your Favorite Pop Songs are Getting Shorter'; Martin Scherzinger, 'The Political Economy of Streaming', in: Nicholas Cook, Monique M. Ingalls, & David Trippett (Eds.) *Music in Digital Culture*. Cambridge: Cambridge University Press, 2019, pp.282–3.
51 Dan Schiller, *Digital Depression: Information Technology and Economic Crisis*. Chicago: University of Illinois Press, 2014, p.107.
52 Sofia Johansson, Ann Werner, Patrik Åker, & Greg Goldenzwaig, *Streaming Music: Practices, Media, Cultures*. London: Routledge, 2018.
53 Williams, *Television*.
54 Johansson, Werner, Åker, & Goldenzwaig, *Streaming Music*.

55 Katz, *Capturing Sound*.
56 Ibid.
57 David Arditi, 'Digital Subscriptions: The Unending Consumption of Music in the Digital Era', *Popular Music and Society* 21, no.3, 2018, pp.302–18; Fleischer, 'If the Song Has No Price, is it Still a Commodity?'.
58 Fleischer, 'If the Song Has No Price, is it Still a Commodity?'.
59 Hesmondhalgh & Meier, 'What the Digitalisation of Music Tells Us About Capitalism, Culture and the Power of the Information Technology Sector'; David Arditi, 'iTunes: Breaking Barriers and Building Walls', *Popular Music and Society* 37, no.4, 2014, pp.408–24.
60 Oneohtrix Point Never, *R Plus Seven*. Warp Records, 2013.
61 Mark Richardson, 'Oneohtrix Point Never, R Plus Seven', *Pitchfork*, 4 October 2013. https://pitchfork.com/reviews/albums/18537-oneohtrix-point-never-r-plus-seven/ [accessed 19 January 2019].
62 The Haxan Cloak, *Excavation*. Tri Angle, 2013.
63 Andrew Gaerig, 'Laurel Halo, Chance of Rain', *Pitchfork*, 20 October 2013, https://pitchfork.com/reviews/albums/18678-laurel-halo-chance-of-rain/ [accessed 19 January 2019]. Laurel Halo, *Chance of Rain*. Hyperdub, 2013.
64 Seth Kim-Cohen, *Against Ambience*. London: Bloomsbury, 2013.
65 Rosi Braidotti, *The Posthuman*. Cambridge: Polity Press, 2013; William Connolly, *The Fragility of Things: Self-Organizing Processes, Neoliberal Fantasies, and Democratic Activism*. Durham & London: Duke University Press, 2013; Timothy Morton, *Realist Magic: Objects, Ontology, Causality*. London: Open Humanities Press, 2013.
66 Mark Andrejevic, 'The Droning of Experience', *The Fibreculture Journal* 25, 2015.
67 Rekret, 'The Head, the Hand and Matter'.
68 Sean Dockray, 'Interface, Access, Loss', in: Marysia Lwandowska & Lauren Ptak (Eds.) *Undoing Property*. Berlin: Sternberg Press, 2013, pp.183–94; Arditi, 'Digital Subscriptions'.
69 Patrick Vonderau, 'The Spotify Effect: Digital Distribution and Financial Growth', *Television & New Media* 20, no. 4, 2017.
70 Patrick Burkhardt, 'Music in the Cloud and the Digital Sublime', *Popular Music and Society* 31, no.4, 2014, pp.393–407.
71 Schiller, *Digital Depression*.
72 Lee Marshall, ' "Let's Keep Music Special. F--- Spotify": On Demand Streaming and the Controversy Over Artist Royalties', *Creative Industries Journal* 8, no.2, 2015, pp.177–89.
73 David Arditi, 'Music Everywhere: Setting a Digital Trap', *Critical Sociology*, 31 August 2017; Vonderau, 'The Spotify Effect'.
74 Marshall, 'Let's Keep Music Special'; Arditi, 'Music Everywhere'; Burkhardt, 'Music in the Cloud and the Digital Sublime'.
75 Marshall, 'Let's Keep Music Special'.
76 The classic articulation of 'real abstraction' is in Sohn-Rethel, *Intellectual and Manual Labour*.
77 Fleischer, 'If the Song Has No Price, is it Still a Commodity?'.
78 I draw here on Jonathan Beller, *The Message is Murder: Substrates of Computational Capital*. London: Pluto Press, 2017.
79 Tiziana Terranova, *Network Culture: Politics for the Information Age*. London: Pluto Press, 2004; Christian Fuchs & Eran Fisher, *Reconsidering Value and Labor in the Digital Age*. London: Palgrave, 2015.

80 Brett Caraway, 'Crisis of Command: Theorizing Value in New Media', *Communication Theory* 26, no.1, 2016, pp.64–81; Dave Beech, *Art and Post-Capitalism: Aesthetic Labour, Automation and Value Production*. London: Pluto Press, 2019, pp.93–103.
81 Andrejevic, 'The Droning of Experience'.
82 Quoted in Vonderau, 'The Spotify Effect'.
83 Eno, Brian, 'Ambient Music'. Liner notes for *Ambient 1: Music for Airports*. LP. Editions E. G., 1978.
84 I draw here on Alexander Galloway, *The Interface Effect*. Cambridge: Polity Press, 2012, p.69.
85 Pearce, 'The Secret Hit-Making Power of the Spotify Playlist'.
86 Pelle Snickers, 'More of the Same: On Spotify Radio', *Culture Unbound* 9, no.2, 2017, pp.184–211.
87 Nick Dyer-Witherford, *Cyber-Proletariat*. London: Pluto Press, 2015; Pasko Billic, 'A Critique of the Political Economy of Algorithms: A Brief history of Google's Technological Rationality', *TripleC* 16, no.1, 2018.
88 Lev Manovich, *The Language of New Media*. Cambridge: MIT Press, 2001, p.223. A point also suggested by Johansson, Werner, Åker, & Goldenzwaig, *Streaming Music*.
89 David Clarke, 'Beyond the Global Imaginary: Decoding BBC Radio 3's Late Junction', *Radical Musicology* 2, 2007.
90 Lawrence Kramer, 'Caliban's Ear: A Short History of Ambient Music', in: Marta Garcia Quinoes, Anahid Kassabian, & Elena Boschi (Eds.) *Ubiquitous Musics: The Everyday Sounds That We Don't Always Notice*. London: Routledge 2013, pp.15–30.
91 On this point see Eric Drott, 'Why the Next Song Matters: Streaming, Recommendation, Scarcity', *Twentieth-Century Music* 15, no.3, 2018, pp.325–57.
92 Crary, *24/7*.
93 Jodi Dean, 'Communicative Capitalism: Circulation and the Foreclosure of Politics', *Cultural Politics* 1, no.1, 2005, pp.51–74.
94 Beller, *The Message is Murder*, p.84.
95 Adorno, *Philosophy of New Music*, p.176, n.4.
96 Okiji, *Jazz as Critique*, p.53.
97 Theodor Adorno, 'Music in the Background', in: *Essays on Music* (Richard Leppert, Ed.). Berkeley & Los Angeles: University of California Press, 2002, pp.506–12, p.509.
98 Leroi Jones (Amiri Baraka), 'The Changing Same (R&B and New Black Music)', *Black Music*. New York: Da Capo 1998, p.186.
99 Baraka, *Blues People*, p.209.
100 Nathaniel Mackey, 'The Changing Same: Black Music in the Poetry of Amiri Baraka', *Boundary 2* 6, no.2, 1978, pp.355–86, quoted on p.381.

3

This is More Than Rap: Labour, Leisure, and Trap

Finally Rich

The logics of the popular are resistant to prophecy. This much is evinced by even a cursory survey of reviews of two debut hip-hop albums, both by Atlanta artists and both released in 2005: Young Jeezy's *Let's Get It: Thug Motivation 101* and Gucci Mane's *Trap House*.[1] Mostly lukewarm, their reception is best characterised by a mild indifference. Whilst the odd critic noted an occasional witty repartee or catchy hook, the consensus was of stale braggadocio, monotony, and undemanding lyrics.[2] But it would be unfair to expect even the most astute listener to foresee just how seismic and abiding the stylistic innovations that these two albums channelled would come to be. For they signalled, it is claimed here, hip-hop's metamorphosis into 'trap'; a signifier for a whole series of formal transformations that can be more or less itemised: the displacement of quotation of soul, funk, and jazz grooves by the synthetic timbres of Roland TR-808 booming kick drums and basslines, the metallic snap of quick decay snare drums and rolling double time hi-hats, ambient synth drones and melodies that evoke horror films, delayed and pitched multi-tracked vocals whose flat delivery and low registers often arrive in halting triplet figures.[3] All in all, to revisit an earlier query, this might be what it sounds like if one plays James Brown in a bank.

Still, to identify these, by now pervasive registers with *Let's Get It* and *Trap House*, involves venturing a periodising claim and, of course, this will always entail something of a wager. This is a gesture made all the more perilous since the elements typically taken to characterise trap might be dissembled along any number of threads discernible prior to 2005. For instance, 808 beats, droning synths, and even triplet rhyme flows are all audible in the mixtapes and albums released locally in the early 1990s by trailblazing Memphis group Three 6 Mafia.[4] We might go back further still, to trace a taste for quicker beats and booming bass to migrations from the Caribbean to Miami in the mid-1980s, in place of the path from Jamaica to the Bronx to which histories of hip-hop are typically restricted.[5] Likewise, trap's Southern-themed street tales and its MCs' sometimes syrupy drawl could be traced at least as far back as Port Arthur, Texas group UGK's 1992 album *Too Hard To Swallow* and the related circle of Houston-based artists who cohered around DJ Screw.[6] Or, as more recent predecessors go, Atlanta rapper T.I.'s 2003 *Trap Muzik* is significant, thematically speaking.[7] Equally, New Orleans rapper Lil Wayne's series of *Carter* mixtapes released through the mid-2000s are notable for wildly improvisational vocal flourishes, phrasing, and vocal scatting since they became conventional in rap music.[8]

In addition, it's pertinent to note that trap would only really register on pop charts through a second generation of producers and artists emerging in the early to mid-2010s. In this respect, the monstrously intense hit singles that Lex Luger produced in 2010 for Waka Flocka Flame ('Hard in Da Paint') and Rick Ross ('B.M.F.') are crucial reference points.[9] So are Atlanta rapper Future's debut commercial album *Pluto* and Chicago artist Chief Keef's *Finally Rich*, each released in 2012, as is Young Thug's noteworthy 2013 mixtape, *1017 Thug*.[10] In the years that followed, releases by Atlanta artists including Young Thug, Future, 2 Chainz, and Migos each charted successively higher and by 2016 rapper Desiigner's hit 'Panda' was the first decidedly trap-sounding song to reach number one on the U.S. pop charts.[11] A few months later Gucci Mane featured on Rae Sremmurd's single 'Black Beatles' and this too charted at number one.[12]

Each of these serves as evidence of trap's ascendancy to hegemony within hip-hop and this paralleled an equally noteworthy development: hip-hop's dominance of pop itself. Indeed, in 2017 it was widely that reported hip-hop had come to supersede rock as the most streamed genre of music in America.[13] That same year Atlanta group Migos's album *Culture* debuted number one on the *Billboard* album charts and 2 Chainz' *Pretty Girls Like Trap Music* debuted at number two, so that it wouldn't be mere hyperbole to proclaim pop as identical to trap.[14] This is an idea underscored by the breadth of mega-stars drawing upon its sonic palette in this period: Lana Del Rey on *Honeymoon* (2015), Lorde on *Sober 2* (2017), Arianna Grande on *Sweetener* (2018), Lykke Li on *So Sad So Sexy* (2018), to name a few.[15]

Sure, the genealogy of trap's ascent could be arranged and recounted along any number of histories. But the gamble animating this chapter is that the content and the impulses that define it emerge as a coherent form in 2005 on *Trap House* and *Let's Get It* and it's through these two albums that we can understand how and why the coordinates of Western popular music were transformed as they were.

The assimilation of trap into the folds of pop supremacy is of interest here not merely for its improbability, however. Rather, it's especially worthy of attention since trap can, at least in its earlier iterations, be defined as a type of work song.[16] At issue, after all, is an expansive term that involves the sites of the preparation and sale of illicit drugs (crack cocaine, in particular). But it also serves as more than a signifier for a means of production and circulation, since it encompasses the existential condition these labours represent. It is the expression of this existential condition which this chapter seeks to examine.

'I Am the Trap'

We can begin to appreciate the relation of work to existence at stake here if we consider the spaces the music inhabits, and on *Trap House* and *Let's Get It*, Gucci Mane and Young Jeezy situate the work of trappin' primarily at two sites: the kitchen and the street corner. References to 'cooking' crack, for instance, abound. This is the process whereby cocaine powder is heated in a mixture of water and baking soda to form a solid substance so that it can be easily subdivided and sold in small pieces at lower prices, and the stove top where this is done is a focal point for both rappers, their culinary artistry a recurring theme. On 'Thug Motivation 101' Young Jeezy has 'my Benihanas on, working two pots'.[17] On 'Trap House' Gucci is 'in the kitchen, but I ain't cookin' dinner' while on 'Pyrex Pot' he's 'got some cocaine jumpin' out the pot, get some cool water, it too damn hot'.[18]

Besides this sort of culinary swaggering, both rappers often boast of their virtuosity and commitment in retailing their wares too. Conceit to large-scale enterprise, for instance, is a common recurrence. Gucci's prices are 'low like Wal-Mart' and when he re-ups 'they bring a tractor-trailer.'[19] Likewise, the Texaco lot off East Atlanta's Bouldercrest Road where Gucci plied his trade as a teen has been the subject of enough lyrics to be well known by fans by now. But commitment to the grinding activity of selling crack, commitment to the street corner, is an especially pronounced theme in Jeezy's work. He's 'on the block, rain sleet, snow, Summer' on 'Trap or Die', he hustles 'from beginning of January to end of December' on 'My Hood.'[20]

Of course, this is not in itself novel artistic material where hip-hop is concerned. Rather, trap music's identification with the drug trade marks it as another iteration of the sub-genre variously known as 'gangsta', 'crack', or 'reality rap'. But *how* trap represents and relates to its context and the stance it adopts is, in important respects, distinct from its predecessors. In order to understand this we must unpack how rap thinks its reality, how it conceives and represents the conditions from which it emerges and where trap departs from hip-hop convention.

To do so demands rejecting attempts to read reality rap symptomatically, to avoid diagnosing it as a merely mechanical replication of its surroundings, and these come in two main forms. First, there's a view of rap as a reflection of African-American social disfunction; a straightforwardly racist accounting that deserves no further assessment. Another more sympathetic, albeit related, line of thought sees reality rap's archetypical figurations as falling all too close to the categories by which the dominant culture has cast Black people. On this view, reality rap's first-person narratives of urban poverty and survival merely reinforce a neoliberal ethos. Here, the rapper merely performs an entrepreneurial discipline, albeit in the only terms available to those excluded from the mainstream, that is to say, in extra-legal economies.[21] To pathologise rap on these terms, however, is still to withdraw all autonomy from the cultural object. It amounts, in other words, to a revocation of the music from the category of art and instead, restricts it to an inert reflection of its context. This is, of course, one way of defining ideology. But to assert such a claim is to pay insufficient attention to the ways in which even the most commercially oriented cultural products can be discerned as the sites of struggle, a point to which we'll return.

Other readings, more attuned to the music's internal tensions, discern in reality rap a more ambiguous position, somewhere between critique and accommodation. Here, the 'gangsta' is both the product and the transcriber of his conditions: he both 'give[s] expressive shape', as Eithne Quinn puts it, to working class Black experience and yet rejects any responsibility for social uplift.[22] This is, it's suggested, to abjure a middle class demand to act as a delegate for his community but it still amounts to an abandonment of an explicitly critical position.[23]

So for some critics the reality rapper offers a first-person account of oppressive social structures that shape working class Black American existence, while for others the music amounts to a social realism that nevertheless identifies too closely with the forces that oppress it. There's a spectrum between critique and accommodation here and this, in turn, is often situated upon a historical vector. On this view, the earliest reality rappers present a life lived outside the law as hostile and discordant to the dominant culture. For instance, on the 1989 album *Straight Outta Compton*, NWA situates itself, most of all, as antagonistic to carceral institutions or, as they put it, 'Fuck tha police'. But by the time NWA member Dr. Dre's *The Chronic* and Snoop Dogg's *Doggystyle* were released in 1992 and 1993 respectively, the argument goes, 'gangsta' is repackaged as a 'simulated liberation', a consumable lifestyle whose emblems are drugs, cars, and women.[24] This is a shift as discernible in lyrics less focused on oppositional sentiment than in celebrating frictionless movement through a city over which the artist claims mastery, as it is in sonic material; Dre and Snoop's relaxed P-Funk grooves displace the frenetic drum loops and dissonant soul samples characteristic of NWA's early work.[25]

But there's still a moralising binary at work in such an accounting, and this tends to weigh down the music under what Kobena Mercer called the 'burden of representation', the singular demand upon Black arts to contribute to social uplift and it situates the critic as moral arbiter above all else.[26] There's also a disavowal that what is at stake is, first and foremost, a cultural form whose pleasures are not reducible to the paradigms of pathology or social function.[27] More convincing analyses are found where hip-hop is situated in African American vernacular traditions, famously characterised by Henry Louis Gates Jr. as 'signifying'; they are modes of communication where meaning is allusive and layered, and where form is dialogic and intertextual.²⁸ In the case of reality rap in particular, the nineteenth century 'badman tales', irreverent and violent set pieces depicting Black male strength and guile, are an especially important reference point.²⁹ As state power displaced the slaveowner's discretionary control over Black people in America, the outlaw anti-heroes on which the tales centred – gamblers, pimps, and bootleggers – came to symbolise acts of resistance deemed essential for survival. Folklore, in other words, acted as an expression of hostility to the post-bellum society.³⁰

Before we explore this theme of symbolic resistance further, it is important to register two fundamental transformations to the 'badman' in the reality rapper's depiction. First, his is a commercial mode of expression dis-embedded from its traditional sites; juke joints, dance halls, and so on. It follows, second, that as a commodity he circulates ever more widely, so the burden placed upon the authenticity of his character grows all the heavier.³¹ The mythologies around the drug money used to found major hip-hop labels including Ruthless, Rap-A-Lot, and Roc-A-Fella records, along with, say, 2Pac and Snoop Dogg's widely publicised legal troubles, or an ultimately tragic yet soap operatic East coast–West coast rivalry, all attest to the escalating stakes of what counts as real in rap throughout the 1990s and 2000s. As its audience grew, so too did the music's detachment from its context, and so its performance of authenticity became all the more severe.

This brings us back to trap which, especially in its early incarnations, makes a claim to authenticity that is both in keeping with reality rap tradition but intensifies it to a level that borders on frenzied desperation. Indeed, if proximity to its source material is the measure of rap realness, then Gucci Mane and Young Jeezy each avow a wholly unmediated mode of expression. In fact, Gucci absolves himself of artistry altogether. Music is, he avers, mainly seed money for his principal enterprise. He's 'a trapper, not a rapper.'³² A similar sentiment is often declared by Young Jeezy who, equally, is motivated by the desire for a perfectly transparent presentation of his milieu. 'This is more than rap', he exclaims at one point, 'this is the streets, I am the trap', he goes on.³³

According to the logics of this sort of metaphysics of presence of the streets, to admit artistry is to risk the exactness of representation of the world for which one is the vessel. Music exists in a state of self-denial where its vocation is the transparent exhibition of experience, and all manner of gossip has been deployed to support such an ideal. For instance, the boxes bursting with bands of hundred-dollar bills pictured on the cover of *Let's Get It* add up to $1.8m provided at a moment's notice by one of Jeezy's associates. The mentorship he received from drug kingpin Big Meech is equally well known.[34] Gucci's relation to the streets is, likewise, central to his mythology. Though the charge of murder levelled against him in the very week that *Trap House* was released was eventually dropped by the Atlanta Police Department, he was nevertheless intermittently incarcerated between 2005 and 2016 for a series of offences.[35]

But let's pause here to return to our earlier question regarding the adequacy of moral assessments of reality rap. In this regard, a fecund line of reasoning is put down in an essay by theorist R.A. Judy for whom such approaches are still too tied to an ontic or everyday understanding of the gangsta. What is at stake instead, Judy argues, is an ontological inquiry, an investigation into what it means to be human itself.[36] On this reckoning, the reality rapper's nihilism, his rejection of any ethical code, sits within a much longer tradition of the aesthetics of refusal, one which Judy, following earlier folklorist framings of hip-hop, traces back to the experience of slavery. In circumstances where the Black person had been reduced to the status of an object, Judy holds, his refusal of the master's power and oppression necessarily entails an embrace of death. For in the condition of enslavement an ethos that welcomes its mortality can resist the complete subjugation of will; thus he becomes 'the human-cum thing that is not subject to work', as Judy puts it.[37]

Several implications follow from this reading. First, we should reject attempts to press the reality rapper into an ethical frame that has no basis in his being. For where the legal recognition a life receives is exhausted by that life's prohibition, the discourse of morality has only limited purchase. Second, we gain a new outlook on the mounting ferociousness of Gucci's and Jeezy's assertions of authenticity where we see that what they convey is not reducible to the literal, which is to say, is in excess of meaning. The point, ultimately, is this: Gucci and Jeezy generate an imagined unity, a shared experience, through a mode of expression which circulates as widely as possible; that is the point of the commodity after all. But this movement also divorces their work from its context and, at its new level of abstraction, only the most intense emotional states of rage and pleasure can persist. In this light, to follow Judy's logic, the rapper should be understood as a system of affects, a terrain of emotional textures rather than a series of literal statements. This is not, however, to jettison analysis of lived experience from our interpretation. Rather, it's to imply that the terms in which we consume trap are more complex and expansive than is often admitted.

'That's My Hood'

Rap music's spatial coordinates are crucial to understanding the dynamics at stake. For while its subjects are sequestered to the spatial limits of the ghetto, it is only when they are abstracted as a commodity that the 'Black noise' they produce can circulate smoothly beyond its borders.[38] Where it's transformed into a commodity, illegality becomes an asset since it's in this context that Black vernacular traditions and styles suit white voyeuristic fantasies for which the ghetto is a place of adventure, extremity, cool criminality, and erotic fantasy.[39] Rap music, in other words, provides an experience of ostensible proximity for the virtual consumption of sites conceived as 'no-go zones' all while permitting the myth of the inner city as a space to be avoided to persist, and to preserving the white consumer from contact with the outlaw subject they consume.[40]

This is to borrow from Adam Krims's study of *Music and Urban Geography*, a work whose central thesis posits the counterpart to the experience of the city as a site of racialised danger and adventure to be the protracted escapism offered to the music's white middle class consumers.[41] For if the ghetto functions as a holding cell for an increasingly superfluous workforce, other zones are given over to flexible accumulation, broadly conceived. Urban infrastructure is diverted to tourism, real estate, service and finance industries just as industrial production withdraws to other sites. Especially intensely registered in the 1990s, what geographer Neil Smith has called a 'revanchist city' deploys a range of strategies – 'three strikes' laws, mandatory minimum sentencing, cuts to welfare – as a means of transferring low-income residents to prisons and outer suburbs.[42] Smith's influential analysis of gentrification as ultimately driven by the need to absorb labour rendered surplus by de-industrialisation and to support colonisation of low-rent areas for property speculation is expedient for understanding the recent history of hip-hop. For under consideration are processes that have fundamentally transformed formerly abandoned zones in, for instance, Harlem, the Bronx, and Brooklyn that had incubated rap in an earlier epoch.

One of the earliest harbingers of this shifting experience of the city as a site primarily devoted to consumption and investment is Notorious B.I.G.'s now classic album, *Ready to Die*. Released in 1994, the album appeared the same year that Rudy Giuliani was elected mayor of New York on a platform of 'pacifying' working class areas. The king of New York rap and 'America's Mayor' are an eccentric pairing only superficially. Archetypal claims to proximity to the streets prevail in *Ready to Die*. But in B.I.G.'s retelling of the rags to riches story there is a recessive experience of time, the streets appear chiefly not as lived present but as memory. We encounter, here, the petrifying logics of gentrification and tourism; where the museum no longer has limits, everything becomes an artefact. The city as a space of angst and terror has been overcome and the present is defined by a new object world, one embellished with finely tailored clothes, dimly lit mansions, and leather interiors. This is all matched by B.I.G.'s own velvet-smooth, breathy vocal flow.

Where the rapper takes up the role of crime boss for whom the ghetto becomes symbolic capital to be cashed in, he operates in a mode analogous to the property speculator for whom exposed brick interiors, out of use signage, salvaged fittings adorning luxury lofts, and trendy bars function as a maudlin record of displaced residents. Thus embroiled in the cleansing of people turned superfluous for the post-Fordist city, the dominant style of hip-hop in the 1990s is metonymic of what developers call 'culture-led regeneration'. From B.I.G. to Jay-Z or 50-Cent, this sort of gentrification rap, whilst gesturing towards the street as a historical vector, came increasingly to mimic capital's own flight from production in the inner city. This is best exemplified in hip-hop's great performative deed in this period, inscribed in the mantra 'I Get Money'. Here, rap generates wealth on the basis of pure diktat, mere speculation, and, in this regard, acts not unlike a finance capital which generates profits in the present by a promise of value to be produced in the future. And so, one might say, whilst finance capital exhibits a desire to free itself from its dependence on labour by generating money merely out of money itself, this is transfigured by the detachment of wealth from toil by the assertion that one simply 'gets', rather than exchanges labour for, money. The rapper and finance capital, in other words, each withdrawn from the circuits of production or from the street, seek to free themselves from the compulsion to labour altogether.

An Artificial Peasantry

The badman anti-heroes of reality rap didn't entirely dissipate into memory in this period, however. Instead, they followed manufacturing capital's own migration from the Northeast and Midwest to the U.S. Sun Belt in the preceding decades. In the late 1990s Southern rappers accounted for about one-third of the hip-hop singles chart, but by 2004 they made up two-thirds and have come to dominate the top ten since.[43] The rationale for capital's increasing shift of operations to the South in the latter half of the twentieth century is well documented: low tax, low union density Southern states with permissive labour and environmental regulations allowed capital to escape ever more recalcitrant workforces in its northern and midwestern U.S. industrial heartlands. Re-locating factories to Southern suburbs also further bolstered the vertical fragmentation of production that we have associated with post-Fordism and which, we have seen, serviced the turn to just-in-time supply chain management and outsourcing characteristic of the current epoch.[44]

So capital moves South because it's in crisis. But to understand why rap followed capital southwards we should return to the spatial logics of its consumption by the dominant culture. In this context, it's worth remarking that the growth of cities in Southern 'right to work' states did not follow a classic core-suburbs model of urban space but rather, as Phil A. Neel shows in his study of urbanisation, took a less concentric path as capital searched for ever lower cost land and labour.[45] The sprawl of industrial space criss-crossed by transit corridors and residential zones this process generates, its crucial to note, also goes hand in hand with a growing suburbanisation of poverty characterised by rising levels of inequality and segregation. This is a phenomenon most clearly emblematised by the explosion in recent decades of new suburban and rural prisons across the

U.S., deployed to warehouse the very workers made surplus by 'lean' production and pushed out of inner cities by gentrification; a suburbanisation of labour by decree.⁴⁶

All of this gestures at the need for an adjustment in the popular representation of working class Black life in Southern rap. Not quite identical to the rural, Southerness nevertheless stands opposed to the urban.⁴⁷ 'Down home', bucolic, lawless, hospitable, the ideology of the South – continuous with slavery – grounded a new site for hip-hop authenticity whilst perpetuating the safe and controlled consumption of Black criminality, all without disrupting the new imaginary of the city as a site of escapism.⁴⁸ Indeed, given lower population density, high levels of urban sprawl, and racial segregation, the setting of Southern cities permitted the rapper's outlaw status to continue to circulate whilst more or less preserving the music's white audience from contact with the subject it consumes, a seclusion less available in New York's rapidly gentrifying boroughs. That a renegotiation of the city and the consumption of racialised criminality is at stake is clear from Southern rap's object world, its displacement of public housing towers and back alleys by low-rise and tract housing, freeway interchanges, and strip mall parking lots. Only this is a suburban universe dissociated from its conventional association with upward mobility.

Several Southern cities and attendant sub-genres vied for rap ascendancy through the early 2000s. New Orleans proffered the whippy halfsteps and swinging refrains of 'bounce', Memphis and Atlanta proposed the insouciant chants of 'crunk', Houston advanced the dreamy disinclination of 'chopped and screwed' music, and so on. This appetite for local scenes is likely partly due to a fall in record industry profits during this period. As revenues were threatened by online downloading in the early 2000s (and accordingly, A&R budgets declined), local, mainly Southern, scenes more or less ignored by the mainstream had developed an independent infrastructure easily adapted to a corporate model where labels outsourced discovery and development to artists themselves and audiences on social media platforms. Yet while each of these local styles contributed motifs that would persist in hip-hop, each had a limited lifespan in the pop music charts and so, in the national and international consciousness too.

That is to say, no local style came to permanent ascendance prior to the rise of trap as it grew in the years following the release of *Let's Get It* and *Trap House*. It's noteworthy that other candidates for hip-hop's post-New York capital anchored their existential principles in revelry, in leisure. Crunk mostly centres on collective abandon in the nightclub, the nucleus of bounce rests with the vocal and bodily dialogue between MC and dancers, the slower tempos and pitched down sound of chopped and screwed music suit the car stereos from which it is broadcast particularly well, and is said to suit Promethazine syrup highs even more so.[49] Trap, on the other hand, is about work. It is set, as we have seen, in the circadian rhythms of the production and distribution of crack cocaine and so, in this sense, amounts to the Monday morning to what had become hip-hop's fantasy of the never-ending holiday. Trap, in other words, is as much about a changing experience of time as it is about a changing negotiation with place.

Bricks Goin' In, Bricks Goin' Out

As work song, trap takes its place alongside a folk tradition of tracklaying, weaving, or cobbling songs and sea shanties; like these, it situates work within a wider cadenced structure. In this case, the work in question is, as we have seen, that of the drug trade. On the opening track to *Trap House* (itself called 'Trap House') Gucci provides something of an interpretive manual for his music. The temporality he invokes is that of ceaseless repetition, a sort of eternal return of the same, where Gucci becomes an appendage to the process of valorisation – whereby money begets more money – upon which his survival is premised: 'junkies goin' in, junkies goin' out ... bricks goin' in, bricks goin' out.'[50] The recurrence of these lines as chorus only serves to underline the perpetual nature of the process whereby everything is abstracted to quantity by money, everything has a value. There's an analogous sentiment discernible in *Let's Get It* where one encounters 'so much white it'll hurt your eyes' and one counts 'so much paper it'll hurt your hands.'[51] So for both, the process under discussion is interminable, ceaseless, and bound to the circulation of money and capital.[52]

What's especially interesting is that in both Gucci's and Jeezy's cases, the archetypal bravado seems so weighed down by its own weariness, the affective register within which it operates is characterised by its flatness as much as by its bluster. If in folk traditions of work song we find a tacit and, at times even explicit, resistance to the alienation of work from pleasure, these binaries are especially complicated in Gucci's and Jeezy's early work, as well as in trap more widely. Understanding these coordinates demands, however, that we look to the wider terms of the racialised nature of the division of labour and leisure in contemporary America.

We have seen in previous chapters that as leisure time is increasingly commodified, colonised by the compulsion to labour, the workday is ever extended, and hyper-precarity makes readiness to work a permanent state of being, while the divisions between labour and leisure grow increasingly nebulous. We have also already examined how music listening increasingly intersects various mechanisms, especially Internet platforms, for the generation of profits. But in the context of exceptionally high rates of unemployment among Black and Brown people, Robin Kelley has argued in an important analysis that play itself is often deployed as a means of survival. That is, where 'free' time expands for the unemployed, stylistic innovation and symbolic creativity of sport or artistic performance grow in significance as entrepreneurial strategies for the avoidance of low wage labour.[53] In this regard, Jeezy and Gucci can be situated within a much longer history of the racialised sale of play as a commodity, only with the proviso that the fantasy on sale here does not amount to the creative expression of the dancer or the athlete, but the representation of dangerous and interminable work.

The routine opposition of labour and leisure is further complicated by the representation of work trap offers. Jeezy presents himself as something of a drug dealing self-help guru ('anything you put ya mind to/put ya grind to' is among the more risible of his formulations). The logic underlying his endlessly reiterated rags to riches tale is a message of meritocratic promise: if you become better drug dealers, you'll no longer have to deal drugs. 'Aye, aye, you gotta believe, you gotta believe', he pleads over the opening beats of 'Thug Motivation 101'. A few lines later, glancing at the marble floors of his mansion, he conjures a childhood memory of scurrying cockroaches. Jeezy's voice is raspy, pressing, insistent, it recalls a low level screaming or dying wish at times. This is an impression amplified by his vocal phrasing which, given its prolonged sentences, is closer to a blues moan than a rapper's rhythm. Having relinquished the complex rhyme patterns by which MCs were once measured, he implies that directness, not vocal 'flow', is to be the vessel of truth. But so clamorous, so insistent, is his perpetual bootstrapping that it loses all credibility. Jeezy's is, in the end, an affective state of attachment to a meritocratic ideal seemingly without any link to a material world. As such, it can only truly aspire to serve the therapeutic function of persevering where one has few if any bases to do so. This is an affective state which Lauren Berlant called 'cruel optimism', one she showed to be coincident with an epoch of crisis.[54] Only in Jeezy's version, his assurances for the future are so insistent that the American Dream he peddles doesn't seem to endure at all; it is already in tatters.

As they do in Jeezy's, groans, grunts, and other improvised noises and phrases ornament Gucci's music too. The sounds of words are stretched to their very limits so that the materiality of language is constantly at stake. But he presents a different affective template, one which is premised upon its emotional flatness. His vocals are placed relatively low in the mix, often doubled and effected, so they can be difficult to discern; his Southern drawl is especially viscous, his voice is nasal and mumbled, and he changes pitch only infrequently. The strikingly matter-of-fact tone by which he delivers stories of drugs and money evokes a cosmic resignation to fate, a pessimistic philosophy of history that seeks to acquiesce to the eternal recurrence of the same: 'bricks goin' in, bricks goin' out.'

It ought to be clear by now that, despite their differences of delivery, Jeezy and Gucci operate within the same expressive core, one where whimsy is precipitously balanced with despair. The intensity of Jeezy's appeal to work, we have seen, betrays a distrust in its own meritocratic contentions. Gucci is less equivocal. His boasts may be outlandish, even giddy. But in opposition to the reality rap tradition to which he and Jeezy belong, Gucci does not set the trap house as memory, as a storehouse of moral or vocational lessons to be drawn upon where necessary. Instead, it is situated in the present as lived reality.[55] The implication, emphasised by his sapless vocal timbre, is that there is simply nowhere else to go. Time, in effect, seems to be arrested. Or, more to the point, he appears to inhabit a temporal warp which resides outside of linear history.[56]

'This Is Hustler Music'

To invoke a temporality where change brings no meaningful transformation, an 'eternal recurrence of the new', to quote Walter Benjamin's formulation, implies the historical experience of capitalism itself.[57] But it would be a mistake to depict Gucci as merely ventriloquising capital's own desire for perpetual, if ever-expanding, persistence. Underlying the ceaseless repetitions which characterise his music vocally and sonically is a clamorous sense of dread, of angst lacking a definitive object on which to be projected. This gets at the transformation implied by trap music over the unruly romps of conventional gangsta rap. At issue is not, as we have seen, the playful defiance of early NWA, nor the frictionless movement and mastery of urban space characteristic of Dr. Dre's post-NWA work. It isn't the nostalgic, but ultimately overcome, memory of the street we discerned in B.I.G. either. Instead, it's the insistent dread of dangerous, dull, and interminable work.

This is an aesthetic transformation underscored by trap's sonic palette. For one thing, this is a style of hip-hop not oriented to what Kodwo Eshun has described as the 'sampladelia of the breakbeat', it is not anchored in the modular quotation of grooves and breaks, it dismisses altogether the comforts of dusty hooks.[58] Instead, trap mines the rhythmic possibilities generated by electronic samplers. Synthesised hi-hats play in double time to booming kick drums and snare snaps, giving the effect of a music that, rather astonishingly, feels both quite slow and fast simultaneously. When hi-hats roll rapidly and wildly, as they often do, the intensity only swells further.

The point can be clarified further if we look to trap's harmonic elements. These are, we have seen, derived in part from techniques associated with horror film in the 1980s, and the moody synths that soundtrack *The Exorcist* and *Halloween* are especially significant reference points. On 'Thug Motivation 101', for instance, producer Shawty Redd deploys screeching, multi-track synth arpeggios we've come to associate with looming terror. On 'Trap House', conversely, Redd uses the sort of warping, siren-like drones that gesture at imminent violence. On other tracks, rapid and repeating piano melodies, swells, and dissonant stabs abound. Between them, they more or less set the template for trap for a decade or more.

Of course, as I already suggested, references to horror film are tropes first developed in this context in crunk music. But the terms by which they're mobilised here are altogether distinct. Crunk is primarily party and club music and it employs the sonic signifiers of horror film in order to place the audience in the role of the killer, the party is their victim. Take

Memphis group Three 6 Mafia's 1997 hit 'Tear Da Club Up': alongside its thumping drums is a short, repeating, spooky piano melody. But the rising horns that lead to the song's chorus release us from the stasis established by the piano and propel us towards the resolution of the chanted refrain of the song's title. The song, in other words, draws its audience to a collective apogee. Conversely, trap has a more languid pace and a flatter vocal delivery. Neither 'Trap House' nor 'Thug Motivation 101' have the sort of rising elements that crunk songs do, there's no way out of the fragmentation set by repeating synth stabs and melodies, nor is there an aural object upon which we might project our dread. One can no longer discern villain nor victim, the source of terror remains opaque, so that angst comes to predominate. The texture in which all this is enveloped only serves to emphasise the point; bright synths and high attack snares or hi-hats are icy cold, metallic, there is very little in the way of harmonic content and the comforting, albeit temporary, resolutions pop songs tend to offer are in short supply.

So the claim I have been developing here, just to emphasise the point, is that the emergence of trap as genre rests with the migration of the popular consumption of Black criminality from the rapidly gentrifying inner cities of the U.S. Northeast. But it is also not reducible to this desire and this requires a further argument still. For if this were all that is at stake, any other Southern micro-genre would have done in its place. Only trap, to quote Jesse McCarthy, 'sounds like what living in contemporary America feels like', which is to say, its very object is the sense of generalised precarity and immiseration that characterises this era of crisis.[59] The music's prevailing mood of cynical yet perpetual and unrelenting attachment to work sounds, in other words, the angst of just that, trapped.

General Taking

We might say that in diverting the popular consumption of Black criminality from hip-hop's rapidly gentrifying Northeastern citadels to the sprawling, suburbanised South, trap offered a spatial fix to the aesthetic economy of rap. But there's a further encounter with systemic attempts to resolve the crises thrown up by a society compelled to produce profits we should consider and this, too, has to do with the music's urban geography.

The trap from which the music draws its designation is, after all, usually a house – typically repossessed from its owner or abandoned by its original residents – repurposed for the production and sale of crack cocaine. Take, as an example, the cover image of *Trap House*: Gucci is pictured standing in a street speaking into a mobile phone, he gives the sideways glance of a demanding deal-maker while behind him stands a two-storey wood frame house; the paint is peeling from its wood siding, its windows are half-boarded up. It's an imagery of working class suburbia that has grown synonymous with Southern hip-hop and serves to announce that we are no longer in the presence of East Coast or West Coast rap's conventional inner city object worlds of back alleys and towering housing projects. But it also implies, I want to suggest, that trap's relationship to the global financial crisis is not only mediated by its relationship to low wage employment, but by its connection to housing too.

In order to begin to unpack such a claim, it's worth considering how the housing market has acted as an important stabiliser for the U.S. economy, both by absorbing surplus capital into the construction industry and through house price inflation that has propped up consumer spending.[60] This financialised real estate economy was premised on overcoming the spatial fixity, the messiness, of the individual home, so that it could circulate as an easily traded commodity.[61] Enter 'tranching': this is the process of standardising, dividing up, and reorganising mortgages that has been fundamental to the growth of secondary and tertiary markets for bank debt and which, it bears remarking, operates not unlike imagery of the ghetto that, dis-embedded from its context, moves freely through the world as a commodity while its inhabitants are confined to strictly defined space. Accordingly, if financialisation transformed the household from the unit of subsistence that it was in Fordism into a balance sheet of assets and liabilities, this finds its echo in the way trap converts the house to a site and theatre of enterprise.[62]

Still, this might seem rather nebulous, perhaps even far-fetched as a mediation between trap and housing markets. It's worth noting, however, that by the time *Trap House* was released in 2005, the 'subprime' mortgage market was reaching its peak and the deluge of foreclosures that would decimate the U.S. beginning in 2007 and the global economy in the years that followed was already underway.[63] This was a market premised on the sale of high interest rate loans for homes in working class minority neighbourhoods; a ponzi scheme designed to generate profit from debt as widely as possible, one that held together so long as house prices rose. As rate hikes increasingly kicked in, however, default rates exploded, asset values collapsed, and the failure to realise value could no longer be deferred.[64] That Gucci, in particular, should somehow anticipate the imagery of the financial crisis is less fanciful when we take into consideration that East Atlanta's Dekalb County, where he lived, had the highest foreclosure rate in Georgia which, in turn, had among the highest rates in America.[65] The point grows ever clearer when we consider that not only is Atlanta amongst the most segregated and unequal cities in America, it was also the first U.S. city to systematically demolish all public housing in the 1990s and shift to a private sector voucher scheme.[66] Housing, in other words, had long been totally subsumed by the market where Gucci's lived experience is concerned.[67]

This brings us back to the aesthetic economy of the house in trap. It's useful, in this regard, to consider Guy Debord's proposition that the suburb generated a 'new artificial peasantry.'[68] His point was that home ownership, by dispersing the city's inhabitants, encourages a narrow-minded solipsism. But Gucci's aestheticisation of the trap house inverts these logics. For where the suburb might've functioned to curb workers' power by scattering them to the isolating logics that bind them to rising asset values, in Gucci's world the home becomes a lawless site of semi-autonomous existence. Indeed, if, as Annie McClanahan has argued in an incisive study of debt, the dominant visual rhetoric of the credit economy has identified the abandoned home with a feral landscape, a collapse of domesticity, and an unruly culture in the process of decay, Gucci might be understood, then, as defying this association of economic decline with ethical failure.[69]

In this respect, 'Trap House' recalls Fred Moten's invitation to understand subprime activity as what he calls, echoing Laura Harris, a 'general taking'. This is a reference to Harris's study of the off-grid aesthetic socialities in favelas and barracks expressed by C.L.R. James and Hélio Oticia which persist through the legacy of confinement and expropriation of Black people from Middle Passage to the present.[70] Harris's analysis permits Moten to grasp the subprime debtor as neither pathological nor as victim but rather, in his words, as the 'guerrilla, establishing pockets of insurgent refuge and marronage, carrying evaluation and disruptively familial extensions into supposedly sanitised zones.'[71] If, then, we understand the subprime crisis as an attack upon domesticity, an incursion from the city to the suburb, especially if, to return to Debord, suburbanisation is typically a rearguard action on behalf of capital, then the abandoned home, the trap, gestures at a mode of life within and against capital and, in turn, denotes the fragility of the imposition of discipline and scarcity the financialised debt economy has sought to exert.

Red Dogs at My Door

So the setting of a music in the trap house can be made to stand, in part, as a signifier for the crisis of a society which has made the home an increasingly speculative venture. But the gothic, brooding intensity of, say, 'Trap House', should also alert us to the fact that, even while we have attended just now to its resistive character, a life lived in illegality is equally characterised by its persecution. This is inevitable where one survives alongside a carceral system whose very function is the preservation of whiteness, which is to say, the system of legal, political, and economic privilege accorded to those who could historically be the bearers of private property and power over racialised others who could not. And, of course, the family home has long stood as among whiteness' most archetypal figures.

We might return here to Jeezy's petition that he *is* the trap, or Gucci's profession that he's 'not a rapper'. Earlier, we interpreted these assertions through the lens of hip-hop's ethics of authenticity, but we might equally apply them here as an invocation of criminality as an existential condition. This is to interpret the trap as an expression of both the 'general taking' of the home, to return to Moten and Harris again, but also as gesturing at the wider ontological condition of homelessness upon which that act of seizure is premised. For the rejection of the law of property and the ideal of domesticity at stake here implies an embrace of dispossession, the state which Moten and Harney call fugitivity, and describe as 'being at ease with the fugitive, at peace with the pursued, at rest with the ones who consent not to be one.'[72]

It's worth noting, in this regard, that there are no explicit references to carceral systems at all in *Trap House* and only three brief mentions in

Let's Get It: Jeezy remarks on a friend in jail on 'Thug Motivation 101', he acknowledges a quotidian police presence on 'Standing Ovation' ('everyday I see feds'), and refers to his own arrest ('Red Dogs at my trap, got me for half a stone').[73] These are, however, anomalous as far as the album's lyrics go. The struggles of avoiding apprehension by the police would become a far more abiding theme on Jeezy's next album and, by the release of *Trap or Die: 3* in 2016, he'd identify with the Black Lives Matter movement and would come to take an increasingly visible role in police abolitionist movements in the years that followed. Similarly, Gucci's struggles with the law would become an abiding theme in his later work, especially as he would be more or less continuously incarcerated from 2005 up to his second studio album, *The State vs. Radric Davis*, in 2009. On the cover of the latter, Gucci is pictured in prison overalls and handcuffs, and he was, indeed, in jail on the date of its release. The relative absence of references to the state's carceral apparatus on *Trap House* and *Let's Get It* thus invites further speculation.

Earlier, we identified whiteness with private property, but if whiteness were a job, to borrow a line from Geo Maher, it would be the police.[74] One is hard pressed to find a better corroboration for Maher's claim than the coincidence of the founding of a police force in Atlanta with the abolition of slavery.[75] This involved the state's seizure of a monopoly on violence from the authority of the slaveowner and in turn, criminality would come to be defined by the former slave's life lived outside the wage. 'The state's function is to annihilate the criminal', as George Caffentzis has put it, 'but [the state's] existence presupposes him.'[76] This is a set of conditions that would undergo its various permutations. For instance, early Georgia courts would enforce misdemeanours against independent modes of survival – hunting or fishing – as a means of entrapping freed slaves; convict leases and chain gangs represented later modes of indentured labour; suburban mega-prisons today offer still another means of partitioning labour on the basis of race. 'Georgia clung to slavery', as W.E.B. DuBois once put it, and we might consider *Trap House* and *Let's Get It* in this context too.[77]

In question, of course, is a popular form whose primary theme is work beyond the bounds of legality and this makes Gucci's and Jeezy's collective silence on the latter worthy of comment. Sure, we might discern in this a wider trend, invoked by rap historian Eric Harvey, whereby opposition to police power recedes in hip-hop as its insistence on its authenticity comes increasingly to the fore.[78] But I would instead like to register this omission as an antagonistic proposition: where the state's violence is an ever-present setting for a population that counts, in part, on an informal economy for its survival, to all but disregard its power also amounts to a refusal of its terms.

We are thus accumulating a seemingly contradictory load of premises: a demand for authenticity, increasingly insistent as the object for which it litigates becomes all the more alien from its origins, an expressive impulse emerging from the experience of being made surplus to the needs of the labour market and so the society along with the state of criminality that is the existential condition that has defined the afterlives of American slavery, the consumption of that criminality by the dominant culture, and the latter's imbrications with the subprime housing market. In its tensions, its different registers and levels of analysis, this variegated terrain only serves to substantiate one of our central assumptions, that culture is always a terrain of struggle, a 'double movement of containment and resistance', to quote from Stuart Hall.[79]

Magic City

There is still another form of work we might consider where trap is concerned and, like drug dealing, it too is both at the margins of the wage and central to the music's mythology: trap circulates primarily in strip clubs. Indeed, so closely has the music been identified with Atlanta's best-known clubs – Magic City, Cheetah, Blue Flame, Follies – that these have become well-known brand names by now. This has been something of a feedback loop: just as the rising significance of strip clubs as reference points coincided with the growth in trap's audience, so too did curiosity grow in the city's sex industry; a fact underscored by the multitude of voyeuristic journalistic accounts it has generated.[80]

At one level, the correspondence between the sex industry and a music whose subject matter is the drug trade arises from a shared economic geography. As a central transport hub, Atlanta is a city through which commodities must move at high rates and fast speeds and this demands the migration of a lot of men to move them. The latter become the vessel for cocaine and also form a market for women's bodies. But there is also a narrower, more functional, relation that has drawn these two forms together and this too revolves around the music's economic occupation since approval from professional dancers is said to be the first measure of artistic achievement.[81] 'If you want to make it in Atlanta,' producer TM88 has said, 'you need to live in Magic City.'[82] This identification of success with Magic City, it bears remarking, is usually traced back to local cocaine kingpin Demetrius 'Big Meech' Flenory Jr. and his BMF syndicate's notoriously extravagant patronage in the early 2000s.[83] That Meech also happened to be Jeezy's backer only draws the links between sex, drugs, and trap ever tighter. But we could also propose a longer history of local Atlanta musics and sex work, one which would begin with the prostitutes working the city's juke joints and take in the city's first ever hip-hop hit: Tag Team's single 'Whoomp (There It Is)' reached number two on *Billboard's* singles chart in 1993 and was produced by Cecile 'The Brain Supreme' Glenn and he, it turns out, was a DJ at Magic City at the time.

Here, we might consider an argument that takes the growing identification of the strip club as part of hip-hop's milieu as evidence of a pornographic gaze, one which restricts the popular representation of Black women to that of a hyper-sexual Jezebel.[84] On this reasoning, contemporary rap tends to restrict representations of women to objects over which men bond and, in the strip club in particular, she provides the site, acts as an ornament, for a homosocial community from which she is excluded.[85] This is what Walter Benjamin called the 'erotology of the damned': the debasement and fragmentation of the body in capitalism, not to mention an eroticisation of money itself as it is placed directly onto the woman, amounts to a diversion of libidinal desire upon the world of objects.[86]

But if, as Hortense Spillers has suggested, the logic of private property invades all kinship relations, if family always implies ownership, this might persuade us to also seek out other lines of argument.[87] We might refer, in this regard, to Leopoldina Fortunati's suggestion that sex work offers women a certain level of autonomy that the indirectly paid sex work of marriage does not.[88] The stripper's or sex worker's shift ends while the wife's work is, all things considered, interminable. This is to reorganise our frame to pose the woman as agent rather than object. 'We use these men, they don't use us,' as one dancer put it.[89]

Others have derived from the figure of the stripper a renewed focus on women's pleasure, one which is not anchored in heteronormative conceptions of desire. Writing on Magic City in particular, L.H. Stallings has proposed a conception of the strip club as a queer space, one which sits beyond the ideology of romance and instead proposes a communal mode of eroticism.[90] Of course, our appraisal should recognise that sex work remains embedded in a racial capitalist society where, for instance, Black strippers tend to earn less than white, which more broadly reflects the tendency to segregate Black women to service occupations.[91] Still, it might nevertheless be understood here as a theatre that upends the domestic and domesticating logics of sexuality and, instead, be deciphered in terms of a proposal for a model of pleasure not anchored in the reproduction of the family nor the moral codes that underlie it.

Stripping might serve, in sum, just as drug dealing does, as a metonym of an allegory for the crisis-era labour we are concerned with; a notoriously dangerous and precarious industry, one into which people enter where more conventional labour markets are less accessible. Still, to dance, as Stallings writes, 'to their own rhythm, not keeping time with a work society that deems them either customer or performer', insinuates a contestation not only of the division of sexual pleasure and performance, but of the separation of labour and leisure more widely.[92]

This returns us to trap which, we have seen, both reflects and problematises wider transformations of the opposition of work and play. To view it in these terms, however, demands rejecting an all-too-common pathologising reception for an understanding of an affective texture which betrays the existential weariness of a precarious and hazardous pursuit of survival. If there is a nihilism to be gleaned in much recent 'crack rap', as its critics regularly assert, it's to be located in its repudiation of a bootstrapping ethos; there is little scope for an ethics where the artist confronts their hero's social disposability so ruthlessly. This, in turn, generates a tension we have explored at length, one around which accounts of the stripper are obliged to oscillate too; for trap only circulates beyond its immediate context by virtue of a commercial logics of abstraction which makes it reducible once again to the racialicing logics of criminality. But here too its conditions are contested, since the extra-legal existence at stake threatens the ideals of domesticity, propriety, and property which would seek to discipline its subjects.

Notes

1. Young Jeezy, *Let's Get It: Thug Motivation 101*, Def Jam Recordings, 2005; Gucci Mane, *Trap House*, Big Cat Records, 2005.
2. See for instance, Sean Fennessey, 'Let's Get It: Thug Motivation 101', *Pitchfork*, 14 August 2005, https://pitchfork.com/reviews/albums/8916-lets-get-it-thug-motivation-101/ [accessed 9 September 2023]; Christian Hoard, 'Let's Get It: Thug Motivation 101', Rolling Stone, 7 August 2005, https://web.archive.org/web/20081227030514/http://www.rollingstone.com/artists/youngjeezy/albums/album/7490389/review/7504105/lets_get_it_thug_motivation_101 [accessed 9 September 2023]; Steve 'Flash' Juan, 'Gucci Mane: Trap House', *RapReviews.Com*, 31 May 2005, www.rapreviews.com/2005/05/gucci-mane-trap-house/ [accessed 9 September 2023].
3. See Justin Adams Burton, *Posthuman Rap*. Oxford: Oxford University Press, 2017; Michael Waugh, '"Every Time I Dress Myself, it Go Motherfuckin' Viral": Post-Verbal Flows and Memetic Hype in Young Thug's Mumble Rap', *Popular Music* 39, no.2, 2020, pp.208–32; Sean M. Kennedy, 'Trap Spaces, Trap Music: Harriet Jacobs, Fetty Wap, and Emancipation as Entrapment', *The Popular Culture Studies Journal* 8, no.2, 2020, pp.68–84.
4. And even in an earlier incarnation as Triple Six Mafia in the early 1990s. See Triple Six Mafia, *Underground Vol.1 (1991–1994)*, Smoked Out Music, 1999.
5. Ronny Sarig, *Third Coast: Outkast, Timbaland, and How Hip-Hop Became A Southern Thing*. New York: Da Capo Press, 2007.
6. UGK, *Too Hard to Swallow*, Jive, 1992.
7. T.I., *Trap Muzik*, Atlantic, 2003.
8. Some of these prehistories are parsed by Regina Bradley in *Chronicling Stankonia: The Rise of the Hip-hop South*. Chapel Hill & London: University of North Carolina Press, 2021.
9. Wacka Flocka Flame, 'Hard in Da Paint', *Flockaveli*. Warner Bros., 2010; Rick Ross, 'B.M.F. (Blowin' Money Fast)', *Teflon Don*. Maybach Music, 2010.
10. Future, *Pluto*, Epic, 2012; Chief Keef, *Finally Rich*, UMGRI Interscope, 2012; Young Thug, *1017 Thug*, RBC Records, 2013.
11. 2 Chainz, *Based on a T.R.U. Story*, Def Jam, 2012; Young Thug, *Barter 6*, Atlantic, 2015; Future, *DS2*, Epic, 2015; Migos, *Yung Rich Nation*, Atlantic, 2015; Desiigner, 'Panda', Def Jam, 2015.
12. Rae Sremmurd, 'Black Beatles' (featuring Gucci Mane), *Sremmlife 2*, Interscope Records, 2016.
13. Daniel Sanchez, 'Hip-Hop Has Replaced Rock as Music's Most Consumed Genre', *Digital Music News*, 4 January 2018, www.digitalmusicnews.com/2018/01/04/hip-hop-rock-2017-biggest-genre/ [accessed 28 October 2021].
14. Migos, *Culture*. Quality Control Music, 2017; 2 Chainz, *Pretty Girls Like Trap Music*. Dej Jam, 2017.
15. Lana Del Rey, *Honeymoon*, Interscope, 2015; Lorde, *Melodrama*, Lava Records, 2017; Arianna Grande, *Sweetener*, Republic Records, 2018; Lykke Li, *So Sad So Sexy*, RCA Records, 2018.
16. Certainly, as it has been popularised, trap's original association with the drug trade diminishes in significance and its relation to labour grows more oblique.
17. Young Jeezy, 'Thug Motivation 101', *Let's Get It*.
18. Gucci Mane, 'Trap House', 'Pyrex Pot', *Trap House*.

19 Gucci Mane, 'Trap House'; 'Hustle', *Trap House*.
20 Young Jeezy, 'Trap or Die'; 'My Hood', *Let's Get it*.
21 Lester K. Spence, *Stare in the Darkness: The Limits of Hip-Hop and Black Politics*. Minneapolis: University of Minnesota Press, 2011, p.28; Burton, *Posthuman Rap*, p.58.
22 Eithne Quinn, *Nuthin' but a 'G' Thang: the Culture and Commerce of Gangsta Rap*. New York: Columbia University Press, 2004.
23 Michael P. Jeffries, *Thug Life: Race, Gender, and the Meaning of Hip-Hop*. Chicago: University of Chicago Press, 2011.
24 Lauren Kojikawa, *Sounding Race in Rap Songs*. Berkeley: University of California Press, 2015, p.113; Kelley, Race Rebels.
25 Quinn, *Nuthin' but a 'G' Thang*.
26 Kobena Mercer, 'Black Art and the Burden of Representation', *Third Text* 4, no.10, 1990, pp.61–78.
27 A point also made by Kelley in *Yo' Mama's Disfunktional!*.
28 Henry Louis Gates Jr., *The Signifying Monkey: A Theory of African American Literary Criticism*. Oxford: Oxford University Press, 2014.
29 A point underlined by Kelley in *Race Rebels* and Quinn in *Nuthin' but a 'G' Thang*.
30 John W. Roberts, *From Trickster to Badman: The Black Folk Hero in Slavery and Freedom*. Philadelphia: University of Pennsylvania Press, 1989, p.204.
31 On this point see Imani Perry, *Prophets of the Hood: Politics and Poetics in Hip Hop*. Durham & London: Duke University Press, 2004; Quinn, *Nuthin' but a 'G' Thang*; and Eric Harvey, *Who Got the Camera? A History of Rap and Reality*. Austin: University of Texas Press, 2021.
32 Gucci Mane, 'Hustle', *Trap House*.
33 Young Jeezy, 'Standing Ovation', *Let's Get It*.
34 Mara Shalloup, *BMF: The Rise and Fall of Big Meech and Black Mafia Family*. New York: St. Martin's Press, 2010.
35 Gucci Mane & Neil Martinez-Belkin, *The Autobiography of Gucci Mane*. New York: Simon and Schuster, 2017.
36 R.A.T. Judy, 'On the Question of Nigga Authenticity', *Boundary 2*, 21, no. 3, 1994, pp.211–30.
37 Ibid., p.212.
38 On this point see Rose, *Black Noise*.
39 Kelley, *Race Rebels*, p.191.
40 Quinn, *Nuthin' but a 'G' Thang*; Kelley, *Race Rebels*; Harvey, *Who Got the Camera?* Of course, white consumption of hip-hop is complex and has many layers. See Kajikawa, *Sounding Race in Rap Songs*; Bakari Kitwana, *Why White Kids Love Hip-hop: Wankstas, Wiggers, Wannabes, and the New Reality of Race in America*. New York: Civitas Books, 2005.
41 Adam Krims, *Music and Urban Geography*. London: Routledge, 2011.
42 Neil Smith, *The New Urban Frontier: Gentrification and the Revanchist City*. London: Routledge, 1996; Krims, *Music and Urban Geography*, ch.4.
43 Murali Balaji, *Trap(ped) Music and Masculinity: The Cultural Production of Southern Hip-Hop at the Intersection of Corporate Control and Self-Construction*. PhD Dissertation, Pennsylvania State University, 2009.
44 Phil A. Neel, *Hinterland: America's New Landscape of Class and Conflict*. New York: Reaktion Books, 2018; Richard Lloyd, 'Urbanisation and the Southern United States',

Annual Review of Sociology 38, May 2012, pp.483–506. By the 1990s over 50% of foreign business investment in the U.S. was directed to Southern states.
45 Neel, *Hinterland*.
46 Gilmore, *Golden Gulag*; Volker Jansse, 'Sunbelt Lock-Up: Where the Suburbs Meet the Super-Max', in: Michelle Nickerson & Darren Dochuk (Eds.) *Sunbelt Rising: The Politics of Space, Place and Region*. Philadelphia: University of Pennsylvania Press, 2011, pp.217–39.
47 See Matt Miller, 'Dirty Decade: Rap Music and the U.S. South, 1997–2007', *Southern Spaces*, 10 June 2008, http://southernspaces.org/2008/dirty-decade-rap-music-and-us-south-1997%E2%80%932007 [accessed 1 November 2021]. I draw here also on Krims, *Music and Urban Geography*.
48 Krims, *Music and Urban Geography*.
49 Certainly, we should be wary of too quickly dismissing complex sub-genres and local traditions. Houston hip-hop has, for instance, reversed the middle class withdrawal to the private space of the automobile by transforming the latter into a public, carnivalesque zone. The reception of bounce, to give another instance, should be understood in terms of the complex dialogic expressive forms which can be understood as generating new modes of kinship against the bourgeois family. These are, in other words, aesthetic practices that operate in the orbit of and against the grain of post-Fordist crisis. But only trap, it is held here, starts explicitly from the problem of work.
50 Gucci Mane, 'Trap House'.
51 Young Jeezy, 'Thug Motivation 101'.
52 It is also, it should go without saying, dangerous work. But, as David Farber argues, the choice of semi-autonomy of crack dealing is often preferable to the low dignity offered by low paid service industry work. See David Farber, *Crack: Rock Cocaine, Street Capitalism and the Decade of Greed*. Cambridge: Cambridge University Press, 2019.
53 Kelley, *Yo Mama's Disfunktional!*
54 Lauren Berlant, *Cruel Optimism*. Durham & London: Duke University Press, 2011.
55 I owe this point to Noah Angell, 'Everything Gucci: The Poetics and Political Economy of Gucci Mane', *Res.*, 13 November 2015, http://beingres.org/2015/11/04/everything-gucci/ [accessed 30 October 2023].
56 On the temporality at stake here, see Moten, *In the Break*, p.11.
57 Walter Benjamin, 'Central Park', *New German Critique* 34, Winter 1985, pp.32–58. Quoted on p.46.
58 Kodwo Eshun, *More Brilliant Than The Sun: Adventures in Sonic Fiction*. London: Quartet Books, 1998.
59 Jesse McCarthy, 'Notes on Trap: A World Where Everything is Dripping', N Plus One 32, October 2018, nplusonemag.com/issue-32/essays/notes-on-Trap/ [accessed November 2018].
60 David Harvey, *Rebel Cities: From the Right to the City to the Urban Revolution*. London: Verso, 2012.
61 Lisa Adkins, Melinda Cooper, & Martin Konings, *The Asset Economy*. Cambridge: Polity Press, 2020; Kevin Fox Graham, 'Creating Liquidity Out of Spatial Fixity' in: Manuel B. Aalbers (Ed.) *Subprime Cities: The Political Economy of Mortgage Markets*. London: Wiley Blackwell, 2012, pp.25–52.
62 Adkins, Cooper, & Konings, *The Asset Economy*.
63 Graham, 'Creating Liquidity Out of Spatial Fixity'.

64 For a good account see McClanahan, *Dead Pledges*.
65 See Mark Duda & William C. Apgar, *Foreclosure Rates in Atlanta: Patterns and Policy Issues*. Washington, DC: Neighborworks America, 2005.
66 See Scott Markley & Makuri Sharma, 'Gentrification in the Revanchiste Suburb: The Politics of Removal in Roswell Georgia', *Southeastern Geographer* 56, no.1, 2016, pp.57–80; Keith Jennings, 'The Politics of Race, Class and Gentrification in the ATL', *Trotter Review* 23, no.1, 2016, pp.1–38.
67 The Sun Valley Apartments off East Atlanta's Bouldercrest Road where he spent his formative years have since been closed down and sold off twice over since Gucci left. Georgia's high foreclosure rates were partly due to some of the most aggressive foreclosure policies in the U.S.
68 Guy Debord, *Society of the Spectacle* (Greg Adargo, Trans.). Detroit: Black & Red, 1977, p.126. On this point see also, Chris Wright, 'Its Own Peculiar Décor: Capital, Urbanism, and the Crisis of Class Politics in the US', *Endnotes* 4, October 2015. https://endnotes.org.uk/translations/chris-wright-its-own-peculiar-decor.
69 See McClanahan, *Dead Pledges*.
70 Laura Harris, *Experiments in Exile: C. L. R. James, Hélio Oiticia, and the Aesthetic Sociality of Blackness*. New York: Fordham University Press, 2018.
71 Moten, 'The Subprime and the Beautiful', p.243.
72 Harney & Moten, *Undercommons*, p.97.
73 The Atlanta Metropolitan police Red Dog unit was an aggressive anti-drug unit established in 1987 to and disbanded in 2011. It's also worth noting the video for 'Trapstar' involves Jeezy's escape from jail.
74 Geo Maher, *A World Without Police: How Strong Communities Make Cops Obsolete*. London: Verso, 2021.
75 Bryan Wagner, *Disturbing the Peace: Black Culture and the Police After Slavery*. Cambridge: Harvard University Press, 2010, pp.131–38.
76 George Caffentzis, *Clipped Coins, Abused Words, and Civil Government: John Locke's Philosophy of Money*. London: Pluto Press, 2021.
77 W.E.B. DuBois, *Black Reconstruction in America*. New York: Free Press, 1998, p.409.
78 Harvey more or less dates this to Dr. Dre's departure from NWA for a solo career that started with *The Chronic* in 1992. See Harvey, *Who Got the Camera?*.
79 Hall, 'Notes on Deconstructing the Popular'.
80 See for instance, Lauren Greenfield (Dir.), *Magic City*, GQ.com, 2015, www.gq.com/video/series/magic-city; Devin Friedman, 'Make it Reign: How an Atlanta Strip Club Runs the Music Industry', *GQ*, 8 July 2015, www.gq.com/story/atlanta-strip-club-magic-city [accessed 31 October 2023]; Chris Dart, 'Inside the Atlanta Strip Club that Supposedly Runs the Music Industry', *The A.V. Club*, 16 November 2015, www.avclub.com/read-this-inside-the-atlanta-strip-club-that-supposedl-1798286442 [accessed 31 October 2023]; Elizabeth Blair 'Strip Clubs: Launch Pads For Hits In Atlanta', *NPR*, 23 December 2010, www.npr.org/sections/therecord/2010/12/23/132287578/strip-clubs-launch-pads-for-hits-in-atlanta? [accessed 31 October 2023].
81 The reality is more complex: aspiring stars would tip the club DJ to play their songs and, in turn, tip the girls to dance when their song comes on.
82 See Friedman, 'Make it Reign'.
83 Shalloup, *BMF*.

84 See Margaret Hunter & Kathleen Soto, 'Women of Color in Hip Hop: The Pornographic Gaze', *Race, Gender & Class*, 2009, pp.170–91.
85 Jeffries, *Thug Life*.
86 Walter Benjamin, *The Arcades Project* (Howard Eiland & Kevin McLaughlin, Trans.), Cambridge: Belknap Press, 1999, p.347, quoted in Esther Leslie, 'Ruin and Rubble in the Arcades' in: Beatrice Hansen (Ed.), *Walter Benjamin and the Arcades Project*. London: Continuum, 2006, pp.87–112.
87 Hortense Spillers 'Mama's Baby, Papa's Maybe: An American Grammar Book'. *Diacritics* 17, no.2, Summer 1987, pp.64–81.
88 Fortunati, *The Arcane of Reproduction*.
89 Taylor Bell, *Hip-Hop's Influence on Stripper Culture: The Era of Cardi B*. BA dissertation, Columbia College Chicago, 2018, https://core.ac.uk/download/pdf/235201789.pdf.
90 L.H. Stallings, *Funk the Erotic: Transaesthetics and Black Sexual Cultures*. Chicago: University of Illinois Press, 2015.
91 Siobhan Brooks, *Race and Erotic Capital in the Stripping Industry*. New York: SUNY Press, 2010. See also Patricia Hill Collins, *Black Feminist Thought: Knowledge, Consciousness, and the Politics of Empowerment*. London: Routledge, 2002.
92 Stallings, *Funk the Erotic*, p.197.

4

So Much Wilder Than Me: The New 'World Music'

Proper Escapism

Ignorance is a condition of exoticism. For where an object is rendered as *exo* – as external or other – the blank space it leaves in its absence activates the imagination. But the construction of a cultural outside becomes all the more aggressive where global space and time are increasingly compressed, where the world has shrunk. The recent renewal of interest in the Cameroonian artist and writer Francis Bebey is an object lesson in such efforts. Here, the elisions come hard and fast: if Bebey is not reduced to a 'protest singer-songwriter', as one *Los Angeles Times* review has it, then it's *The Guardian* clumsily twisting his biography, or retailers muddling it further.[1] The new consumer of Bebey's music would be hard pressed to discover a rather extraordinary life. Following completion of his studies in his native Douala, then Mathematics and broadcasting in Paris and New York, he would work as a freelance journalist across Africa and on the basis of which he'd publish his first book, *Radiobroadcasting in Black Africa* in 1963.[2] Four novels, including the prize-winning *Agatha Mudio's Sons*, would follow along with a children's book, several volumes of poetry, and a major study, *African Music: A People's Art*, all mostly published around the same period that he worked at UNESCO's music programme in the late 1960s and early 1970s, and then a period as a full-time musician beginning in the mid-1970s.[3] But polymathy shades into eccentricity through the occlusion of detail, and so it happens that an opus once placed alongside the great chroniclers of African decolonisation, Mongo Beti or Chinua Achebe, say, is reduced to an outlandish novelty act: 'proper escapism', 'oddball', 'one-of-a-kind.'[4]

This rather austere caricature of Bebey that tends to circulate in the Anglophone West has its origins in two posthumous collections of recordings originally released on his own Ozileka label following his departure from UNESCO in 1974 and reissued in 2011 and 2014 on the French label, Born Bad Records. The detail these provide the consumer is parsimonious, amounting to a brief anecdote from Bebey's son, Patrick, whilst the presentation of his musical output is organised by a commitment to eccentricity rather than comprehensiveness. On the 2011 collection, *African Electronic Music: 1975–1985*, Bebey's more conventional pop fusions of synthesisers and keyboards with West African instruments and rhythms are put aside in favour of his most outlandish experiments in electronic composition.[5] The 2014 compilation, *Psychedelic Sanza 1982–1984*, showcases Bebey's inventive amplification of West African thumb piano and here too the selections gravitate towards his less conventional, weirder experiments with West African and Western pop convention.[6] Bebey's resounding vocal growls punctuate succinct choruses, distorted bass, and economical drumming, and are packaged and circulated with paltry little text, only perpetuating the cargo cultish framing of his electronic music all the more. Sure, lazy exoticism is not all that remarkable. But the modest revival of interest in Bebey in recent years bears further scrutiny to the extent it reflects a wider shifting interpretive frame, a whole set of changing coordinates of the musical production of otherness and difference.

A new culture of decontextualisation and eccentricity takes hold. Take, as another example, the DRC-based group Konono No.1 who, active since the 1970s, released a first album in the West, *Congotronics*, on the Belgian label Crammed Discs in 2005.[7] The group's wildly thunderous and distorted sound, anchored in DIY-amplified thumb piano backed by steady drumming, garnered rave reviews and tour gigs. 'Tough, ultra loud industrial electronica', wrote *DJ Mag*; 'echoes of European techno', said *The Guardian*; *The Wire* compared the group to post-punk; and *The Independent* called them 'Africa's Velvet Underground'.[8]

The latter is an especially common analog; it was deployed again in 2007, in the press releases for two critically acclaimed Tuareg bands from Mali: Group Doueh and Group Inerane have each been compared to the Velvet Underground by their label, Sublime Frequencies.[9] Both groups play what's sometimes called 'Desert Blues', a music that translates a traditional Tuareg lute playing for electric guitar and it's the unusual tunings and distorted sound this generates that has attracted comparisons with Western underground groups.[10] Or consider Syrian wedding singer Omar Souleyman, another Sublime Frequencies artist first released in the West in 2007, who plays an upbeat dance style typical of his local Sha'bi music.[11] Souleyman's fast-paced, high-energy keyboard riffs and pulsing electronic drums were easily consumed by Western audiences as 'Syrian techno'.

In the years that followed, a steady stream of unusual global popular music hybrids have come to be staples of critics' annual best-of lists and festival lineups. A collection of heavily compressed audio files of Malian pop titled *Music From Saharan Cellphones* inaugurated the Portland-based Sahel Sounds label in 2011; its most well-known artist, Mdou Moctar, is often called 'Hendrix of the Sahara'.[12] That same year Awesome Tapes From Africa was founded; its biggest release, however, came with the 2015 reissue of Ghanaian hip-house artist Ata Kak's *Obaa Simba*, originally self-released in the mid-1990s and whose rapping style is compared to 'a high-pitched, motor-mouthed rapping Lil Wayne, Young Thug, and Spongebob Squarepants.'[13] A reissue of previously mostly unknown Nigerian musician William Onyeabor on Luaka Bop in 2013 is lauded for its synth-based disco and compared to Funkadelic, while Charanjit Singh's 1982 experiment with Roland drum and bass synthesisers, *Synthesizing: Ten Ragas to a Disco Beat*, is retrospectively celebrated for having anticipated acid house.[14]

But these are merely illustrations of a still wider field united by, on the one hand, their origins in Third World or diaspora communities and, on the other, a Western consumption of eccentricity stabilised by its framing through existing categories: a peculiar subordination of difference to identity, a containment of musical imaginaries by the construction of a folk-other which the first part of this chapter seeks to unpack. In the chapter's second part, this ceaseless pursuit of an Other at the limits of existing stylistic categories is placed in relation to the imperial postures of the collector and tourist and their consumption of meals, travelways, and artefacts, most of all. Here we will confront a broader negotiation of aesthetic and economic value in the quest for the exotic and, in particular, the ways in which these practices reflect a fractured constellation of distinct but overlapping historical modes of experience and, in turn, express a wider demand for flexibility and adaptability in light of contemporary social and economic change.

The Will to Hybridity

Infamously conceived as a category in the late 1980s by a group of record company executives in search of new markets, 'world music' is a genre defined, more or less, by the racialisation of the artists it's designed to encompass. No doubt, pop musical exoticism could be traced back much further, but among the distinguishing features of its most significant iterations in the 1980s was its premise upon an ideal of collaboration.[15] An ostensibly authentic incorporation of global folk musics into Western pop operated through the figure of the Western celebrity's partnership with often anonymous local artists, mere figures for a timeless set of musical traditions, of which Paul Simon's work with South African musicians on *Graceland* and Ry Cooder's with Cuban musicians on *Buena Vista Social Club*, are the best-known iterations.[16] These associations sought both to signal a more 'respectful' appropriation of non-Western cultural forms, while also drawing from the latter a ballast against the threat posed to rock music's master narratives of rebellion and authenticity by its growing identification with commercialism.

Over the decade or so that followed, crossovers between Western and non-Western musics intensified, and a new array of global pop hybrids garnered commercial success. The Belgian group Zap Mama (that combined West African singing styles with RnB and hip-hop production) and Apache Indian (a British artist blending ragga and bhangra) are typical of 1990s world music fusions. These were contemporary too with a litany of dance musics known as 'world beat' exhibiting a penchant for the quotation of ethnographic field recordings, hand drumming, wooden flutes, or digeridoo.

It's noteworthy that, as these cultural hybridities expanded, so were their theorisations coming to circulate ever more widely as well. Perhaps most significant in this respect was Homi Bhabha's influential accounting of cultural 'in-betweenness'. As ever-expanding liminal spaces between cultures emerged, Bhabha reasoned, so too could old hierarchies be made to waver, fixed identities to fragment, and disavowed knowledges to emerge.[17] And while endorsements of hybridity, transnationality, and migration did register opposition to neoliberal discourses and enduring imperialism, they tended to do so in broad, civilisational terms that obscured the historical processes by which these are conditioned.[18]

On this latter point, Gayatri Chakravorty Spivak has suggested that the 'self-declared hybrid' remains 'in the service of *neo-colonialism*' since, to the extent it entails an aestheticised view of hybridity, it overlooks the asymmetry that generates liminal spaces to begin with.[19] Bringing Spivak's argument to bear directly on world music hybrids in the 1990s, Ashwani Sharma suggests that ornamentation of Western pop with Third World cultural forms amounts to the incorporation of difference 'within the terroristic violence of racialised capitalism.'[20] World music, in other words, amounts to a strategy for the containment of difference, for it can value alterity only to the degree it can be experienced through 'universally valid commercial units of culture.'[21]

Raw as Hell

These arguments imply the universalising effects of global capitalism: difference becomes a merely generic claim, a 'real universality', in Étienne Balibar's words, where the concrete processes of accumulation come to incorporate all corners of the world.[22] This oscillation between universal and particular is reflected in the very logic of world music which is premised, on the one hand, upon the practical universality of the pop song, by now a component of practically every culture. On the other hand, nationalism and the survival of pre-capitalist practices mean local variations on a global form continue to emerge.[23] But the new world music at issue in this chapter operates with changing coordinates of authenticity and hybridity, and this is apparent if we attend to its sonic semantics, its textural composition. Throughout the 1980s and 1990s world music favoured glossy audio production that would downplay technical interventions. Studios designed to neutralise reverb and echo thus registered on recordings merely as an absence. That is, to veil the existence of the studio is for the recording to stage only itself, and in this way to effect a sense of liveness, of proximity. But this is a set of techniques whose returns diminish as they're ever more identified with commercial artifice and, in this respect, the crackles on Bebey's home recordings or the warps from his use of a tape-over-tape recording technique, the buzzing magnetic mics devised by Konono No.1 for the likembe, the low fidelity of open air recordings of Group Inerane and Group Doueh, or the highly compressed and gnarled audio files collected for *Music From Saharan Cellphones*, are all reflective of a wider rejection of sonic slickness.[24]

As we've already seen, it's sometimes suggested that the new world music echoes the DIY aesthetics of underground music of recent decades and thus serves to confirm that the music remains uncontrived, spontaneous, raw.[25] Indeed, the latter is an especially ubiquitous descriptor. According to their label, Group Doueh plays 'raw and unfiltered music' and Group Inerane is 'raw as hell'.[26] Ata Kak recalls 'DIY machine soul' to one journalist, Omar Souleyman is 'raw, joyous, danceable' for another, and Konono No. 1 plays a 'raw, noisy variant' of traditional music.[27] Makeshift adaptations to limited technical conditions, in other words, corroborate the absence of commercial ambitions so that mediation and sonic infidelity come to signify the music's proximity to the listener.[28]

To be sure, such tactics are continuous with strategies of earlier world musics. The qualities associated with authenticity are still projected upon a racialised other whose music is imagined to emerge spontaneously out of an organic aesthetic community. Only, where sanitised folkloric sounds or 1990s hybrids now seem contrived and mechanical, the collector or record label works all the more insistently to generate a state of exteriority for the music. This is especially evident where labels restrict access to technological infrastructure so that artists continue to use outmoded gear when they reach Western markets. Slapdash, anachronistic album cover design is pervasive too. In any case, the global South remains confined to the object world of sleepy memory. It lags incessantly behind, a relic of another epoch, 'a timewarp of permanent underdevelopment and poverty'.[29]

My Own Meaning

Whilst the desire to preserve uneven technological access animates the qualities associated with new world music authenticity, there are still other constraints we should observe here, and these hinge on a politics of knowledge. Consider that access to these obscure global popular musics was made possible by an explosion of blogs in the mid-2000s. Prior to a clampdown on intellectual property offences that drove music consumption to streaming platforms, file hosting software such as DivX, Megadownload, and Mediafire made it possible for Web users to circulate previously hyper-obscure, long out of print recordings. Whilst these were often shared with little to no information, normally for the simple reason that communities of amateur collectors were often short of it in the first place, this state of affairs contributed to the sense of their singularity and, in turn, seemed to sediment into a genre convention.

We have already considered the aggressive exclusion of liner notes to the reissues of Bebey's music, but this is a pretty standard practice. In tracking the reception of Konono No.1 for instance, ethnomusicologist David Font-Navarrete points to a widely circulated attribution of the group's origins in 'Bazombo trance music', a wholly phantastic form that has served as alibi for meaningful assessment of the group's modernist interpretations of folk forms.[30] But this evacuation of context amounts to a wider strategy made explicit by the Sublime Frequencies; label co-founder Alan Bishop who once asserted that knowledge of local musics detracts 'from the expressive capabilities of the vocalizing or of the sound itself, which allows me to create my own meaning for it, which elevates it into a higher piece of work for me.'[31]

What are we to make of this suspension of exegesis, this attack upon history and context along with the internment of the music in distant time and place it entails? One proposition has been to look to Web 2.0 economies. For where streaming platforms offer unprecedented access to cultural material, the argument goes, epistemic strategies of new world music preserve underground sensibilities; invoke independent record shops, cassette trading and the amateurish journalism of the fanzine.[32] There are still other questions at issue here, besides the projection of analog institutions onto the digital, however. Sure, the music serves, in an era where consumption is mainly online, to generate a sense of discovery by a process of re-enchantment; it constitutes the cultural object and its producer as other. But this pursuit of the foreign by the cultivation of aura, it bears reiterating, differs in important respects from the celebratory multiculturalism of global hybridity evinced by earlier world musics. For one thing, in the process of its exotification, it foregrounds the agency of the collector and dismisses the work of the artist by way of a depiction of musical spontaneity; labels are often better known than their artists, whilst press releases recount curators' heroic searches through markets and bazaars for elusive recordings or years' long attempts to locate the personnel behind rediscovered albums.

1492

The standards of aesthetic judgement definitive of the recirculation of recordings at issue here can be traced, in part, to the principles of 'crate digging'. This refers to the collection and recontextualisation of rare soul, funk, and jazz originating with hip-hop, especially as that practice roamed ever wider, to encompass global popular musics through the late 1990s and early 2000s: African funk, Turkish psychedelia, Bollywood soundtracks, or Ethiopian jazz. But hip-hop's archival reconstructions are premised upon a mining of the music for rhythmic breaks and grooves so that its appraisal of recorded music rests with the extent to which it can be subsumed to hip-hop's own aesthetic hierarchies; recontextualisation amounts to the subsumption of one genre by another.

While hip-hop's art of collection bears an inclination to obscurity and rarity of its sources, new world music adds to this its own principle of eccentricity. Its singular, hyper-local, and obscure character rebounds against its consumption as Western genre (indie rock or techno, say), so it is both reconciled with, yet outside, Western music systems. This balancing act between the singular and general, it is held here, constitutes the primary strategy for the preservation of exoticism where the latter's historical conditions, of a spatial exteriority to 'civil' society and capital, grows all the more difficult to conceive.

We can get at the eccentricity of the new world music if we compare Bebey with his friend and fellow Cameroonian-French migrant, Manu Dibango. The latter achieved global popularity in the early 1970s with his 'Soul Makossa', a straight ahead jazz-funk tune that bears little relation to the local Dualan dance after which it is named. The song was a major international sensation following its popularisation by influential DJ David Mancuso around 1973, and it found a still wider audience through its adaptation by Michael Jackson in 1982 for 'Wanna Be Startin' Something' and has recurred in a number of variations and quotations since. If Dibango's sound is a hybrid, this is registered on 'Soul Makossa' mainly by the heavily reverbed Dualan lyrics which echo around its driving beat and saxophone. This is a world music that leans far more on the side of the familiar than the foreign, however. Bebey, on the other hand, is not so easily reducible to existing forms. The cultural mixtures he effects are often awkward and fit prevailing styles only uncomfortably. The terms on which traditions meet are less stable since, unlike in Dibango's work, there isn't a consistent cultural dominant into which musical elements are to be integrated and this generates the stranger, less easily categorisable sorts of sonic combinations fashionable today.

The decades separating Dibango's 'Soul Makossa' from the reissues of Bebey signal disparate strategies of cultural hybridity and the reception of these, in turn, denote the shifting strategies by which a Western subject seeks pleasure in a tightly managed loss of self in the other, a primitivism that can be traced back to the beginning of a conception of history itself. Indeed, when Enrique Dussel called 1492 – the year of Columbus's arrival in the Caribbean – 'the date of the "birth" of modernity', his point was that the sense of a progressive movement through time was premised upon the 'discovery' of its other, a being continually situated at the onset of history.[33] Colonialism, in other words, has always functioned as a machine for the production of a modern sense of self.

In this regard, it's worth remarking that the consolidation of a modern society of property owners operates by attributing qualities it sees as both natural and as lost to all those it excludes from civil society. To desire to be opened up to the other, therefore, is both to be made ecstatic, but it also implies, each time, the necessity to leave that state in the name of maturity and the deferral of pleasure demanded of the productive subject. One is both lost in an other but only to be ever more secured as a sovereign, self-possessed self in the process. Hal Foster refers to this oscillation as the 'ambiguity' of the primitivist encounter, and for which, we might add, music has been an especially privileged medium of expression.[34] From Rousseau to Nietzsche, philosophers have identified the origins of language and music in primitive speech-song. Insofar as it once functioned as the direct expression of spontaneous desire, then it can continue to stand as a memory of a necessarily eclipsed experience, especially where it's identified with folk cultures.[35] There's a pseudo-universalist foundation to the contemporary subject we can glimpse here: the global circulation of music suggests we are all somehow the same despite our differences. But folk cultures also stand for an innocence the modern self has transcended and outgrown and this development, in turn, generates a traumatic sense of loss that propels the desire for the other. And this returns us, finally, to the new world music. For where musical exoticism appears overly contrived, all-too propelled by commercial ambition, then a new exteriority must be devised by novel processes of mediation if the pleasures of the primitivist encounter are to persist.

The Man of Any Past

So, one should be endlessly on guard of a tendency, so deeply entrenched, to relegate non-Western peoples and cultures to a timeless and homogeneous state of humanity. But we should also attend to developments other than those arising from Eurocentric impulses, for these suggest models of aesthetic experimentation not reducible to a Western subject in search of temporary respite from the burdens of their hegemony. Bebey's 1969 study, *African Music*, is an instructive departure point in this regard.[36] That book is anchored in the premise that, given its pursuit of formal aesthetic pleasure, Western music abandons the expressive character still preserved in an African music integrated with everyday life. This entails distinct standards of judgement: technique for the European and the capacity to express emotion for the African. It further informs Bebey's two-pronged pedagogical ethos: to 'open the ears' of the Western audience to the universality of African forms as well as the regeneration of African music as it comes into contact with the West.[37] Bebey calls for a careful 'marriage' or 'melding' of cultures that breathes new life into African folk forms; a search for still vital elements within African and European musical cultures.[38] A good deal of his musical output might be interpreted along these lines too. Combinations of traditional instruments, an electrified thumb piano, or a BaBenzele single pitch flute with programmed drums or bass might indeed figure in Bebey's ideal of cultural union. Most spectacular of all though are the unsettling psychedelic roars which ornament a number of Bebey's thumb piano compositions; so loud they rumble distorted.

But this is a philosophy whose impulses are all the clearer for being made literal in Bebey's novels. Each of his fictional works deals with social tensions between traditional and modern institutions in decolonising West African states and can be read as cautionary tales of the moral corruptions where imbalances between Europe and Africa occur. *The Ashanti Doll*, published in 1973 but set in Accra following Kwame Nkrumah's ascension to power – a period in which Bebey worked in Ghana as a journalist – is set against the backdrop of the withdrawal of one market trader's permit when her daughter marries an opposition party deputy.[39] The betrayal of market traders by the ruling party stands in for the corruptions that arise when a state loses touch with its established constituencies and these sorts of imbalances between tradition and modernisation drive a whole series of subplots: an educated friend of the illiterate protagonist grows jealous and attacks her, an aunt marries a polygamist only to abandon her sexual mores. Indeed, the novel's resolution hinges on the union of the innocent and unschooled Edna and the idealist young bureaucrat, Spio. Published three years later, *King Albert* is organised by the same structuring principle. It portrays the rivalry between an elderly traditional businessman, Albert, and the stylish, Western-educated Bokounou over both the affections of a young woman and an electoral contest for the state's first parliamentary assembly.[40] In a competition conditioned, on the one hand, by a modern polity and the rites of marriage, on the other, Albert is victorious only once he comes to gradually acquiesce to the modernising social developments around him.

How then does such a culturally dialogical ethos shape Bebey's approach to musical composition? Take 'New Track', now among Bebey's best-known songs. Layers of sound, traditional and contemporary, are stacked upon one another as if music were architecture. An amplified thumb piano accompanies a thumping bass drum, a West African wood block beat, and a bouncing bassline; a combination ornamented by some outrageously screeching synth sounds. Half-sung, half-spoken lyrics are pulled to the front of the mix, expressing a beguiling demand for change: 'I want a banana, more freedom, and dance on a new track'.

The point is often equally apparent from Bebey's lyrics. On the song 'La Condition Masculine' – first released in 1981 and included on the 2011 reissue *Psychedelic Sanza* – Bebey stages a tongue in cheek role reversal whereby a husband complains that his wife has stopped obeying him since she discovered the 'feminine condition'. Another such exchange occurs on 'Un Petit Ivorien' from 1979, when a young, naïve boy, condescended to by tourists, recovers his self-assurance when he begins to see their shallowness. This sort of lesson, where folkish wisdom sees through the pretenses of urban sophistication, is also the message on 'The Coffee-Cola Song'. Electronic drums, a plucky guitar, and plonking synth accompany a Ba-Benzele flute, its single bopping note see-saws with Bebey's vocal:

> There are people in town, man
> Crazy people in town
> Eating bread and butter and drinking coffee-cola
> They believe we are wild, man
> They believe we are wild
> Just because we don't use any money and we don't drink coffee-cola
> But if you could see how they live
> Then you'll discover how savage they are
> So much wilder than me.[41]

On the ballad 'Pygmy Love Song', swelling psychedelic synths lay the ground for a pair of dueling flutes which, Bebey explains in *African Music*, express a couple's union for the Ba-Benzele. It's a rather fitting theme for a saccharine tune that begins: 'My heart is full of love...'[42] and whose chorus consists in the Ba-Benzele yodelling technique often deployed by Bebey. It would seem, in light of these dialogical and reclamatory commitments, that anthropologist Steven Feld's consideration of Bebey as reiterating the 'industrialization of desire for pleasure in participation in spiritual difference', is rather heavy-handed and off-track.[43] Feld is referring here to the decades-long saga of primitivist caricatures and appropriations of the Ba-Benzele, from Brian Eno and Jon Hassell to Madonna. That's not to say we cannot discern an essentialising tendency in Bebey's work, it's just he anchors the preservation of the essence of African culture in a distinct assimilationist ethos that demands further consideration.

Here, we should consider Bebey's acknowledged veneration of Léopold Sédar Senghor, founding figure of the Negritude movement.[44] Indeed, Bebey plainly adopts Senghor's vitalist terms to conceive African culture as expressive of a 'life force' which animates all being.[45] So, just as for Senghor rhythm is 'the architectural structure of our being', for Bebey it is a privileged vessel for the 'expression of life force'.[46] We find parallels in their sorting of African and European art too, though for the more philosophically inclined Senghor, these are ontological principles derived from the philosophy of Henri Bergson.[47] But while Bergson sought a mode of cognition opposed to Cartesian rationalism, Senghor argues that a supra-rational, immediate, and sensuous grasp of being is already present in African culture. 'Emotion is Negro, just as reason is Hellenic', he has famously declared.[48]

This brings us back to the charge of cultural essentialism. For just as Theodor Adorno has argued that, despite its probing of the limits of logic, Bergson's attempt to retrieve a knowledge in excess of reason was always destined to hypostatise into yet another abstract principle, so we might claim that Senghor and Bebey operate with a discourse still defined by European traditions of knowledge.[49] Not only do they homogenise African musical traditions, the argument goes, but in the process they reproduce Europe's own self-mythologising repression of sensuality too.[50]

Could one nevertheless defend Bebey's valorisation of cultural traits on the grounds they were sought to sustain decolonial movements beyond the restricted terms of nationalism and not merely the revival of anachronisms?[51] Certainly, these are terms implied by Jean-Paul Sartre who, in a famous essay, views Negritude as the expression of a peasantry in revolt against Western technical culture.[52] Or does it instead, as Frantz Fanon claims in reply, amount to a poetry for which the past supplants revolt in the present? 'In no way', Fanon writes in *Black Skin, White Masks*, 'should I dedicate myself to the revival of an unrecognized Negro civilization. I will not make myself the man of any past. I do not want to exalt the past at the expense of my present or my future'.[53] And by the publication of *Wretched of the Earth*, Fanon is all the more adamant: the valorisation of pre-colonial histories expresses the desire for recognition by the coloniser on the latter's terms. And of the inner life of the nation, it can only clutch at its garments: '[t]he sari becomes sacred, and shoes that came from Paris or Italy are left off in favour of pampooties'.[54]

Attending to this knotty debate here should, at the very least, attune us to the distortions effected through the contemporary circulation of Bebey's work; the smothering of the processes of decolonisation of which he was a noteworthy participant. Equally, we should rebuff readings which would lump him with a wider exoticising gaze, for his work is better understood as bringing the ancestral into the history of the new African state. Certainly, a tendency to cultural essentialism is evident in Bebey's writing on music, only we might understand his integration of ethnic musical traditions as strategically deployed for a nation-building project in an ethnically divided Cameroon.[55] In this way we are better to interpret Bebey's work, his literary output as well as his music, as politically conciliatory.[56] Or, we might follow Gary Wilder's recent account of Negritude as a reclamation rather than a rejection of the forms that mediated their subjection. 'Rather than counterpose autarchic notions of Africa, the Caribbean, or blackness to a one-dimensional figure of France,' he writes, '[Senghor and Césaire] claimed within "France" those transformative legacies to which they were rightfully heirs.'[57] The charge of essentialism only holds, on these terms, if viewed through the lens of a nationalist project rather than a theory of modernity itself, one which puts in question the very categories of Europe and Africa. Of course, as Fanon's remarks imply, the dialogical image of culture touted by Bebey, and for that matter Senghor too, might remain constrained by an idealist view of social change, all too heedless to a whole series of unequal exchanges: economic, political, legal, and so on.

But this is a point of debate which is not resolvable solely at the level of culture alone; it stands here to underline the extent to which the political impulses underlying Bebey's work are obliterated by his consumption today. With nowhere to go, his politics can only register as another of his strange quirks and participate in the mystification necessary for his frictionless and easy consumption. Yet we should also acknowledge that Bebey's work is not exhausted by these deliberations. There is a remainder, an excess that withdraws; everything is not simply present and available in Bebey's music and this is partly what gives it its power. This is particularly evident in the cryptic growls with which he punctuates some of his thumb piano compositions in the early 1980s – the enthralling polyrhythms of 'Bissau' in particular – somewhere between a moan and a scream. We have already mentioned the screeching synthesiser on 'New Track', which announces its contemporaneity and otherworldliness all at once. The comic role reversals and pursuit of irony, which we've encountered in 'Coffee-Cola Song', permeate his music and his literature as well, often disrupting what starts off as a narrow didacticism. Laughter, Bebey writes in *King Albert*, is a means of human relation: it 'keeps without difficulty in the shade of the dull days, behind the dreary mist of the winter season, or sheltered from resounding mockery... This laughter is probably the gift which we offer most graciously to our fellows, when the circumstances of life lead us to think of offering them anything.'[58]

All of this begs the question of why, four decades later, in the context of an ongoing neocolonial recidivism where a conciliatory cultural politics seems all the less salient, that interest in Bebey and the new world music, more broadly, has blossomed. We have seen that the answer, in part, rests with an ongoing crisis and negotiation with authenticity in popular music, especially as this plays out in its circulation on digital platforms. Where new global hybridities present novel sonic textures that elide immediacy and context, this suggests a changed nexus of knowledge and power generating cultural exteriority.

New Venom

The resuscitation of Bebey into a world where his work can no longer claim its primary truth means it ends up as mere kitsch, curiosity, a hollow theatre of a now vacuous and wacky 'protest music'. Obviously, at one level this mode of consumption is conditional upon globalisation, typically presented as a series of inevitable technological processes that, for the Third World, brought down the price of raw materials and so generated impossible debt burdens which, in turn, led to restructuring by the International Monetary Fund's Structural Adjustment Programs which dictated neoliberal reforms that more or less eradicated the state and consigned society to the vicissitudes of the market. Global unevenness and inequality are, as we have seen, a material feature of new world music too, expressed in its instrumentation, its audio quality, its packaging. But we have also seen that the vertical fragmentation of production on a global scale in recent decades has implied the restructuring of the world system and thus increasingly multiplex relations of core to periphery. This 'marginalization of the center', to use Ashwani Sharma's phrase, compels the curatorial pursuit of cultural exteriority, for an outside, ever further towards sonic eccentricity.[59]

For its advocates, there's something inherently progressive to be gleaned from all this. The labels in question operate outside the hegemonic systems of the record industry, their margins are small and the terms of record deals tend to be transparent by most accounts. Curation is driven by an ethos of inclusion, 'exposure', preservation of overlooked cultural artefacts, and the expression of some self-awareness regarding the irrefutable inequalities between label and artist is typical.[60] 'Punk ethnography', 'guerilla' or 'salvage' ethnomusicology: the terms used to describe the processes at work here imply a wider aesthetic philosophy.[61] Such a claim calls for some further examination.

It would seem apt, in this light, to consider the idea of 'salvagepunk' circulated by China Mieville and Evan Calder Williams in the late 2000s.[62] The post-apocalyptic aesthetic with which Mieville and Calder Williams are concerned, images of a world emptied of people where rusted cars and collapsed skyscrapers dominate a desolate landscape and of which the *Mad Max* films are emblematic, figures the inherently catastrophic nature of capital's logics of accumulation. Capital, the argument runs, stops at nothing in the pursuit of its own expansion, not even, it grows increasingly evident today, the collapse of the planetary ecosystem which is among its ultimate conditions. As a concept, salvagepunk is at once descriptive and prescriptive.[63] It submits that apocalypse is the existent organisation of the world rather than its impending horizon. This is to reject a developmental vision of history for an already existent ruined battleground of scattered processes of survival.[64] It's also to dismiss, for Mieville and Williams, nostalgia for revolutionary conditions that are no longer operative or all too heteronomous with the present; a melancholia that earlier we identified in the work of Mark Fisher. Instead, it follows, we should be attuned to the possibilities inherent within capital's destructive processes. Objects might be repurposed or redeemed, new use values, 'new venom', in Williams's words, might be wrought from the apparently obsolete.

There are obvious parallels between salvagepunk and the new world music and this is not only because the music is valorised partly for its make-do character. It also involves an analogous rejection of principles of development: where linear history erodes, so new musics are recovered from any point in the past five decades or so. This reflects the wider temporal logics of the uneven development of contemporary capitalism which we outlined in this book's first chapter. The society might proceed 'forwards' in terms of technological advances but might also move 'backwards', as it were, where cheap, anachronistic techniques and methods of production could be leveraged across spatially dispersed markets through global communications and transport infrastructure. The twentieth century 'standard' of secure, permanent, unionised employment becomes an exception as anachronistic forms of wage contract, more contingent and erratic, become the dominant means of survival. Rather than the completion of capital's historical advance, we're confronted with a series of self-differentiating temporalities, a fractured constellation of distinct but overlapping frames of historical experience.

But recovery of outmoded commodities in search of new use also points to other premises. Amiri Baraka, to take one example, argued for the origins of jazz in the salvage of European instruments to new ends, and this is a tradition of re-appropriation that continues through, for instance, hip-hop's deployment of the turntable or house and techno's annexation of drum and bass synthesisers.[65] We might also consider Walter Benjamin's scattered reflections on the figure of the collector who, on his account, releases the object from the grip of reification, 'divests things of their commodity character by taking possession of them'.[66]

But Benjamin also offers a still significant caution in this respect, especially relevant to the collector of world music. The collector's act of decommodification, the 'connoisseur's value' effected by his idiosyncratic aesthetic economy, to use another phrase of Benjamin's, is a Sisyphean task.[67] The object's re-circulation as exchange value is an ever-looming horizon. This is a logic that also organises Will Straw's account of the subjectivity of the record collector; caught in the inherent temporal disjunction between the cultural object's economic value and its existence as an object of desire.[68] That is, from the viewpoint of the market, the recording has a deeply transitory character, desire for it is expressed only once, in the act of exchange. Yet from the perspective of the collector, the object is cured of its fragility and its ephemerality – a result of the seriality of its production – and is transformed by a new spatiality once it finds its place in the collector's classificatory schema. So, to return to the new world music, the collector's re-presentation of the cultural object rescues it but only by situating it within a new order which gives it new value and from which it might be commodified once again and, in turn, demands the process of discovery starts over if exteriority, an outside, is to be brought inside once more.

Solace in the Tacit

This is all to say that collection is a ceaseless pursuit whose telos never arrives, since the collector's seizure of their object at once summons and withdraws its singularity. The process must always begin anew. And it's in this regard that the collector inhabits a temporal space that they share with a related figure: the tourist. Both are driven, after all, by the boundless global quest for the exotic, the novel, the not-yet-possessed. We should observe the contradictory logic of the transitory in their pursuit of auratic experience here. On the one hand it demands their mastery over their environment, the abstraction of their object from its context, whether artefact, meal, or travelway. On the other hand, only an imperial mode of being that inevitably destroys its object generates the experience they desire.[69]

In this regard, the changing coordinates of tourism in the current epoch are instructive for our analysis of the new world music's pursuit of authenticity. Where post-war mass tourism involved a suspension of everyday obligation through an infantilising handover of responsibility to the travel agent, hotel clerk, steward, and so on, tourist activity today grows ever less spectacular as it intersects ever more tightly with everyday life and for ever more people.[70] Think, for instance, of the ubiquitous planning of meals, the consumption of hyper-localised craft products, or visits to recently established urban heritage zones.[71] As they occupy ever more of quotidian experience, these demand ever more romanticism, ever more reflexive negotiation of the codes of consumption to effect the power of their paltry rituals. The tourist's gaze, in other words, inevitably depletes the authenticity of its object and is compelled to work harder for its sustenance.[72]

This is an issue emblematised by the room-sharing platform Airbnb, whose trademark is its invitation to 'live like the locals', a promise bearing little fruit where either the locals live ever more like we do, or where one's temporary neighbours turn out to be other Airbnb guests gazing disappointingly back at us. The work through which one thus locates 'authentic' sites to visit grows ever more taxing, demands ever more nuance and negotiation as it's progressively subsumed to processes of exchange. Of course, Airbnb's expanding dominance of the hotel industry is itself emblematic of a spatialisation of economic crisis. The growing numbers of people willing or compelled to rent their homes to strangers speaks to a state of affairs where asset values rise while the value of labour-power doesn't. To be sure, there's a link implied here between the diminishing character of work and ongoing negotiations with authenticity. It's a relationship we can glimpse, for example, in those lists of life hacks that pervade social media: a coat hanger becomes a bookstand, an old pen preserves a phone charger, a bread clip saves a pair of sandals; economic insecurity is aestheticised as a performance of elegance and ingenuity.[73] Certainly, these are merely iterations of a wider contemporary 'craft mentality' which renews romantic allusions to pre-industrial experience.[74]

This search for 'solace in the tacit', as one critic puts it, is discernible in the curation of the new world music as well, to return to our central claim, just as it is in the tourist's ever more frenzied movement through the world.[75] What is the consumption of wired-up thumb pianos, makeshift amplifiers, jerry-rigged studios, and improvised distribution networks if not continuous with nostalgia for the hand-carved trinket, a locally woven textile, tinkling with a broken motor or mending a torn shirt? The homemade, whether a ceramic bowl or an analog tape recording, draws upon a communal imaginary which emerges in a wider context where global commodity chains and disposability prevail. The presentation of a folk-other demands, it turns out, hard work.

The link between new world music and the craft economy is all the more palpable where we take into account the widely documented explosion of an artisan economy following the global financial crisis of 2008.[76] Kirstin Munro and Chris O'Kane have proposed that this amounts to a 'new spirit of capitalism'.[77] This phrase refers to Luc Boltanski and Eve Chiapello's influential study of what they called an aesthetic critique of the society.[78] On their argument, a new justificatory spirit for capitalist society succeeds by responding to the moral precepts of 1960s and 1970s countercultures. That is, Boltanski and Chiapello show that by portraying lifetime employment and a social safety net as stifling and oppressive, capital successfully presented declining working conditions as liberating and fulfilling. Equally, for Munro and O'Kane, the craft business is presented as a self-employment morally distinct from capitalism at the very epoch where 'creative' labour produces cultural and informational goods crucial for the contemporary economy.

That is, the convergence of styles of cultural and occupational performance we have identified between contemporary 'artisan' labour and new world music reflects a wider context where creativity becomes the affective imperative of post-Fordist labour; where generalised insecurity blurs distinctions between the working lives of 'creatives' and those working outside traditional Fordist arrangements, note Munro and O'Kane. As a matter of fact, ingenuity, flexibility, and adaptability define both the stylistic markers of the new world music artist as well as the demands of an increasingly precarious labour market. Indeed, precarity-become-spectacle is, all in all, a pretty good summation of what's involved here and, in this respect, it's significant to note that artisanal work might stand as the horizon of contemporary occupational desire as well. It insinuates, after all, a sense of community between producer and consumer, alludes to an experience of the unity of head and hand prior to the subsumption of the body to the dictates of the machine and the mechanised organisation of time. It might be apparent that these are qualities we have associated with the experience of music, too. But so long as they remain premised upon mechanisms of exchange, the unity upon which they're established remains ever fractured and this delimits the myopia of dominant modes of new world music consumption too.

Notes

1. Randall Roberts, 'In Rotation: Francis Bebey's "African Electronic Music, 1975-1982"', *Los Angeles Times*, 21 June 2012, https://latimesblogs.latimes.com/music_blog/2012/06/in-rotation-francis-bebeys-african-electronic-music-1975-1982.html [accessed 26 May 2022]; Rob Fitzpatrick, 'The 101 Strangest Records on Spotify: Francis Bebey – African Electronic Music 1976–1982', *The Guardian*, 30 January 2013, www.theguardian.com/music/music blog/2013/jan/30/101-strangest-spotify-francis-bebey [accessed 29 June 2022].
2. Francis Bebey, *La Radiodiffusion En Afrique Noire*. Issy-les-Moulineaux Seine: Editions Saint-Paul, 1963.
3. For a more detailed bibliography, see David Ndachi Tagne, *Francis Bebey*. Paris: L'Harmattan, 1993, pp.8–10; Fernand Nathan, *Francis Bebey: Ecrivain et Musicien Camerounais*. Paris: Editions Fernand Nathan, 1979, pp.6–9; René Balbaud, 'Francis Bebey', *Africa Report* 15, no.8, 1970, and daughter Kidi Bebey's memoir, *My Kingdom for a Guitar*. Bloomington: Indiana University Press, 2021.
4. RwdFwd, 'Francis Bebey' https://rwdfwd.com/products/francis-bebey-psychedelic-sanza-1982-1984; Forced Exposure, 'Francis Bebey', www.forcedexposure.com/Artists/BEBEY.FRANCIS.html; Fitzpatrick, 'The 101 Strangest Records on Spotify'.
5. Francis Bebey, *African Electronic Music 1975–1982*. Born Bad Records, 2011.

6 Francis Bebey, *Psychedelic Sanza 1982–1984*. Born Bad Records, 2014.
7 Konono No.1, *Congotronics*. Crammed Discs, 2005.
8 Colm O'Loughlin, 'On Our Radar: The Music You Must Hear', *DJ Mag*, 8 June 2008, https://djmag.com/node/1228 [accessed 4 July 2022]; Alex Petridis, 'Assume Crash Position', *The Guardian*, 4 April 2006, www.theguardian.com/music/2006/apr/04/popandrock1 [accessed 4 July 2022]; Rob Young, 'Konono No.1', *The Wire* 253, March 2005, p.52; Robin Denselow, 'Konono No. 1: Africa's Velvet Underground', *The Independent*, 7 April 2006, http://www.independent.co.uk/arts-entertainment/music/features/konono-no-1-africa-s-velvet-underground-6104367.html [accessed 4 July 2022].
9 Group Doueh, *Guitar Music From the Western Sahara*. Sublime Frequencies, 2007; Group Inerane, Guitars From Agadez (Music of Niger). Sublime Frequencies, 2008. See also, Justin F. Farrar, 'Group Doueh', *Broward Palm Beach New Times*, 27 September 2007, www.browardpalmbeach.com/browardpalmbeach/Print?oid=6313024 [accessed 4 July 2022]. Sublime Frequencies compares Group Inerane to Velvet Underground in the press notes to Group Inerane, *Guitars From Agadez Volume 3*, Sublime Frequencies, 2010.
10 Michael E. Veal, 'Dry Spell Blues: Sublime Frequencies Across the West African Sahel', in: Micheal E. Veal & E. Tammy Kim (Eds.) *Punk Ethnography: Artists & Scholars Listen to Sublime Frequencies*. Middletown: Wesleyan University Press, 2016, pp.210–36, p.223.
11 Omar Souleyman, *Highway to Hassake (Folk and Pop Sounds of Syria)*. Sublime Frequencies, 2007.
12 *Music From Saharan Cellphones, Vol.1*. Sahel Sounds, 2011.
13 Ata Kak, *Obaa Sima*. Awesome Tapes From Africa, 2015. Mikey IQ Jones, 'The Incredible Story of Ata Kak's *Obaa Sima*, the Original Awesome Tape From Africa', *Fact*, 3 October 2015, www.factmag.com/2015/03/10/the-incredible-story-of-ata-kaks-obaa-sima-the-original-awesome-tape-from-africa/ [accessed 4 July 2022].
14 William Onyeabor, *Who Is William Onyeabor?* Luaka Bop, 2013; Charanjit Singh, *Synthesizing: Ten Ragas to a Disco Beat*. Bombay Connection, 2010.
15 Simon Frith, 'The Discourse of World Music' in: Georgina Born & David Hesmondhalgh (Eds.) *Western Music and Its Others: Difference, Repetition and Appropriation in Music*. London: University of California Press, 2000, pp.305–22.
16 Paul Simon, *Graceland*. Warner Bros., 1986; Buena Vista Social Club, *Buena Vista Social Club*. World Circuit, 1997.
17 Homi Bhabha, *The Location of Culture*. London: Routledge, 1994.
18 Ashwani Sharma, 'Sounds Oriental: The (Im)possibility of Theorizing Asian Musical Cultures' in: Sanjay Sharma, John Hutnyk, & Ashwani Sharma (Eds.) *Dis-Orienting Rhythms: The Politics of the New Asian Dance Music*. London & New Jersey: Zed Books, 1996, pp.15–31; Neil Lazarus, *The Postcolonial Unconscious*. Cambridge: Cambridge University Press, 2012.
19 Gayatry Chakravorty Spivak, *A Critique of Postcolonial Reason: Toward a History of the Vanishing Present*. Cambridge: Harvard University Press, 1999, p.361 [emphasis in original].
20 Sharma, 'Sounds Oriental', p.16.
21 Veit Erlmann, 'The Politics and Aesthetics of Transnational Musics', *The World of Music* 35, no.2, 1993, pp.3–15, quoted on p.9.
22 Étienne Balibar, *Politics and the Other Scene*. London: Verso, 2012, pp.147–49.

23 Peter Manuel, 'Modernity and Musical Structure: Neo-Marxist Perspectives on Song Form and its Successors', in: Regula Burckhardt Qureshi (Ed.) *Music and Marx*. London: Routledge, 2002, pp.45–62.
24 Eric J. Schmidt 'Arid Fidelity, Reluctant Capitalists: Salvage, Curation, and the Circulation of Tuareg Music on Independent Record Labels', *Ethnomusicology Forum* 28, no. 3, 2019, pp.260–82.
25 This is the claim made by, for instance, Schmidt 'Arid Fidelity, Reluctant Capitalists'; David Novak, 'The Sublime Frequencies of New Old Media', *Public Culture* 23, no.3, 2011, pp.601–34; and Michael E. Veal & E. Tammy Kim (Eds.) *Punk Ethnography: Artists & Scholars Listen to Sublime Frequencies*. Middletown: Wesleyan University Press, 2016.
26 Group Doueh, *Guitar Music From The Western Sahara*; Group Inerane, *Guitars From Agadez Volume 4*. Sublime Frequencies, 2011.
27 Jones, 'The Incredible story of Ata Kak's *Obaa Sima*'; Malcolm Jack, 'Review: Omar Souleyman – Oran Mor Glasgow', *The Scotsman*, 10 December 2011, www.scotsman.com/arts-and-culture/review-omar-souleyman-oran-mor-glasgow-1651187 [accessed 30 June 2022]; Peter Margasak, 'Konono No. 1', *Chicago Reader*, 10 November 2005, https://chicagoreader.com/music/konono-no-1-2/ [accessed 30 June 2022].
28 This is the central argument of Novak, 'The Sublime Frequencies of New Old Media', and throughout Veal & Kim (Eds.) Punk Ethnography.
29 Michael Taussig, *Mimesis and Alterity: A Particular History of the Senses*. London: Routledge, 1993, p.232.
30 David Font-Navarrete, '"File Under Import": Musical Distortion, Exoticism, and Authenticité in Congotronics'. *Ethnomusicology Review* 16, 2011, pp.1–19.
31 Andy Beta, 'An Interview With Alan Bishop', The Believer, 1 July 2008, https://culture.org/an-interview-with-alan-bishop/ [accessed 30 June 2022].
32 Novak, 'The Sublime Frequencies of New Old Media'; Simon Reynolds, 'Xenomania: Nothing is Foreign in an Internet Age', *MTV*, December 2011, www.mtviggy.com/articles/xenomania-nothing-is-foreign-in-an-internet-age/ [accessed 20 December 2011]. See also Schmidt 'Arid Fidelity, Reluctant Capitalists' and Novak, 'The Sublime Frequencies of New Old Media'.
33 Enrique Dussel, 'Eurocentrism and Modernity (Introduction to the Frankfurt Lectures)', *Boundary 2* 20, no.3, 1993, pp.65–76.
34 Hal Foster, 'The "Primitive" Unconscious of Modern Art', *October* 34, 1985, pp.45–70.
35 Timothy D. Taylor, *Beyond Exoticism: Western Music and the World*. Durham & London: Duke University Press, 2007; Richard Middleton, 'Musical Belongings: Western Music and Its Low-Other', in: *Western Music and Its Others: Difference, Representation, and Appropriation in Music*. Berkeley and Loss Angeles: University of California Press, pp.59–85.
36 Francis Bebey, *African Music: A People's Art* (Josephine Bennett, Trans.). New York: Lawrence Hill, 1975.
37 Ibid., p.18.
38 Ibid., pp.126–28.
39 Francis Bebey, *The Ashanti Doll* (Joyce A. Hutchinson, Trans.). London: Heinemann, 1978.
40 Francis Bebey, *King Albert*. Westport: L. Hill, 1981.
41 Francis Bebey, 'Coffee-Cola Song', *African Electronic Music*.

42 Francis Bebey, 'Pygmy Love Song', *Psychedelic Sanza*.
43 Steven Feld, 'Pygmy Pop: A Genealogy of Schizophonic Mimesis', *Yearbook for Traditional Music* 28, 1996, pp.1–35; Steven Feld, 'A Sweet Lullaby for World Music', *Public Culture* 12, no.1, 2000, pp.145–71.
44 See, for instance, Richard Bjornson, *The African Quest for Freedom and Identity: Cameroonian Writing and National Experience*. Bloomington: Indiana University Press, 1991.
45 Leopold Sédar Senghor 'African-Negro Aesthetics', (Elaine P. Halperin, Trans.) *Diogenes* 16, no.4, 1956, pp.23–38.
46 Senghor, 'African-Negro Aesthetics', p.33; Bebey, *African Music*, p.3. For an account of Senghor's views on music see Tsitsi Ella Jaji, *Africa in Stereo: Modernism, Music and Pan-African Solidarity*. Oxford: Oxford University Press, 2014.
47 See Leopold Sédar Senghor, 'Negritude: A Humanism of the Twentieth Century' in: W. Carty & M. Kilson (Eds.) *The African Reader: Independent Africa*. New York: Vintage, 1970, pp.179–92.
48 Léopold Sédar Senghor, 'What the Black Man Contributes' in: Robert Bernasconi (Ed.) *Race and Racism in Continental Philosophy*. Bloomington: Indiana University Press, 2003, pp.287–301. Quoted from p.288.
49 Theodor Adorno, *A Metacritique: Studies in Husserl and the Phenomenological Antinomies* (Willis Domingo, Trans.). Cambridge: The MIT Press, 1984, pp.45–47.
50 On the critique of Bebey along these lines, see Kofi Agawu, 'The Invention of African Rhythm', *Journal of the American Musicological Society* 48, no.3, 1995, pp.380–95 and Kofi Agawu, *Representing African Music: Postcolonial Notes, Queries, Positions*. London: Routledge, 2013, pp.32, 57, 107.
51 This is implied by Donna V. Jones, *The Racial Discourses of Life Philosophy: Négritude, Vitalism and Modernity*. New York: Columbia University Press, 2010; F. Abiola Irele, *The Negritude Moment: Explorations in Francophone African and Caribbean Literature and Thought*. Trenton: Africa World Press, 2011. See also, Gary Wilder, *Freedom Time: Negritude, Decolonization and the Future of the World*. Durham & London: Duke University Press, 2015.
52 Jean-Paul Sartre, 'Black Orpheus' in: *'What Is Literature?' And Other Essays*. Cambridge: Harvard University Press, 1988.
53 Frantz Fanon, *Black Skin, White Masks* (Charles Lam Markmann, Trans.). London: Pluto Press, 2008, p.226.
54 Frantz Fanon, *Wretched of the Earth*. New York: Grove Press, 1963, p.220. Or, as Amilcar Cabral puts it: 'a return to one's origins is not, nor can it be, in itself an *act of struggle* against foreign domination (colonial and/or racist), nor does it necessarily mean a return to traditions'. See Amilcar Cabral, *Resistance and Decolonisation* (Dan Wood, Trans.), London: Rowman & Littlefield, 2016, p.166.
55 Anja Brunner, 'Popular Music and the Young Postcolonial State of Cameroon, 1960–1980', *Popular Music and Society* 40, no.1, 2017, pp.37–48.
56 Bebey has been criticised for failing to publicly condemn the Ahidjo regime. Richard Bjornson reports that Bebey was jeered by young people at a concert in Cameroon for this reason, though Kidi Bebey insists this was due to mistaken association with the ruling Ahidjo regime. See Bjornson, *The African Quest for Freedom and Identity*, n.22, p.483,

and Bebey, *My Kingdom for a Guitar*, p.196. Indeed, Kidi Bebey's memoir suggests that, given the public dissidence of Bebey's brother Marcel Bebey Eyidi (eventually leading to the latter's arrest and torture), Francis's position in Cameroon was highly precarious.

57 Wilder, *Freedom Time*, p.7.
58 Bebey, *King Albert*, p.158.
59 Sharma, 'Sounds Oriental', p.18.
60 Others, however, have called for the return of recordings to Africa pillaged by collectors in recent years and sold for exorbitant prices over online networks. On this point see Boima Tucker, 'The Scramble for Vinyl', *Africa is a Country*, 14 September 2010, https://africasacountry.com/2010/09/the-scramble-for-vinyl [accessed 3 July 2022]; Abigail Gardner & Gerard Moorey, 'Raiders of the Lost Archives', *Popular Communication* 14, no.3, 2016, pp.169-77; Lari Aaltonen, 'Crate-Digging Columbuses and Vinyl Vespucci's: Exoticism in World Music Collections', *Intercultural Masquerade: New Orientalism, New Occidentalism, Old Exoticism* (R Marchart, F. Dervin, & M. Gao, Eds.). New York: Springer, 2016, pp.67-80.
61 Andrew C. McGraw, 'Radio Java' in: Michael E. Veal & E. Tammy Kim (Eds.), *Punk Ethnography: Artists and Scholars Listen to Sublime Frequencies*. Middletown: Wesleyan University Press, 2016, pp.323-39, p.326.
62 Evan Calder Williams, *Combined and Uneven Apocalypse*. London: Zero, 2011; China Mieville, 'The Limits of Utopia', *Salvage*, 1 August 2015, https://salvage.zone/the-limits-of-utopia/ [accessed 4 July 2022].
63 Zak Bronson, 'Living in the Wreckage', *Los Angeles Review of Books*, 12 February 2016, https://lareviewofbooks.org/article/living-in-the-wreckage/ [accessed 19 November 2022].
64 Williams, *Combined and Uneven Apocalypse*, p.237.
65 Baraka, *Blues People*; Shuja Haider, 'Dropping Acid', Logic, 1 January 2019, https://logicmag.io/play/dropping-acid/ [accessed 4 July 2022].
66 Benjamin, *The Arcades Project*, p.9.
67 Ibid.
68 Will Straw, 'Music as Commodity and Material Culture', *Repercussions* 7-8, Spring-Fall, 1999-2000, pp.147-72.
69 See Mary Louise Pratt, *Imperial Eyes: Travel Writing and Transculturation*. London: Routledge, 1992.
70 John Urry & Jonas Larsen, *The Tourist Gaze 3.0*. London: Sage, 2011.
71 Ibid.
72 Marco D'Eramo, *The World in a Selfie: An Inquiry into the Tourist Age*. London: Verso, 2021.
73 On this point see Raymond Malewitz, *The Practice of Misuse: Rugged Consumerism in Contemporary American Culture*. Stanford: Stanford University Press, 2014.
74 See Doreen Jakob, 'Crafting Your Way Out of the Recession? New Craft Entrepreneurs and the Global Economic Downturn', *Cambridge Journal of Regions, Economy and Society* 6, no.1, 2013, pp.127-40; Susan Luckman, 'The Aura of the Analogue in a Digital Age: Women's Crafts, Creative Markets and Home-Based Labour After Etsy', *Cultural Studies Review* 19, no. 1, 2013, pp.249-70.

75 Dennis Stevens, 'Validity is in the Eye of the Beholder: Mapping Craft Communities of Practice' in: Maria Elena Buszek (Ed.), *Extra/Ordinary: Craft and Contemporary Art*. Durham & London: Duke University Press, 2011, pp.43-58, quoted on p.45.
76 Jakob, 'Crafting Your Way out of the Recession?'
77 Kirstin Munro & Chris O'Kane, 'Autonomy and Creativity in the Artisan Economy and the New Spirit of Capitalism', *Review of Radical Politics Economics* 49, no.4, 2017, pp.582-90.
78 Luc Boltanski & Eve Chiapello, *The New Spirit of Capitalism* (Gregory Elliott, Trans.). London: Verso, 2005.

5

Machine Memory Triumphs in Multiplicity: Nature and Technique

Delete Beach

Since the 2010s, partly as microphone technologies have become more accessible and portable, the deployment of environmental soundscape as musical embellishment has become more frequent; a fact typically registered by critics as evoking a concern with climate crisis.[1] Anthony Child's *Electronic Recordings from Maui Jungle* (2015), Elysia Crampton's *Moth/Lake* (2016), Egyptrixx's *Pure, Beyond Reproach* (2017), Mica Levi's *Delete Beach* (2017), KMRU's *Logue* (2021), to mention some favourite instances, exemplify a recurring formula: the sonic texture of a landscape – a rushing river, lapping waves, or buzzing insects, say – opens a track but more or less rapidly recedes behind synths, drones, or programmed drums, so that explicitly 'natural' sound is quickly silenced or fades into background, a reiteration of the industrial domination of environment, albeit in aesthetic form.[2]

But if the relation of technology to nature plays out as an analogy where natural sound is deployed as ornament, the questions it raises – What purposes animate such pursuits? What vocation do they imply for recorded sound? What relation between the didactic and the aesthetic do they propose? – appear all the slipperier where field recording has come to signify, especially since the late 2000s, a genre in its own right. This is a development epitomised in the growing renown of Chris Watson, the form's best-known contemporary practitioner. Reputed for the technical sophistication of his close-proximity recordings of soundscapes, Watson started out, following his departure in 1981 from post-punk band Cabaret Voltaire, to produce sound for TV programming, including the BBC's famed *Planet Earth* series of wildlife documentaries. As his reputation grew in the late 1990s and early 2000s, his standing gradually shifted from that of an engineer to that of an artist: his recordings were released as stand-alone albums while commissions for artistic installations became more frequent. Watson's rise reverberated across a wider group of environmental field recordists in experimental music and art circles active around this period (of which Peter Cusack, Jana Winderen, Andrea Polli, and Francisco López are amongst the best known), while the assemblage of books, feature articles, and exhibitions on the subject multiplied steadily and studios and research centres obtained a growing share of dwindling arts and university funding.[3]

Of course, the compulsion to record the soundscape is coincidental with the history of recording technology itself. The earliest phonographs, for instance, were prominent tools in the capture of wildlife and indigenous cultures by naturalists and ethnographers alike.[4] But in the context of rapidly accelerating ecological crisis to which environmental field recordings are often understood to be responding in some way, the sonic presentation of nature increasingly strains against its own limits. For one thing, a non-denotative aesthetic form is at stake here, so that ambiguity is a structural inevitability. For another, the object in question is the planetary ecosystem; it operates at the most disparate scales and its boundaries are impossible to delineate definitively. These issues speak to intersecting crises of knowledge and the aesthetic which will demand further unpacking as we proceed.

But there is still another, wider concern that underlies these questions since they all evidently amount to two terms and this will form the central concern of this chapter. That is, the concept of nature is at issue here, yet so also are the means of its representation: the technologies that make it available for consumption in the first place. There's a tendency, in this regard, in recent environmental field recording for a play with mediation; the sonic textures produced by experiments with different microphones and the transmission of otherwise undetectable sounds using hydrophones and contact microphones have been especially abiding interests. But these practices typically exhibit a rather unstable position for the techniques they deploy, a fact underlined by their unreflective links to military and extractive logics, in particular.

This reflection on mediation and technology in light of ecological crisis will occupy the first part of this chapter as it takes in the recent history of the sonic representation of nature, while in its second part we will consider something of the obverse to the field recordist's desire for an authentic presentation of soundscape: the fantasy of an identification of the human with technology. Here, we take up electronic musics associated with the short-lived intellectual and aesthetic fashion known as 'accelerationism', of which we will take the artists Holly Herndon, James Ferraro, and Daniel Lopatin as exemplary. As a set of ideas, accelerationism is sufficiently ambiguous to have stood both as an appeal for repurposing automation and related techniques for progressive ends as well as an expression of the profound disappointment for technology to have failed, until now, to liberate humanity. The 'entanglement' with environment which animates field recording and the identification with automation expressed in accelerationist musics might seem to represent disparate aesthetic strategies, but both grapple with parallel questions of sovereignty over technique which we'll unpack in what follows. That is, as we'll see, both submit experimentation with technological mediation as an encounter with agency and this takes the form of experimentation with sonic contingency; of a restoration of play with chance, error, or accident that is otherwise subdued in a digital age where listening is both ubiquitous and automated. But both do so by way of dispositions whose sonic landscapes are peculiarly depopulated and whose textures are ultimately disturbingly frictionless.

Desire of Place

We can begin by observing that the question of technological capture is a definitive one for field recording insofar as its self-understanding is derived from its opposition to the studio. The latter, as we saw in the previous chapter, is premised upon its withdrawal; the staging of 'live' performance historically involved the minimisation of the mediations that make it possible. Conversely, where a recording feigns to capture a 'field', its site and processes become its explicit object. The difference here, as Mitchell Akiyama notes, might amount mainly to rhetoric – anything can become a studio or a field after all – but a peculiar identification with its site characterises the field recording nonetheless.[5]

This is a still hazy framing of the sonic representation of nature. We can parse it further by comparing two conceptual approaches to soundscape recording. To begin, a theory of acousmatic formalism, associated most of all with French composer Pierre Schaeffer, rejects reference to sonic sources in order to consider sound in itself. Schaeffer pursues a *musique concrète*, in other words, an approach that demands of its audience a 'reduced listening' that attends to the formal properties of the sound object.[6] The coordinates of Schaeffer's practice centred on new studio technologies as they emerged in the middle of the twentieth century: tape looping, time stretching, and pitch shifting. A growing ability to manipulate sound helped to detach it from whatever caused it and, in this regard, Schaeffer's influential 1948 recordings, *Cinq Études de Bruits*, present a cacophonous series of indiscernible thumps, whistles, and bangs whose sources in trains, pianos, or saucepans are discernible only from the compositions' titles.[7]

Seemingly opposed to Shaeffer's project lies the work of acoustic ecology, first developed under the auspices of the World Soundscape Project (WSP) at Simon Fraser University in Canada in the 1960s, led by Murray Shafer, Barry Truax, and Hildergard Westerkamp, since it explicitly hinges on sound's referential properties. Rather than Schaeffer's interest in sound's formal properties, acoustic ecology is compelled by what critic David Toop describes as a 'desire of place'. It seeks to evoke the atmosphere of its sources; the field recording is merely supplementary to the originary object it invokes, an 'adjunct to the ear', to use Schafer's phrase.[8] This is to imply, in turn, a sonic realism; an objectivity committed to sound's 'own integrity', as Westerkamp has said.[9] An ethics follows from such a metaphysics too, since the project of extending the sources of musical composition beyond the human to the ecosystem is intended to compel the latter's preservation; an imperative evident, for example, in Westerkamp's influential 'Beneath the Forest Floor', her 1992 study of an old-growth forest in the Pacific Northwest.[10] Running water is looped into rhythmic patterns, bird calls are drenched in reverb or have their pitch changed to conjure more harmonic tones, while the soundscape's vulnerability is summoned by the grating howl of a logger's chainsaw. A commitment to the sites upon which it operates here works by isolating the musical qualities of 'natural' sound.

This opposition between acousmatic formalism and sonic realism, between sound-in-itself and sound-as-reference, emerges in the 1960s, but its persistence up to the present is palpable if we look to the recent work of artist Francisco López who, echoing Schaeffer, describes his work as attending to 'the transcendental dimension of the sound matter itself'; a move he characterises as a 'deactualization' of reference to a natural object.[11] On *Wind*, an hour-long, unedited, and unprocessed recording of air moving through Argentine Patagonia released in 2007, long silences are punctuated by the crushing lacerations of intense gusts as they make contact with López's microphones.[12] *La Selva: Sound Environments from a Neotropical Rainforest*, first recorded in the late 1990s, leans ever slightly more to the lyrical: noisy choruses of frogs and running water are discernible amongst more anonymous tumbling and clacking.[13] López's handling of urban environments has a still more enigmatic, haunting character; machinic hums generate a gloomy ambient droning on *Buildings [New York]*, while elsewhere he renders undefinable, crushing walls of noise (*Untitled #104*).[14] López calls for 'blind listening', and he offers little in the way of image or text to supplement his work, which he explicitly opposes to the WSP, and Schafer in particular. 'The tuning', he writes, in reference to Schafer's book of that title, 'is basically a "silencing", as if noise were an evil condition in itself and also an exclusive feature of a post-industrial human-influenced world.'[15] Here, López echoes other critics of the moral hierarchy underlying much of acoustic ecology: its conflation of quietude with nature and of noise with industrialisation expresses a metaphysical ideal of pure sonority, one which tends towards a nostalgic authoritarianism.[16]

But if sound's relation to its referential object remains a source of contention in the present, we should also observe recent shifts in the renewal of these issues, since they harbour wider historical transformations in the relation to non-human nature. In particular, we should observe how ecological crisis inflects the consumption of nature as an aesthetic object. In this regard, it's notable that despite his commitment to formalism López nevertheless betrays his own variation on sonic realism where he betrays that a grasp of the depth and complexity of natural sound functions as a moral basis for his acousmatic techniques:

If our reception of nature sounds were more focused on the environment as a whole, rather than on the organisms we perceive to be most similar to us ...

we would be more likely to take the bioacoustics of plants into account. Further, a sound environment is the consequence not only of all its sound-producing components but also of all its sound-transmitting and sound-modifying elements.[17]

This argument for a more faithful representation of environment, we will later speculate, grows more inevitable where that object is perceived as threatened by ecological catastrophe. That is to say, the asceticism submitted by sonic formalism seems less adequate as an artistic strategy where its natural sonic sources are in the process of being annihilated. But López's occasional slips into realism, his gestures towards a mythical causal object, also signal an existing rapprochement between formalism, on the one hand, and contemporary soundscape recordists, on the other hand.[18]

Put otherwise, if Westerkamp and other practitioners of acoustic ecology extend the activity of composition to the soundscape as such, more recent work presses the point even further, so that mediation itself becomes the agent of composition. In this regard, Chris Watson exhibits a reflexivity and play with sonic media anathema to earlier acoustic ecology; ever so slightly lyrical effects are evoked through time-compressions and edits that draw out the almost rhythmic and tonal qualities of the sites he records, even if his sources tend to remain oblique, their identity established mainly through track titles and accompanying notes. Instead of the sites themselves, the gravitational centre of Watson's work, the source of the pleasures it advances, emerges from recording technologies that transcend the limits of the naked human ear to transport the listener to wholly impervious spaces: hydrophones, miniature, and contact microphones offer an otherwise inaccessible proximity to wildlife. *Outside the Circle of Fire* stages the rumbling purr of a leopard and the snaps of vultures feeding on a zebra carcass, *Ant-Steps* captures the marching of insects, on *Weather Report* one hears the creaks of a shifting glacier.[19] This modification on acoustic ecology's pursuit of sonic integrity is effected by the microphone's migrations across scale and geography and these are themes also discernible in the way Peter Cusack situates his work at the intersections of natural and industrial zones. His 2012 collection *Sounds From Dangerous Places*, for instance, presents electricity flowing into the Chernobyl exclusion zone, marine life at polluted Italian dockyards, or machinery in the Caspian oil fields in Azerbaijan.[20]

Watson and Cusack thus epitomise how an earlier pursuit of an unspoilt nature is qualified, if not quite abandoned altogether, in contemporary field recording. Yet the space it leaves behind is filled by an ambiguous ideology of ruins and catastrophe which, across all its varied modulations of scale and magnitude, presents its sites with a perplexing indeterminacy.[21] It's in this vein we should absorb Cusack's confessional attachment to environmental destruction which, he says, 'can be both sonically and visually compelling, even beautiful and atmospheric. There is often an extreme dichotomy between an aesthetic response and the knowledge of danger.'[22] Scenes of annihilation, whether executed by vultures or oil rigs, are set in curiously depopulated zones, where the inhuman and organic are made discernible at various scales, but agency and historicity – especially economic interests – are occluded. It's in service to this inhuman framing that the earlier realist ethos we've examined recurs as a commitment to 'atmosphere'. Cusack describes his works as a 'sonic journalism', a 'bearing witness', by which field recordings 'transmit a powerful sense of spatiality, atmosphere and timing'.[23] Watson invokes a 'memory effect. It's my recall of memory and feelings about the sense and spirit of that place that I try and reconstruct in my compositions'.[24] Thus modified by a crisis at once ecological and of nature as object, aesthetic moralism persists: Watson complains of noise pollution in interviews whilst Cusack bemoans the 'homogenisation of the soundscape'.[25] Together they evince the moral hierarchy we'd already discerned in the work of acoustic ecology; a metaphysical ideal of pure sonority and the evacuation of social forces upon which this is premised.

Only a God Can Save Us

If, in the course of tracing trajectories in sonic realism, we have discerned a destabilisation of the object of environmental field recording, then we should also remark that this has gone hand in hand with a foregrounding and inflation of the listening subject as the basis of attempts to secure the 'field' as an artistic medium. This is a motif that has recurred its way into cliché: Cusack invokes listening as a 'relational frame'; Andrea Polli describes it as an 'immersive' act that 'provokes an emotional reaction'; Watson references 'a sublime stillness'; Leah Barclay asserts 'embodied connections with the environment.'[26] This emphasis on a disposition that cultivates identification with sonic sources is in keeping with a wider predilection we have already encountered of scholarly accounts to theorise the properties of listening and sound as inherently emancipatory and a wellspring of agential reserve. Sound can 'open the narrow confines of the political'; it situates us beyond 'distinctions between culture and nature, human and nonhuman, mind and matter, the symbolic and the real'; it's a 'material agency in itself', it 'engages us in sensual and sensory affective processes to situate us in fields of distributed subjectivities'.[27]

In an earlier chapter we have suggested, along these lines, that the theorisation of sound in an ontological register tends to be deployed for a dispersal of the sovereign subject by privileging affective experience as anterior to rational cognition. Sound, on this view, acts as a favourite medium for access to pre-human indeterminacies and intensities and so, we've maintained, is inclined to stand as an alibi for the failure to examine the social forces mediating relations of human and non-human processes in the first place. We can unpack this claim further if we consider a periodising argument, traceable to influential works in Science and Technology Studies by both Donna Haraway and Bruno Latour who, each writing in the early 1990s, took advances in synthetic biology, bio-informatics, and cybernetics as evincing a state of 'hybridity' or posthumanity that erodes modern dualisms of mind and body, the natural and the cultural, and brings forth the immediacy of the material world.[28] There's a risk of primitivism in such a claim as we have already unpacked in chapter one: where immediacy is endorsed, the innocence of thought is implied. And it's within this wider ambient atmosphere of ontological hybridity that field recording, conceived as by-passing cognitive abstraction to address feeling as such, is viewed by its proponents as an especially prescient means of alerting us to the urgency and scale of ecological crisis by transcending the limits of anthropocentrism.

Such ideas are typically framed by the related notion of the 'Anthropocene'; the idea that human forces have so significantly altered the planetary ecosystem that the Earth's geophysical composition has been permanently altered; nature itself is 'hybrid' now. Notwithstanding the mystifying integration of the agents of environmental destruction into a single actor deemed to be humanity as such, the significance of

Anthropocene discourses for field recording rests with the implication that ecological crisis entails epistemic crisis too.[29] For where the geological timespan of the planet intersects human history, the argument goes, two disparate temporalities blur; ecology operates at scales in excess of human cognition. Ecological crisis imparts 'hyperobjects', to refer to one influential analysis, that stress representational systems of meaning to their limits and, in turn, imply a new significance for pre-cognitive, affective reception of natural phenomena.[30] Given its framing of ecological crisis in existentialist terms, it's an argument that recalls philosopher Martin Heidegger's influential account of technological domination of the Earth as conditioned by a metaphysical disposition – associated with Descartes – that takes the world as its personal object and resource.[31] Where the processes associated with ecological destruction are put down to a subjective constitution anchored in anthropocentric hubris, for that reason, we can only conclude as Heidegger did in another context, that 'only a God can save us', since capacity for change is situated at the level of a shapeless planetary ethos.[32]

We should pause here to register the politically disabling effects of such a stance, more or less dominant in popular responses to climate change: an imaginary centred on a looming apocalyptic horizon tends to disavow potentials for agency in the present and continuities with social hierarchies from the past. To claim that the field recording operates at the level of affect is to hold out for it a defiance to anthropocentric hubris and cultivate 'entanglement' with a complex ecological infrastructure. This is a perspective, as we have already seen, that finds its aesthetic expression in its taste for depopulated, inhuman landscapes alongside its pursuit of pure sonority. In this regard, Watson's recording of the otherwise imperceptible movements of the Vatnajökull icecap in Iceland, to take a better-known example, compresses time to intimate myriad and ongoing movements and transformations concealed by its apparent stasis and solidity.[33] This is to narrativise an otherwise inaccessible sonic object and so, relate its colossal scale to the localised frame of the listener. Thus does a theory of affect conceive subjective entanglement on a planetary level of the Anthropocene and so rekindle the power of aesthetic experience: by evoking the incapacity to cognise ecological destruction. A natural sublime is preserved following the eradication of ideals of nature; a sense of greatness and boundlessness is upheld despite the domination of the planetary ecosystem, but only by inviting the spectator to participate in the destruction of the natural object. That is, whilst nature might be fully dominated and mastered, the process of crisis and catastrophe is not: the uncanniness of crisis itself is pressed in to do the work of the sublime; of compelling awe and wonder.

A Real Interaction

Until now we have surveyed the depoliticising effects of the aesthetisation of nature and its collapse in contemporary field recording, but a further reappraisal of the concept of nature is called for here, since it's on these terms that the aesthetic and ontological strategies in question hinge, and it's in this light we should consider Raymond Williams's argument that modern symbolic interaction between nature and culture is a 'function of an increasing real interaction'.[34] That is, the objectification and abstraction of 'nature' are understood by Williams as a reflection of real transformations in the relation between humans and their environment, ones wrought by the forcible separation of direct producers from their means of production. Williams thus poses capitalism, and the processes of 'so-called primitive accumulation' – whereby dispossession, enclosure, and colonialism set labour 'free' to pursue its survival through a wage – as central to any understanding of 'nature'. Once it's mediated by private property in this way, then nature can begin to appear, as Alfred Schmidt puts it, as an 'abstract-in-itself', a lifeless, mechanical object external to humanity, endlessly available for conscious intervention.[35]

We can further refine this history of the objectification of nature by returning to the account of gender and racial inequality presented in chapter one. There, we looked to scholars who have sought to locate the experiences of women and colonial subjects as inextricable from processes of primitive accumulation by their confinement to reproductive and domestic work or a spectrum of modes of forced labour.[36] The sorting of gendered and racialised populations is relevant here insofar as it is tied to the emergence of modern categories of nature and culture. For as nature is progressively constituted as an object for the modern acquisitive subject, so too women could be objectified as 'natural' producers of children, racialised people treated as 'natural' labour. The point here, in short, is that claims for overcoming dualist conceptions of humanity and nature at the level of subjective affect, ontological entanglement, or hybridity upon which the reception of environmental field recording are premised, overlook a whole history of real interactions that constitute and reinforce the categories of nature and culture in the first place.

To observe the historical conditions for the objectification of nature in this way is to see claims to 'entanglement' as voluntarist, idealised. For where access to the recorded sound of the environment is mediated by regimes of private property, its aesthetic powers remain inextricable from a racialised and gendered global division of the pleasures and the pain music and media industries engender. Indeed, we can consider that the overwhelming majority of the world's intellectual property is held in a small number of overdeveloped states in the global North, while the hardware and infrastructure upon which the music industry relies are produced, assembled, and disposed of in the global South, where labour costs are low and environmental regulations lax. These are processes organised, of course, mainly along neo-colonial lines and looking at the contemporary music industry in the widest possible terms – as well as mass media, communications infrastructure, and technoscience more broadly – we can perceive the reorganisation of an autonomous mind exercising its powers over a world it conceives as available for enclosure. Not a state of hybridity or entanglement with non-human nature then, but rather the pervasiveness of modern dualisms of mind and world on a neo-colonial scale.[37]

It Does Not Hear as do Ears

But, to return to field recording, there is a further formal affinity with capital's consumption of the 'free gifts' of nature we should examine. After all, doesn't the field recordist adopt an acquisitive gaze, one which treats the world as a reservoir of potential sound-value to be enclosed and accumulated? 'It's a method of extraction I suppose,' Watson once told an interviewer.[38] For if the moral foundations of capitalism rest with the idea, first formulated by John Locke, that enclosure is legitimated by the mixing of one's labour with the Earth – what I labour upon becomes mine, and the notion that nature would otherwise lie untouched and, in Locke's words, become 'waste' – the reverberations of the logics of property with the practice of field recording resound rather forcibly.[39] They resonate even more so when we reckon with the extent to which the earliest field recording practices are imbricated in the colonial systematisation and classification of indigenous speech and song.[40] Likewise, if we take John Lomax's recordings of African American folk song to stand as the first field recordings made for their own sake, an imperial gaze grows all the more palpable when we recall that these were mainly produced in Southern American prisons, where socially segregated inmates were especially fecund stores of musical traditions to be mined.[41]

Along the same lines, it's significant that recordists' growing capacity to represent the soundscape with ever more precision and sophistication is itself a product of the very mastery of nature to which it is, usually explicitly, opposed. Microphone technologies, for instance, advanced rapidly given arms races in communications, sonar, and radar during the World Wars.[42] These developments, in turn, are punctuated by the fact that the most widely ever circulated environmental field recordings, *Songs of the Humpback Whale*, became available given the U.S. Navy's release of classified recordings in the 1960s. Likewise, this martial entanglement is discernible in the frisson of naughty excitement expressed in Peter Cusack's introduction to Watson's *Ant-Steps*; a recording that employs ultra-sensitive microphones developed by the U.S. Army capable of detecting the footsteps of a single insect: 'the military purpose of the device remains a mystery', Cusack writes, 'Watson was instructed never to look inside'.[43]

More recent developments in field recording might be put down to advances in mobile rather than military technologies. Hand-held portable microphone and editing applications are now ubiquitous; a state of affairs that returns us to the indeterminacy between studio and field we noted earlier. For where increasingly hi-fidelity recordings can take place anywhere, evocation of place becomes ever more foregrounded in recorded music. But it might also be apparent that mobile communications technologies that extend the space of the studio to the point of its dissolution are also those that have been central to the contemporary extension of the working day, not to mention the growing surveillance and discipline of labour, for while studio and field, music and sound, grow indistinct, so too does the indeterminacy of labour and leisure follow a parallel logic.

So just as we have seen that the contemporary ubiquity of music consumption through streaming platforms intensifies the control and colonisation of the soundscape, expansive sonic quotation of environmental objects amounts to a romantic gesture, a revival of references to vital forces opposed to mechanical processes. Where the soundscape is overwhelmingly submitted to control, so sonic contingency must be intentionally generated. 'Nature repels intentionality', it's been suggested; it stands for indeterminacy and for excess just as the 'field' has stood for a rhetorical appeal to spontaneity.[44] This is a set of relationships that have to do with the ontology of the recording itself. In this light, Gilbert Simondon has proposed the recording as a formally distinct form of memory: '[m]achine memory triumphs in multiplicity and disorder; human memory triumphs in the unity of forms and in order'.[45] Making a corollary claim, Friedrich Kittler notes the boundary between noise and meaning is contingent upon its medium: '[t]he phonograph does not hear as do ears that have been trained immediately to filter voices, words, and sounds out of noise; it registers acoustic events as such'.[46] Thus does a new experience of contingency, of accident, re-emerge in an increasingly colonised soundscape, through the subsumption of nature by the recording. And so, a shifting relation of nature and machine, contingency and necessity, appears in an epoch where the experience of ecological chaos prevails all the more.

Between Reason and Imagination

Viewed in this light, the appeal to natural beauty disguises mediation insofar as it appears as external to history. But it also stands in for an excess over existent society. How we imagine our relation to non-human nature thus also reflects how we conceive possibilities for meaningful social change. So it is that, concurrent with the pursuit of a pre-reflexive relation to both sound and environment, there emerged an obverse impulse for their philosophical mastery. In the widely circulated volume *#Accelerate#*, published in 2014, Ray Brassier calls for 'an overcoming of the opposition between reason and imagination'.[47] In the same volume, Nick Srnicek and Alex Williams demand 'a promethean politics of maximal mastery over society, and its environment'.[48] In a related text, Aaron Bastani champions a 'fully automated luxury communism' for which toil and scarcity are overcome by 'reprogramming the gifts of nature'.[49] On 'xenofeminist' iterations of what's come to be known as the 'accelerationist' argument, 'the emancipatory potential of technology' would abolish biological gender difference too.[50]

So where the conception of nature is at stake, some theorists endorse an ontological humility that de-centres the human agent while others call for a still more hubristic rationality. Both are ultimately engaged in a mystification albeit in opposing ways. For the accelerationist, it is only by abjuring the modesty and political parochialism that restricts technological imaginaries that we can develop an emancipatory imaginary necessarily 'at ease with a modernity of abstraction, complexity, globality and technology'.[51] The point, therefore, is to accelerate, as the title of the manifesto penned by Williams and Srnicek has it: 'to preserve the gains of late capitalism while going further than its value system, governance structures and mass pathologies allow'.[52] Where irrationalities generated by capitalist competition inhibit the full development of technological potential, we are called upon to speed up, to 'repurpose' innovation to push beyond capitalism's limits to free humanity.

These are seductive proposals, for sure, but to grasp their philosophical principles we should consider the precursors that animate them. Two sets of ideas are especially significant in this regard, of which the first are the Italian Marxist 'post-Operaismo' interpretations of Marx's so-called 'Fragment on Machines', particularly those proffered by Antonio Negri and Paolo Virno.[53] An increasingly automated system of production, the argument goes, also grows increasingly dependent on the intellectual, affective, communicative capacities and knowledges that circulate throughout society. These 'general productive forces of the social brain', as Marx has it, no longer need capital to organise them as factory labour did so that capital increasingly exists as a mere fetter on this 'general intellect', whose liberation is imminent.[54] For the accelerationist, therefore, it remains merely to 'accelerate', to intensify the contradictions, in part, by redirecting technological development for human flourishing rather than capital accumulation.

While its political economy is derived from idiosyncratic albeit influential readings of Marx, accelerationism's rhetorical charge derives from reactionary philosopher Nick Land, head of the influential Cybernetic

Culture Research Unit at Warwick University in the 1990s. Drawing on a peculiar concoction of cyberpunk literature, 1990s rave culture aesthetics, and contemporary French philosophy, Land developed a view – one hesitates to call it a theory given its muddled logics – premised on the notion of the human as a fetter to technological development. Only the destructive, inhuman power of capital ceaselessly liberates us from technological obsolescence; even the human itself is outmoded. This is Land's 'machinic desire', one that anticipates capital as the vessel for the displacement of the human by the machine and, in turn, the transcendence of capital too.[55]

In sum, accelerationism seeks to confront what it sees as an ineffective and fading left, wrought by tribal attachments and a fear of political scale with a Promethean meta-narrative of rationalism-cum-social dynamism. This is an admittedly truncated account, but it suffices here to outline the basic point, that at issue is a Mephistophelean logic; yet it's one for which the machine, not the labourer, is the gravedigger of capital. Instead of entanglement, mastery over nature is called for here. Yet both strategies are animated by the desire to transcend the antagonisms that shape this relation in the first place.

The Despotism of Capital

Given her endorsement of Williams and Srnicek's work and her collaboration with Reza Negarestani, another prominent accelerationist philosopher, the electronic artist Holly Herndon has often been associated with accelerationism. Most of all though, it's the tenor of didactic optimism with which Herndon confronts technological change in her work that conforms to accelerationist principles. Herndon's purpose is, to use her formulation, to 'direct the conversation', and in earlier work this revolved mainly around anxiety over web surveillance.[56] The 2012 album *Movement*, for instance, involved experiments with Max/MSP software patches to trigger particular sonic processes on the basis of data derived from Herndon's web-browsing habits.[57] On the 2015 album *Platform*, the first single 'Home' is accompanied by a video that transforms PowerPoint graphics used by the NSA and recovered by Edward Snowden, into patterns of emojis raining down on Herndon.[58] Indeed, references to web surveillance are frequent, and performances have included projecting audience data gleaned from social media in real-time on stage. Such concerns are more or less bounded by liberal anxieties over privacy and individual liberty, just as Herndon's pronouncements regarding developments in Artificial Intelligence (AI) and Machine Learning centre on artist autonomy and intellectual property; always stopping short of a critique of the sovereign artist or a rejection of property itself, however.

But Herndon's trepidations around technological control are offset by more alluring technophilic strains in her work, and these are especially condensed in her presentation of voice. For if the grain of the voice, its singular texture, summons the singing body, as per Roland Barthes's well-known formulation, then Herndon's vocal techniques gesture at a cyborg anatomy.[59] Phrasing is chopped up and multiplied into choral shapes, synth patches modulate vocals towards what Adam Harper describes as the 'small-scale uncanniness' of a monstrous throat, neither quite human nor quite robotic either.[60] Oddly halting operatic harmonies, shifts in tone at granular elliptical rhythms, all produce tenderness and fervour inextricable from mineral affect. Herndon's voice, in short, is truly a bearer of both feeling and the machinic.

We might consider antecedents to such a strategy in order to unpack its implications. Writing of the widespread imaginaries housed in synthetic vocal effects in Black popular RnB of the late 1990s and early 2000s – Jodeci, Missy Elliott, the Neptunes – Alexander Weheliye invokes a mutually constitutive relation, where the machinic and human provenance of the voice amplify rather than interrupt one another; an amalgam neither nostalgic for naturalistic presence nor in pursuit of evisceration in the machine, but for which the RnB song becomes an expansive field of impersonal desire.[61] A case might be made that Herndon's arpeggiated synthetic vocal work approximates dispersals of the desiring subject observed by Weheliye. Certainly, to the extent that her fractal approach to song construction is reflective of a wider cyborg apparatus evocative of the period – Fever Ray, Arca, or SOPHIE are other examples – then we should note the abiding, albeit typically overlooked, influence of RnB. Their vocal styles are synthetic and modular, somewhere at the intersection of the feminine and the machinic, so that desire is redistributed beyond the bounds of the normative gendered body. Except Herndon's alchemising of human and machine tends also to be restrained by normative convention and compelled by didacticism so that its transgressive elements are not always sustained: 'Lonely At the Top', a track on *Platform*, caricatures an ASMR recording for a presumably overworked executive or artist in a rather puerile gesture of subcultural politics; 2019 album *Proto* is premised upon a collaboration with 'Spawn', an 'AI baby' that Herndon and partner Mat Dryhurst 'gave birth to'.[62] Besides the dubitable heteronormativity which merely reproduces the idealised nuclear family in the form of speculative technology, there's also a humanising exegetical impulse that's even more pronounced in her and Dryhurst's release of 'Holly+' in 2022; a deepfake software that transforms any voice into the timbre of Herndon's in real-time, 'encouraging people', as they note, 'to experiment with a new technology'.[63]

There's an admirable optimism and spirit of collaboration in Herndon's work, yet we should also perceive here the ideal of technological 'repurposing' championed by Williams and Srnicek and other accelerationists, but brought to bear directly upon the field of music. This is a view, we have seen, premised upon a clean extraction of technological latency from its subordination to narrowly instrumentalising logics.[64] So, on the one hand, 'Holly+' makes AI 'relatable'; on the other hand, Herndon and Dryhurst advocate for blockchain to decentralise control of culture industry revenues (and so protect artists' intellectual property). We can detect in such a conceptual architecture the techno-vitalism that others have ascertained in accelerationism, more broadly; an imaginary for which technological forces are, as it were, outside capital and can be 'repurposed' for other functions, and which posits for itself a deracinated perspective from which to envisage that the tools in questions aren't saturated with political imperatives.[65] Ultimately, the point is that technology is never merely the organisation of materiality, but a social relation above all.[66] This is not to stake liberation upon freedom from technique, but it does imply a demand for more careful accounting of the dependencies that any given technology inculcates.

We can return, in this context, to an earlier discussion of the automation of music-making, from the industrial production of pianos to music streaming, in terms of capital's 'real subsumption', and more thoroughly unpack this category, developed in an unpublished chapter of *Capital*.[67] There, it is used by Marx to refer to processes where capital doesn't merely integrate existing labour processes (what Marx calls 'formal subsumption'), but where the labour process has been subordinated to and reshaped by capitalist production. Capital, in other words, transforms its milieu to its own requirements; labour confronts a world alien to it. This is what, in an influential exposition, Jacques Camatte described as 'the despotism of capital', where domination by 'dead' over living labour, machine over human prevails, we are governed by the petrification of past exploitation to which we are compelled to submit our bodies and minds in order to survive.[68]

But what exactly are the implications of viewing technology as the congealed monuments to capital's taking control over labour in this way? Most of all, it implies that digital tools and techniques intrinsically consolidate and synthesise the racial and gendered sorting of populations for production and, considered in this light, the discrete, modular sets of tools upon which the accelerationist technological imaginary is premised amounts to a conceptual architecture with a creaking edifice. Amongst the most significant historical evidence for such an argument rests with the Russian revolutionary adoption of Taylorist principles of scientific management of industrial production, likely the grandest socialist 'repurposing' – to stick with accelerationist nomenclature – ever attempted. The Leninist turn to labour discipline, Robert Linhart shows in his extraordinary study of the subject, was justified on the grounds that newly won efficiencies in production would free the masses to participate in the direction of the state. Yet in practice it meant workers' submission to an authoritarian production process and their isolation from the institutions of power.[69] Equally, more recent scholarship has shown how disciplinary logics are engineered directly into the form and function of the technical object, as when algorithms optimise for racially discriminating patterns of past users; from protocols for the calculation of financial risk to predictive policing.[70] 'The algorithm's reliance on historical category', to use Ramon Amaro's phrase, is exacerbated by the deep integration of economic and technological rationality, a line of argument that might be extended to suggest that computation, insofar as it codes disparate phenomena into quantity – into 1s and 0s – in order to make them commensurable, is formally analogical with the capitalist subsumption of quality to quanta of value.[71]

Given this assessment, it's tempting to describe the accelerationist imaginary, following Dave Beech, as an aristocratic view for which work is suitable for anyone but itself.[72] The transcendence of manual labour appears, in other words, as part of a longer history where autonomy is premised on the surrogate effect of servants, slaves, wives, and, later, industrial workers; less-than-human others subjected to repetitive, gruelling labour.[73] Its prescient, therefore, to note the imbrications of the Promethean heroisation of technological reason with early modern philosophies – Descartes, above all. In this regard, Silvia Federici has suggested that the Cartesian institution of an ontological division between the purely mental and purely physical domains, and the mechanical vision of the body it implies, should be construed in terms of the suppression of feudal social relations.[74] From this perspective, the central accomplishment of the age of reason entailed posing the body as intelligible and, thus, as an object that could be subordinated to uniform and predictable forms of behaviour, a claim that's not dissimilar to an intuition found in Alfred Sohn-Rethel's critique of epistemology, wherein the Cartesian representation of the world as *res extensa* is correlated to the limitations of capitalist control over pre-industrial production. Sohn-Rethel's contention is that the epistemic project of modern science and philosophy is inseparable from the need to posit a mental labour autonomous from manual labour since it permits the imposition of abstract knowledge over labour and, thus, of control by automation over artisanry.[75] What we have to retain from all this, then, is that the desire to 'master' nature has always been a project of social control, and extricating it will not merely be a matter of cognition nor reducible to will alone.

We have thus far put off any historically contextualising claims regarding accelerationism, but we can now venture one here. For detectable in its expressions of machinic desire are the wider conditions of capitalist crisis: the decelerating pace of growth, as we saw in earlier chapters, is the result of overcompetition. It is not the speed of innovation and advance of automation, but economic over-capacity, cash with nowhere to invest profitably, that generates mass and under-development. We should observe in both the desire and the anxiety that orbit around the displacement of the human by the robot, accordingly, the symptoms of a process where capital has declining prospects for profitable investment, and more and more of us become surplus to requirement. Not enough market dynamism, in other words, rather than too much technological innovation.

What's most striking about the historicity of accelerationism, however, is the brevity of its popularity; even some of its key proponents have adopted more sceptical positions given the increasingly irrefutable evidence that capacities of AI and machine learning tend to be exaggerated and that declarations of fully automated production in certain sectors conceal dependence on low paid labour elsewhere.[76] We might put the transience of accelerationism down to its origins in social media, a realm where nifty slogans circulate quickly and widely, but whose lifespan tends to be abbreviated. More importantly, it's given its lack of a subject, its absence of an agent of social change, and so its reliance upon the imaginaries of its proponents, that techno-utopianism so easily slips into its opposite.

Enlightened Cynicism

This brings us to another dimension of accelerationist discourse established, especially stridently, by Benjamin Noys: the profound disappointment that animates it.[77] One way of articulating the accelerationist's core argument is to say that, while capitalism has intensified, it no longer accelerates; its profits are derived from rentierism, not innovation. Critics have discerned nostalgia for a Fordist era of rising productivity in such a claim; a sensibility expressed, for instance, in Williams and Srnicek's exultation of long-abandoned socialist experiments with cybernetic models of distribution.[78] Here is the melancholy longing for lost futures of a once living modernism we have already encountered in chapter one via the work of Mark Fisher. But what stands out here is the way in which the end of history is reiterated time and again, as if embodying the state of exhaustion it seeks to designate. When Fredric Jameson first discerned in postmodern culture a rearward looking 'nostalgia mode' he dated it to the run-up to the 1980s, while Fisher's iteration of the claim at times locates it in Thatcherism and at others with Blairism.[79] Still more recently it has been deployed as a frame for the reception of electronic music sub-genres in the 2010s, Vaporwave in particular. The latter, a small, mainly online community of artists and fans – performances and hard copy releases were rare – became especially outsized in its significance since it served so widely as a screen upon which critics could project theses about the traumas of late capitalism, the demise of aesthetic authenticity, and, more broadly, a rehearsal of the end of history that invites further examination.

As a collection of signifiers, Vaporwave orbits equivocation; between edifying and commercial intention, between music and Muzak, there's an ambiguity usually read as symptomatic of a capitalist colonisation of the life-world so complete as to have vanquished any scope for authenticity or critique. Certainly, these are terms one might attribute to the psychic investment in any number of popular musics in the past half-century or so, except that with Vaporwave there's a knowingness so severe, a self-parody so layered, that a newly intensified moral ambiguity emerges.

Such a constrained hyper-reflexivity is best emblematised by two of Vaporwave's founding documents, Daniel Lopatin's 2010 album, *Chuck Person's Eccojams Vol.1*, and James Ferraro's *Far Side Virtual* from 2011.[80] Both are characterised by oddly pitched, looping and echoing quotation and imitation of 1980s and 1990s commercial musics: smooth jazz, easy listening, corporate training video soundtracks, especially. Yet whilst Ferraro has primarily engaged in tongue in cheek pastiche of the sounds of digital living – software jingles or muzakal tropes are abundant in his work – Lopatin has been all the more interesting for blurring the lines between samples, synthesised, and acoustic instruments; plucked and bowed strings, reed, harpsichord, marimba, experiments with texture that cohere into lush harmonies, that disintegrate into fluttering polyphony, tittering arpeggios.

Both Ferraro and Lopatin operate, in keeping with accelerationist principle, according to a wholly modular relation to the recent history of music and soundscape. Genre elements and epochs are placed upon a spinning wheel of sonic fragments to be drawn seemingly at random, an approach that also serves to describe any number of electronic music artists from the early to mid-2010s, including the whole gamut of what was referred to as deconstructed club music. But we should observe as well that such a segmental relation to genre, rhythm, and style reverberates with the terms by which we have already described the ascendance of ambient as a meta-genre; a principle governing frictionless relations between stylistic registers effected by the transformations wrought by streaming platforms upon song-form. Except that the artists with which we're concerned here deploy these techniques to a new degree of intensity, a wayward and chaotic display of technical wizardry pushes pop to the limits of its conventions, by cycling through its parts, styles, and conventions ever more impatiently, yet without seeking to exceed them.

In this respect, we might conceive of accelerationism as an attempt to recover sonic contingency and errancy in light of the hegemony of the streaming platform. We have already suggested the desire that animating field recording can be interpreted along similar lines, whereby nature stands as a rhetorical appeal to spontaneity. Only where we consider more experimental electronic music from the early 2010s, and Lopatin's and Ferraro's kaleidoscopic carnivals of frayed commercial utopias most of all, these are frequently made to stand as figures of accelerationism, where it's conceived as a response to the state of ennui brought about by capital's seemingly unceasing advance on whatever might exceed it. One critic describes Lopatin's work as 'a study in futuristic doom told with a smirk'.[81] For another, Vaporwave reveals 'the lies and slippages of modern techno-culture and its representations, or as its willing facilitators'.[82] Another, still, discerns 'simultaneous critique and parody of consumers'.[83] Others, finally, see the music as 'about the impossibility of the critical task itself' or 'an aestheticization of the feeling of estrangement'.[84] All in all, where consumption is all too knowing, critique oscillates endlessly with identification.

It's important to note some of the dimensions of gender at work here: the enthusiasm of Herndon's liberal ethos of access and education is countered by the cold masculinist detachment typical of Vaporwave. Of course, cynicism is a common means of preserving the masculinist ideal of the sovereign artist all too aware of his collapsing dominion, but it's a tactic which leads one down an ethico-political cul-de-sac which has its most substantive articulation in Steven Shaviro's book-length study of accelerationist aesthetics which, like our own, hinges upon the notion of real subsumption by capital. Only Shaviro draws his understanding from Negri, Virno, and other philosophies of the 'Fragment on Machines', which take the displacement of the individual by automation as implying that capital – having absorbed the skills of living labour – has become the society's sole driving force. In this regard, Shaviro follows Negri in referring to the transformation from formal to real subsumption simply as 'biopower', a command over life itself. For once capital penetrates the whole of society; Negri's argument goes, 'the entire society becomes one enormous factory, or rather, the factory spreads throughout the whole of society. In this situation, production is social and all activities are productive.'[85]

Made to stand for the character of contemporary society itself, this looser conception of real subsumption can serve to depict feelings of malaise, powerlessness, and alienation.[86] For Shaviro, it does the conceptual work of confirming the colonisation of all aspects of life, all that remains is the 'valuation and evaluation of everything' and so 'transgression is entirely negative.'[87] This is an argument expressed in accelerationist aesthetics too, for which the pursuit of transgression beyond convention inevitably produces more material for capital to colonise; artworks can offer only more of what already is. At best, they register their complicity. 'The only way out is the way through', Shaviro holds, for where capital is viewed to have subsumed the whole of the society, only capital's own 'creative destruction', its perpetual dissolution of all social institutions, can be a source of enthusiasm. In such a state, where cultural expression is restricted to conveying its exhaustion, nihilism prevails. Hence Shaviro's endorsement of 'enlightened cynicism' which presses the monstrous terms of the culture industry to their limits. What else can one do, after all, except convey one's political impotence, revel in the excesses of commercial society, take relief in its hollowness, where exceeding the limits of the present is impossible?

But this sort of cynical enlightenment entails a rather bewildering series of claims, premised upon the inflation of some of the processes of the culture industries to the level of life itself. One is reminded of the architects of neoliberalism who, in their polemics against the welfare state, sought to displace class analysis by conflating labour with capital, and thus reconceptualising working life not as exploitation, but rather as a series of investments in oneself.[88] This account of the becoming-entrepreneurial of the neoliberal self does register a contemporary disposition, only when it's taken too literally it presents a rather truncated frame of reference which reduces every aspect of existence to a domain of human capital. Such a formulation might name a particular tendency, operative since the 1980s, whereby the management of risk is increasingly shifted from the firm and the state onto the individual worker compelled to manage their life as if they too were each a firm and life merely a series of investments. But to see the hegemony of this view as evidence for capital's final conquest of antagonism over-inflates the scope and scale of the defeat of the Fordist social contract in the first place.

As we saw in an earlier chapter, the protections offered to the Fordist worker were historically fleeting and restricted by the categories of race and gender. The point is not to dismiss the historic concessions won by industrial labour in the capitalist core countries in the twentieth century, but to contextualise these in a wider and longer history which encompasses the wider hierarchies upon which these were partly premised. To do so serves to emphasise a longer continuity in the gendered and racialised antagonisms, the inequalities, the abjection, definitive of the contemporary in place of a picture that sees only the smooth and linear advance of market control.

Indeed, to posit the completion of capitalist subsumption only serves to emphasise further the impression of an altogether disembodied, immaterial imaginary for which the consumption and not the manufacture of the objects of a digital economy takes centre stage and, further, is refracted in what remains out of frame in accelerationist aesthetics too. The landscapes, both sonic and visual, that appear in the work of Lopatin, Ferraro, and Herndon take the form of a disorderly mass of ever-so-slightly obsolete leisure products: laptop computers, games and software, daytime TV, or shopping malls. This out of time symbolic topography might pry open a crevice of critical distance to signal the tawdriness of the rewards of middle class life. But it also obscures the lithium and copper mines, the chipboard assembly plants, or E-waste dumps upon which these also are premised.[89] This is a relatively prosaic point, for sure, but it gestures at the absent tension in these works and, on this latter point, Larne Abse Gogarty has described a wider contemporary aesthetic strategy by the delightfully acerbic formulation of a 'flat unmediated aspirational nihilism', whose piling up of consumer objects, of styles, and of epochs leaves everything 'up for grabs, with no consequences to how this arrangement emerges.'[90]

This is a mode of presentation, then, whose very ambiguity, its accumulation of objects oscillating between the possible emblems of techno-domination and techno-utopia, conveys an absence at the core of an imaginary for which the activity and products of technology can be the agent of meaningful social change. And so, finally, there's a symmetry here with the ontology of entanglement whose own response to ecological crisis rests with an ethical disposition, an embodied attunement, even if the latter is premised upon what it ultimately grasps as the inadequacy of rational thought over affect. Both occlude the very thing which makes them possible: mind over body, body over mind, mastery over nature or identification with it; what is evaded in either case are the textures of desolation, suffering, and oppression which have given the relation of mind to body or human to nature their material conditions. This occlusion generates an empty space that the focus on technique and mediation tries to fill. But this always remains a one-sided view, restricted to the consumption of technology, while its wider conditions always remain out of frame.

Tell him I'm gone, Oh boys, tell him I'm gone

Here, where cultural forms orbit around their deferral of a confrontation with their conditions, is as good a place as any to draw an end to our episodic survey of work and song in the present. It returns us to one of the animating impulses for this book: that starting from the wage-relation furnishes an understanding of song with specific threads to follow; as a refusal of work, on the one hand, and as a mediator between music and society, on the other hand. Whilst our analyses have been selective – there's no reason to elude one's subject-position or the parochialism of taste in a work such as this – and have eschewed completeness or a comprehensive account of the present, the fundamental principles derived ought to be unambiguous nonetheless. Still, where an analysis proceeds by way of example, as the chapters here have, the work has no inherent endpoint and further illustrations are always available.

A supplementary study might look to the unforeseen taste for Korean pop across Asia beginning around 2007 and exploding in the West around a decade later, or it could take in the unlikely superstardom of a young country and western singer-songwriter (Taylor Swift) or of the member of an RnB group (Beyoncé) around the same period. A conception of the dancing body invites further assessment as well, especially given that it proposes an experience of movement and gesture not dictated by the machine. Dance music has been a crucial site for explorations of queerness over recent decades and this, too, invites further speculation here. Likewise, one might examine the fragmentary medleys of so-called 'deconstructed club' music which came to prominence around a decade ago, the local micro-genres (Jersey club or footwork, say), or forms emerging from the global South and diaspora communities (kuduro, amapiano, gqom, for instance), which have circulated through nightclubs globally. So too the polysemy of sex and work, from James Brown's 'shake your money maker' to DJ Assault's 'work that body', that refuses to countenance any detachment of the political from the erotic. These will have to be the subject of another study but, at least, they should evoke here a conviction which has motivated this book; for they signal a rejection of the separation of pleasure and the political and the refusal of the subordination of one to the other. Most of all, this is a refusal of which song continues to be a bearer.

Notes

1. See for instance, April Clare Welsh, 'Bird Sound Power: How Björk, Equinoxx and more Embraced Field Recording in 2017', *Factmag*, 14 December 2017, www.factmag.com/2017/12/14/field-recording-music-2017-bjork-equiknoxx/ [accessed 31 October 2023]; Lottie Brazier, 'How Musicians are Using Field Recordings to Capture the Politics of Place', *Pitchfork*, 3 April 2018, https://pitchfork.com/thepitch/how-musicians-are-using-field-recordings-to-capture-the-politics-of-place/ [accessed 31 October 2023].
2. Anthony Child, *Electronic Recordings from Maui Jungle*. Editions Mego, 2015; Elysia Crampton, *Moth/Lake*. Boomkat, 2015; Egyptrixx, *Pure, Beyond Reproach*. Halocline Trance, 2017; Mica Levi, *Delete Beach*. DDS, 2017; KMRU, *Logue*. Injazero, 2021. For a longer list see Rory Gibb, A.M. Kanngieser, & Paul Rekret, 'In Sonic Defiance of Extinction', *Transmediale Magazine*, 2018, pp.26-30.
3. In recent years this canonical history has been revised to include significant developments by previously overlooked women composers, such as Pauline Oliveros and Annea Lockwood.
4. Kheshti, *Modernity's Ear*; Joeri Bruyninckx, *Listening in the Field: Recording and the Science of Birdsong*. Cambridge & London: MIT Press, 2018.
5. Mitchell Akiyama, *The Phonographic Memory: A History of Sound Recording in the Field*, PhD Dissertation, McGill University, 2015.
6. See Pierre Schaeffer, *Treaty on Musical Objects: An Essay Across Disciplines* (Christine North & John Dack, Trans.). Berkeley: University of California Press, 2017.
7. Pierre Schaffer, *Cinq Études De Bruits: Étude Aux Objects*. INA-GRM, 1948.
8. David Toop, *Haunted Weather: Music, Silence and Memory*. London: Serpent's Tail, 2004; R. Murray Schafer, *The Soundscape: Our Sonic Environment and the Tuning of the World*. Rochester: Destiny Books, 1977, p.208, quoted in Akiyama, *The Phonographic Memory*.
9. Hildergard Westerkamp in Andra Shirley Jean McCartney, *Sounding Places: Situated Conversations Through the Soundscape Compositions of Hildergard Westerkamp*, PhD Dissertation, York University, 1999, p.141.
10. Hildergard Westerkamp, 'Beneath the Forest Floor', *Transformations*. Empreintes Digitales, 1996.

11 Francisco López, 'Blind Listening' in: D. Rothenberg & M. Ulvaeus (Eds.) *The Book of Music and Nature: An Anthology of Sounds, Words, Thoughts*. Middletown: Wesleyan University Press, 2001, pp.163–68, p.163.
12 Francisco López, *Wind [Patagonia]*. And/OAR, 2007.
13 Francisco López, *La Selva*. V2_Archief, 1998.
14 Francisco López, *Buildings [New York]*. V2_Archief, 2001; Untitled # 104. Alien8 Recordings, 2000.
15 Francisco López, 'Environmental Sound Matter', CD *La Selva: Sound Environments From a Neotropical Rainforest*. V2_Archief, 1998. Quoted in Makis Solomos, 'A Phenomenological Experience of Sound: Notes on Francisco López', *Contemporary Music Review* 38, no.1–2, 2019, pp.94–106.
16 Marie Thompson, *Beyond Unwanted Sound: Noise, Affect, and Aesthetic Moralism*. London: Bloomsbury, 2017. See also Jonathan Sterne, 'Soundscape, Landscape, Escape' in: Karin Bijsterveld (Ed.) *Soundscapes of the Urban Past: Staged Sound as Mediated Cultural Heritage*. Bielefeld: Transcript Verlag, 2013, pp.181–94.
17 López, 'Blind Listening'.
18 The reference to a 'mythical object' is from Brian Kane, *Sound Unseen: Acousmatic Sound in Theory and Practice*. Oxford: Oxford University Press, 2016.
19 Chris Watson, *Outside the Circle of Fire*. Touch, 1998; Chris Watson, 'Ant-Steps', *Interpreting the Soundscape*. Leonardo Music Journal, 2006; Chris Watson, *Weather Report*. Touch, 2003.
20 Peter Cusack, *Sounds from Dangerous Places*. ReR Megacorp, 2012.
21 On this point see Jeff Kinkle & Alberto Toscano in *Cartographies of the Absolute*. Winchester: Zero Books, 2015, pp.226–28.
22 Peter Cusack, *Sounds From Dangerous Places*. Berlin: ReR MegaCorp, 2012, p.viii.
23 Peter Cusack, *Field Recording as Sonic Journalism*, n.d., https://ualresearchonline.arts.ac.uk/id/eprint/9451/1/Cusack,%20Sonic%20Journalism.pdf.
24 Chris Watson quoted in Ableton, 'Sounds Outside: The Art of Field Recording', *Ableton.com*, 20 June 2016, www.ableton.com/en/blog/art-of-field-recording/ [accessed 31 October 2023].
25 Luke Turner, 'Chris Watson on Recording the Music of the Natural World', *The Quietus*, 24 January 2013, https://thequietus.com/articles/11222-chris-watson-interview [accessed 31 October 2023]; Peter Cusack, 'CD Companion Introduction: Interpreting the Soundscape', *Leonardo Music Journal* 16, 2006, pp.69–70.
26 Cusack, *Sounds From Dangerous Places*; Andrea Polli & Leah Barclay quoted in Angus Carlyle & Cathy Lane, *In The Field: The Art of Field Recording*. London: Uniform Books, 2011.
27 Salome Voeglin, *The Political Possibility of Sound: Fragments of Listening*. London: Bloomsbury, 2019, p.37; Cox, 'Beyond Representation and Signification'; Kassabian, *Ubiquitous Listening*.
28 See Donna Haraway, *Simians, Cyborgs, and Women: The Reinvention of Nature*. London: Routledge 1991; Bruno Latour, *We Have Never Been Modern*. Cambridge: Harvard University Press 1991; and my account of these claims in Paul Rekret 'Seeing Like a Cyborg? The Innocence of Posthuman Knowledge' in: David Chandler & Christian Fuchs (Eds.) *Digital Objects, Digital Subjects: Interdisciplinary Perspectives on Capitalism, Labour and Politics in the Age of Big Data*. London: University of Westminster Press, 2019, pp.81–94.
29 Dipesh Chakrabarty, *The Climate of History in a Planetary Age*. Chicago: University of Chicago Press, 2021.

30 Timothy Morton, *Hyperobjects: Philosophy and Ecology After the End of the World*. Minneapolis: University of Minnesota Press, 2013.
31 Martin Heidegger, 'The Age of the World Picture' in: *The Question Concerning Technology & Other Essays* (William Lovitt, Trans.). London: Garland, 1977, pp.115-54.
32 Martin Heidegger, 'Only a God Can Save Us: The Spiegel Interview (1966)' in Thomas Sheehan (Ed.) *Heidegger. The Man and the Thinker*. Piscataway: Transaction Publishers, 1981, pp.45-67.
33 Chris Watson, 'Vatnajökull', *Weather Report*.
34 Raymond Williams, *Problems in Materialism and Culture*. London: Verso, 1980, p.83.
35 Alfred Schmidt, *The Concept of Nature in Marx*. London: NLB, 1971, p.82.
36 Silvia Federici, *Caliban and the Witch: The Body and Primitive Accumulation*. New York: Autonomedia, 2004; Davis, *Women, Race & Class*.
37 I develop these arguments in Rekret, 'Seeing Like a Cyborg?'.
38 Ableton, 'Sounds Outside'.
39 John Locke, *Two Treatises on Government. Volume V, The Works of John Locke in Ten Volumes*. Darmstadt: Scientia Verlag Aalen, 1963, pp.207-485.
40 Kheshti, *Modernity's Ear*.
41 On this point see Akiyama, *The Phonographic Memory*; Patrick B. Mullen, *The Main Who Adores the Negro: Race and American Folklore*. Chicago: University of Illinois University Press, 2008.
42 Friedrich Kittler, *Gramophone, Film, Typewriter* (G. Winthrop-Young & M. Wutz, Trans.). Stanford: Stanford University Press, 1999.
43 David Rothenberg, 'Nature's Greatest Hit: The Old and New Songs of the Humpback Whale', *The Wire*, September 2014 www.thewire.co.uk/in-writing/essays/nature_s-greatest-hit_the-old-and-new-songs-of-the-humpback-whale [accessed 31 October 2023]; Peter Cusack, 'Interpreting the Soundscape', *Leonardo Music Journal* 16, 2006, pp.68-70.
44 Theodor W. Adorno, *Aesthetic Theory* (Robert Hullot-Kentor, Trans.). London: Bloomsbury, 2004, p.94.
45 Gilbert Simondon, *On the Mode of Existence of Technical Objects* (Cecile Malaspina & John Rogove, Trans.). Minneapolis: University of Minnesota Press, 2016, p.137.
46 Kittler, *Gramophone, Film, Typewriter*, p.23.
47 Ray Brassier, 'Prometheanism and its Critics' in: Robin Mackay & Armen Avanessian (Eds.) *#Accelerate#: the Accelerationist Reader*. Falmouth: Urbanomic, 2014, p.487.
48 Alex Williams & Nick Srnicek, '#Accelerate: Manifesto for an Accelerationist Politics' in: Robin Mackay & Armen Avanessian (Eds.) *#Accelerate#: The Accelerationist Reader*. Falmouth: Urbanomic, 2014, p.360.
49 Aaron Bastani, *Fully Automated Luxury Communism*. London: Verso, 2019, p.160.
50 Laboria Cuboniks, *Xenofeminism: A Politics for Alienation* (n.d.), (https://laboriacuboniks.net/manifesto/xenofeminism-a-politics-for-alienation/); Helen Hester, *Xenofeminism*. London: Polity Press, 2018.
51 Williams & Srnicek, '#Accelerate', p.354.
52 Ibid.
53 See Karl Marx, *Grundrisse: Foundations of the Critique of Political Economy* (Martin Nicolaus, Trans.). London: Penguin, 1993, pp.690-712; Paolo Virno, *A Grammar of the Multitude* (Isabella Bertoletti et al., Trans.). New York: Semiotexte, 2004; Michal Hardt & Antonio Negri, *Empire*. Cambridge: Harvard University Press, 2000.

54 Marx, *Grundrisse*, pp.694, 705.
55 Nick Land, 'Machinic Desire' in *Fanged Noumena: Collected Writings 1987–2007*. Falmouth: Urbanomic, 2011, pp.319–44.
56 Holly Herndon, 'Holly Herndon', *Red Bull Music Academy*, 2014, www.redbullmusicacademy.com/lectures/holly-herndon-tokyo-2014 [accessed 31 October 2023] quoted in Travis Jeppesen, 'The New Gods in the Machine: Holly Herndon's Vehicularity', *Afterall* 41, Spring/Summer 2016, pp.80–89.
57 Holly Herndon, *Movement*. RVNG. Intl., 2012.
58 Holly Herndon, *Platform*. 4AD, 2015.
59 Roland Barthes, 'The Grain of the Voice' in *Image – Music – Text* (Stephen Heath, Trans.). London: Fontana, 1977.
60 Adam Harper, 'How Internet Music is Frying Your Brain', *Popular Music* 36, no.1, 2017, pp.86–97.
61 Alexander Weheliye, 'Feenin: Posthuman Voices in Contemporary Black Popular Music', *Social Text* 20, no.2, 2002, pp.21–47.
62 Holly Herndon, 'Proto', www.hollyherndon.com/proto. I take the formulation of alchemising of body and machine from Benjamin Noys, *Malign Velocities: Acceleration and Capitalism*. Alresford: Zero Books, 2014.
63 Jordan Darville, 'Holly Herndon Announces New Voice Instrument and "Digital Twin" Holly+', *The Fader*, 14 July 2021, www.thefader.com/2021/07/14/holly-herndon-holly-plus [accessed 31 October 2023].
64 On this point see David Cunningham, 'A Marxist Heresy? Accelerationism and Its Discontents', *Radical Philosophy* 191, May/June 2015, pp.29–38.
65 I draw here on Cunningham, 'A Marxist Heresy?' and Jasper Bernes, 'Planning and Anarchy', *South Atlantic Quarterly* 119, no.1, 2020, pp.53–73.
66 See Alberto Toscano, 'Lineaments of the Logistical State', *Viewpoint Magazine*, 28 September 2014, https://viewpointmag.com/2014/09/28/lineaments-of-the-logistical-state/ [accessed 31 October 2023].
67 Marx, *Capital, Volume 1*, pp.943–1084.
68 Jacques Camatte, *This World We Must Leave, and Other Essays* (Alex Trotter, Ed.). New York: Autonomedia, 1995.
69 Robert Linhart, *Lénine, Taylor, les Paysans*. Paris: Seuil, 1976x see pp.91–94.
70 Neda Atanasoski & Kalindi Vora, *Surrogate Humanity: Race, Robots, and the Politics of Technological Futures*. Durham & London: Duke University Press, 2019.
71 Ramon Amaro, *The Black Technical Object: On Machine Learning and the Aspiration of Black Being*. London: Sternberg Press, 2023; Seb Franklin, *The Digital Disposed: Racial Capitalism and the Informatics of Value*. Minneapolis: University of Minnesota Press, 2021.
72 Beech, *Art and Post-Capitalism*, p.86.
73 Atanasoki & Vora, *Surrogate Humanity*, p.18.
74 Federici, *Caliban and the Witch*; Davis, *Women, Race & Class*.
75 Sohn-Rethel, *Intellectual and Manual Labour*, pp.113, 122, 141, 179–80.
76 Lauren Kelly, 'Re-Politicising the Future of Work: Automation Anxieties, Universal Basic Income, and the End of Techno-Optimism', *Journal of Sociology* 59, no.4, 2022, pp.828–43.
77 Noys, *Malign Velocities*.
78 Cunningham, 'A Marxist Heresy?'.

79 See Jameson, *Postmodernism*; Fisher, *Capitalist Realism*.
80 *Chuck Person's Eccojams Vol.1*. The Curatorial Club, 2011; James Ferraro, *Far Side Virtual*. Hippos in Tanks, 2011.
81 Sophie Kemp, 'Love in the Time of Lexapro EP', *Pitchfork*, 2018 https://pitchfork.com/reviews/albums/oneohtrix-point-never-love-in-the-time-of-lexapro-ep/ [accessed 31 October 2023].
82 Adam Harper, 'Vaporwave and the Pop-Art of the Virtual Plaza', Dummy, 12 July 2012, www.dummymag.com/news/adam-harper-vaporwave/ [accessed 31 October 2023].
83 Ken McLeod, 'Vaporwave: Politics, Protest, and Identity', *Journal of Popular Music Studies* 30, no.4, 2018, pp.123–41, p.124.
84 James Parker, 'Internet Club', *Tiny Mix Tapes*, 2012 www.tinymixtapes.com/music-review/internet-club-vanishing-vision [accessed 31 October 2023]; Alican Koc, 'Do You Want Vaporwave or Do You Want The Truth?' *Capacious* 1, no.1, 2017, pp.57–76.
85 Antonio Negri, *The Politics of Subversion: A Manifesto for the Twenty-First Century* (J. Newell, Trans.). London: Polity Press 2005, p.204.
86 Anthony Iles & Mattin, 'Introduction', *Abolishing Capitalist Totality: What is to be Done Under Real Subsumption?* Berlin: Archive Books, 2024.
87 Steven Shaviro, *No Speed Limit: Three Essays on Accelerationism*. Minneapolis: University of Minnesota Press, 2015.
88 On this point see Michel Foucault, *The Birth of Biopolitics: Lectures at the College de France, 1978–1979* (Graham Burchell, Trans.). Basingstoke: Palgrave MacMillan, 2007.
89 On this point see Dyer-Witherford, Cyber-Proletariat, pp.104–12.
90 Larne Abse Gogarty, *What We Do Is Secret: Contemporary Art and the Antinomies of Conspiracy*. London: Sternberg Press, 2023.

Bibliography

Aaltonen, Lari, 'Crate-Digging Columbuses and Vinyl Vespucci's: Exoticism in World Music Collections', in: R. Marchart, F. Dervin, & M. Gao (Eds.) *Intercultural Masquerade: New Orientalism, New Occidentalism, Old Exoticism*. New York: Springer 2016, pp.67–80.

Abel, Mark, *Groove: An Aesthetic of Measured Time*. Leiden: Brill, 2016.

Ableton, 'Sounds Outside: The Art of Field Recording', *Ableton.com*, 20 June 2016. https://www.ableton.com/en/blog/art-of-field-recording/ [accessed 31 October 2023].

Adkins, Lisa, Melinda Cooper, & Martin Konings, *The Asset Economy*. Cambridge: Polity Press, 2020.

Adorno, Theodor, *Philosophy of New Music* (Robert Hullot-Kentor, Ed. & Trans.). Minneapolis: University of Minnesota Press, 2006.

Adorno, Theodor, *Aesthetic Theory* (Robert Hullot-Kentor, Trans.). London: Bloomsbury, 2004.

Adorno, Theodor, 'On the Social Situation of Music' in: Richard Leppert (Ed.), Susan H. Gillespie (Trans.) *Essays on Music*. Berkeley & Los Angeles: University of California Press, 2002, pp.288–317.

Adorno, Theodor, 'Music in the Background', in: *Essays on Music* (Richard Leppert, Ed.). Berkeley & Los Angeles: University of California Press, 2002, pp.506–12.

Adorno, Theodor, *Essays on Music* (Richard Leppert, Ed.). Berkeley & Los Angeles: University of California Press, 2002.

Adorno, Theodor, 'Free Time' in: *The Culture Industry*. London: Routledge, 1991.

Adorno, Theodor, *A Metacritique: Studies in Husserl and the Phenomenological Antinomies*. Willis Domingo (Trans.). Cambridge: MIT Press, 1984.

Adorno, Theodor, *Introduction to the Sociology of Music* (E.B. Ashton, Trans.). New York: Seabury Press, 1976.

Agawu, Kofi, *Representing African Music: Postcolonial Notes, Queries, Positions*. London: Routledge 2013.

Agawu, Kofi, 'The Invention of African Rhythm', *Journal of the American Musicological Society* 48, no.3, 1995, pp.380–95.

Akiyama, Mitchell, The Phonographic Memory: A History of Sound Recording in the Field, PhD Dissertation, McGill University, 2015.

Amaro, Ramon, *The Black Technical Object: On Machine Learning and the Aspiration of Black Being*. London: Sternberg Press, 2023.

Anderson, Paul Allen. 'Neo-Muzak and the Business of Mood', *Critical Inquiry* 41, no.4, 2015, 811–40.

Andrejevic, Mark. 'The Droning of Experience', *The Fibreculture Journal* 25, 2015.

Angell, Noah, 'Everything Gucci: the Poetics and Political Economy of Gucci Mane', *Res.*, 13 November 2015, http://beingres.org/2015/11/04/everything-gucci/ [accessed 30 October 2023].

Arditi, David, *Getting Signed: Record Contracts, Musicians, and Power in Society.* Cham: Palgrave MacMillan, 2020.

Arditi, David. 'Digital Subscriptions: The Unending Consumption of Music in the Digital Era', *Popular Music and Society* 21, no.3, 2018, pp. 302–18.

Arditi, David. 'Music Everywhere: Setting A Digital Trap', *Critical Sociology*, 31 August 2017.

Arditi, David. 'iTunes: Breaking Barriers and Building Walls', *Popular Music and Society*, 37, no.4, 2014, pp.408–24.

Arthur, Christopher J., 'The Practical Truth of Abstract Labour' in: R. Bellofiore, G. Starosta, & P. Thomas (Eds.) *Marx's Laboratory: Critical Interpretations of the Grundrisse.* Leiden: Brill, 2013, pp. 101–20.

Atanasoski, Neda & Kalindi Vora, *Surrogate Humanity: Race, Robots, and the Politics of Technological Futures.* Durham & London: Duke University Press, 2019.

Balakrishnan, Gopal, 'Speculations on the Stationary State', *New Left Review* 59, September/October 2009.

Balaji, Murali, Trap(ped) Music and Masculinity: The Cultural Production of southern Hip-Hop at the Intersection of Corporate Control and Self-Construction. PhD Dissertation, Pennsylvania State University, 2009.

Balbaud, René, 'Francis Bebey', *Africa Report* 15, no.8, 1970.

Balibar, Étienne, *Politics and the Other Scene.* London: Verso, 2012.

Banaji, Jairus, 'The Fictions of Free Labour: Contract, Coercion, and So-Called Unfree-Labour', in *Theory as History: Essays on Modes of Production and Exploitation.* Leiden: Brill, 2010, pp.131–54.

Banaji, Jairus, *Theory as History: Essays on Modes of Production and Exploitation.* Leiden: Brill, 2010.

Baraka, Amiri, *Blues People: Negro Music in White America.* New York: Harper Perennial, 1999.

Baraka, Amiri (Leroi Jones), 'The Changing Same (R&B and New Black Music)', *Black Music.* New York: Da Capo, 1998.

Barker, Thomas P. 'Spatial Dialectics: Intimations of Freedom in Antebellum Slave Song', *Journal of Black Studies* 46, no.4, 2015, pp.363–83.

Barrett, Michele & Mary McIntosh, *The Anti-Social Family*. London: Verso, 2015.

Barthes, Roland, *Image – Music – Text* (Stephen Heath, Trans.). London: Fontana, 1977.

Bastani, Aaron, *Fully Automated Luxury Communism*. London: Verso, 2019.

Bebey, Francis, *La Radiodiffusion En Afrique Noire*. Issy-les-Moulineaux Seine: Editions Saint-Paul, 1963.

Bebey, Francis, *African Music: A People's Art* (Josephine Bennett, Trans.). New York: Lawrence Hill, 1975.

Bebey, Francis, *The Ashanti Doll* (Joyce A. Hutchinson, Trans.). London: Heinemann, 1978.

Bebey, Francis, *King Albert*. Westport: L. Hill, 1981.

Bebey, Kidi, *My Kingdom for a Guitar*. Bloomington: Indiana University Press, 2021.

Beech, Dave, *Art and Post-Capitalism: Aesthetic Labour, Automation and Value Production*. London: Pluto Press, 2019.

Bell, Taylor, *Hip-Hop's Influence on Stripper Culture: The Era of Cardi B. Dissertation*, Columbia College Chicago, 2018, https://core.ac.uk/download/pdf/235201789.pdf.

Benanav, Aaron, *Automation and the Future of Work*. London: Verso, 2020.

Benjamin, Walter, *The Arcades Project* (Howard Eiland & Kevin McLaughlin, Trans.). Cambridge: Belknap Press, 1999.

Benjamin, Walter, 'Central Park', *New German Critique*, 34, Winter 1985, pp.32–58.

Bennett, Toby, *Corporate Life in the Digital Music Industry: Remaking the Major Record Label from the Inside Out*. London: Bloomsbury, forthcoming.

Bensaïd, Daniel, *Marx for Our Times: Adventures and Misadventures of Critique* (Gregory Elliott, Trans.). London: Verso, 2010.

Beller, Jonathan. *The Message is Murder: Substrates of Computational Capital*. London: Pluto Press, 2017.

Berlant, Lauren, *Cruel Optimism*. Durham & London: Duke University Press, 2011.

Bernes, Jasper, 'Planning and Anarchy', *South Atlantic Quarterly* 119, no.1, 2020, pp.53–73.

Beta, Andy, 'An Interview With Alan Bishop', *The Believer*, 1 July 2008, https://culture.org/an-interview-with-alan-bishop/ [accessed 30 June 2022].

Beta, Andy, 'Fourth World in the 21st Century', *Resident Advisor*, 12 June 2017, www.residentadvisor.net/features/2984 [accessed January 19, 2019].

Beta, Andy, 'How a Digital Rabbit Hole Gave Midori Takada's 1983 Album a Second Life', *The New York Times*, 24 May 2018. www.nytimes.com/2018/05/21/arts/music/midori-takada-through-the-looking-glass.html [accessed January 22, 2019].

Bhabha, Homi, *The Location of Culture*. London: Routledge, 1994.

Billic, Pasko. 'A Critique of the Political Economy of Algorithms: A Brief history of Google's Technological Rationality', *TripleC*, 16, no.1, 2018.

Bjornson, Richard, *The African Quest for Freedom and Identity: Cameroonian Writing and National Experience*. Bloomington: Indiana University Press, 1991.

Blair, Elizabeth, 'Strip Clubs: Launch Pads For Hits In Atlanta', *NPR*, 23 December 2010, www.npr.org/sections/therecord/2010/12/23/132287578/strip-clubs-launch-pads-for-hits-in-atlanta? [accessed 31 October 2023].

Boggs, James, *Pages From a Black Radical's Notebook: A James Boggs Reader* (Stephen M. Ward, Ed.). Detroit: Wayne State University Press, 2011.

Boltanski, Luc & Eve Chiapello, *The New Spirit of Capitalism* (Gregory Elliott, Trans.). London: Verso, 2005.

Boon, Marcus, *The Politics of Vibration: Music as a Cosmopolitical Practice*. Durham & London: Duke University Press, 2022.

Born, Georgina & David Hesmondhalgh (Eds.), *Western Music and Its Others: Difference, Repetition and Appropriation in Music*. London: University of California Press, 2000.

Boyle, Michael Shane, 'Performance and Value: The Work of Theatre in Karl Marx's Critique of Political Economy', *Theatre Survey* 58, no.1, 2017, pp.3-23.

Bradley, Regina, *Chronicling Stankonia: The Rise of the Hip-hop South*. Chapel Hill & London: University of North Carolina Press, 2021.

Braidotti, Rosi. *The Posthuman*. Cambridge: Polity Press, 2013.

Brar, Dhanveer Singh, *Teklife/Ghettoville/Eski: The Sonic Ecologies of Black Music in the Early 21st Century*. London: Goldsmiths Press, 2020.

Brassier, Ray, 'Prometheanism and its Critics' in: Robin Mackay & Armen Avanessian (Eds.) *#Accelerate#: the Accelerationist Reader*. Falmouth: Urbanomic, 2014.

Braverman, Harry, *Labour and Monopoly Capital: The Degradation of Work in the Twentieth Century*. New York: Monthly Review Press, 1998.

Brazier, Lottie, 'How Musicians are Using Field Recordings to Capture the Politics of Place', *Pitchfork*, 3 April 2018, https://pitchfork.com/thepitch/how-musicians-are-using-field-recordings-to-capture-the-politics-of-place/ [accessed 31 October 2023].

Brenner, Robert, *The Economics of Global Turbulence: The Advanced Capitalist Economies from Long Boom to Long Downturn, 1945–2005*. London: Verso, 2006.

Bronson, Zak, 'Living in the Wreckage', *Los Angeles Review of Books*, 12 February 2016, https://lareviewofbooks.org/article/living-in-the-wreckage/ [accessed 19 November 2022].

Brooks, Siobhan, *Race and Erotic Capital in the Stripping Industry*. New York: SUNY Press, 2010.

Brouillette, Sarah, 'On Art and Real Subsumption', *Mediations* 29, no.2, 2016, pp.169–76.

Brown, Nathan, 'Postmodernity, Not Yet: Toward a New Periodisation', *Radical Philosophy* 2, no.1, February 2018, www.radicalphilosophy.com/article/postmodernity-not-yet.

Brunner, Anja, 'Popular Music and the Young Postcolonial State of Cameroon, 1960-1980', *Popular Music and Society* 40, no.1, 2017, pp. 37-48.

Bruyninckx, Joeri, *Listening in the Field: Recording and the Science of Birdsong*. Cambridge & London: MIT Press, 2018.

Bull, Michael. *Sound Moves: Ipod Culture and Urban Experience*. London: Routledge, 2007.

Burdon, George, 'Immunological Atmospheres: Ambient Music and the Design of Self-Experience', *Cultural Geographies* 30, no.4, April 2023.

Burkhardt, Patrick. 'Music in the Cloud and the Digital Sublime', *Popular Music and Society* 31, no.4, 2014, pp.393-407.

Burton, Justin Adams, *Posthuman Rap*. Oxford: Oxford University Press, 2017.

Cabral, Amilcar, *Resistance and Decolonisation* (Dan Wood, Trans.). London: Rowman & Littlefield, 2016.

Caffentzis, George, *Clipped Coins, Abused Words, and Civil Government: John Locke's Philosophy of Money*. London: Pluto Press, 2021.

Caffentzis, George, *No Blood For Oil: Essays on Energy, Class Struggle, and War 1998-2016*. New York: Autonomedia, 2017.

Camatte, Jacques, *This World We Must Leave, and Other Essays* (Alex Trotter, Ed.). New York: Autonomedia, 1995.

Caraway, Brett, 'Crisis of Command: Theorizing Value in New Media', *Communication Theory* 26, no.1, 2016, pp.64-81.

Carlyle, Angus & Cathy Lane, *In The Field: The Art of Field Recording*. London: Uniform Books, 2011.

Chakrabarty, Dipesh, *The Climate of History in a Planetary Age*. Chicago: University of Chicago Press, 2021.

Chandler, Nahum Dimitri, *X: The Problem of the Negro as a Problem for Thought*. New York: Fordham University Press, 2014.

Clarke, David. 'Beyond the Global Imaginary: Decoding BBC Radio 3's Late Junction', *Radical Musicology* 2, 2007.

Cohen, Norm, *Long Steel Rail: The Railroad in American Folksong*. Urbana: University of Illinois Press, 2000.

Collins, Patricia Hill, *Black Feminist Thought: Knowledge, Consciousness, and the Politics of Empowerment*. London: Routledge, 2002.

Connolly, William, *The Fragility of Things: Self-Organizing Processes, Neoliberal Fantasies, and Democractic Activism*. Durham & London: Duke University Press, 2013.

Cooper, Melinda, *Family Values: Between Neoliberalism and the New Social Conservatism.* New York: Zone Books, 2017.

Cooper, Melinda, 'Workfare, Familyfare, Godfare: Transforming Contingency into Necessity', *South Atlantic Quarterly* 111, no.4, 2012, pp.643-61.

Cooper, Melinda & Angela Mitropoulos, 'The Household Frontier', *Ephemera: Theory and Politics in Organization* 9, no.4, 2009. pp.363-68.

Cox, Christoph, 'Beyond Representation and Signification: Toward a Sonic Materialism'. *Journal of Visual Culture* 10, no.2, 2011, pp.145-61.

Crary, Jonathan, *24/7: Late Capitalism and the End of Sleep.* London: Verso, 2013.

Cunningham, David, 'A Marxist Heresy? Accelerationism and Its Discontents', *Radical Philosophy* 191, May/June 2015, pp.29-38.

Cusack, Peter, *Sounds From Dangerous Places.* Berlin: ReR MegaCorp, 2012.

Cusack, Peter, 'CD Companion Introduction: Interpreting the Soundscape', *Leonardo Music Journal* 16, 2006, pp.69-70.

Cusack, Peter, 'Interpreting the Soundscape', *Leonardo Music Journal* 16, 2006, pp.68-70.

Cusack, Peter, *Field Recording as Sonic Journalism*, n.d., https://ualresearchonline.arts.ac.uk/id/eprint/9451/1/Cusack,%20Sonic%20Journalism.pdf.

Dart, Chris, 'Inside the Atlanta Strip Club that Supposedly Runs the Music Industry', The A.V. Club, 16 November 2015, www.avclub.com/read-this-inside-the-atlanta-strip-club-that-supposedl-1798286442 [accessed 31 October 2023].

Darville, Jordan, 'Holly Herndon Announces New Voice Instrument and 'Digital Twin' Holly+', *The Fader*, 14 July 2021, www.thefader.com/2021/07/14/holly-herndon-holly-plus [accessed 31 October 2023].

Davis, Angela Y., *Women, Race & Class.* New York: Vintage Books, 1983.

Dayal, Geeta, 'Ambient Pioneer Midori Takada: "Everything on Earth Has a Sound"', *The Guardian*, 24 March 2017, www.theguardian.com/music/2017/mar/24/midori-takada-interview-through-the-looking-glass-reissue [accessed 27 October 2023].

Dean, Jodi, 'Communicative Capitalism: Circulation and the Foreclosure of Politics', *Cultural Politics* 1, no.1, 2005, pp.51-74.

Debord, Guy, *Society of the Spectacle* (Greg Adargo, Trans.). Detroit: Black & Red, 1977.

Denning, Michael. *Noise Uprising: The Audiopolitics of a World Musical Revolution.* London: Verso, 2015.

DeNora, Tia. *Music and Everyday Life.* Cambridge: Cambridge University Press, 2003.

Denselow, Robin, 'Konono No. 1: Africa's Velvet Underground', *The Independent*, 7 April 2006, www.independent.co.uk/arts-entertainment/music/features/konono-no-1-africa-s-velvet-underground-6104367.html [accessed 4 July 2022].

Devine, Kyle, *Decomposed: The Political Ecology of Music*. Cambridge & London: MIT Press, 2019.

D'Eramo, Marco, *The World in a Selfie: An Inquiry into the Tourist Age*. London: Verso, 2021.

Dinerstein, Joel, *The Origins of Cool in Postwar America*. Chicago: University of Chicago Press, 2017.

Dinerstein, Joel, *Swinging the Machine*. Boston: University of Massachusetts Press, 2003.

Dockray, Sean. 'Interface, Access, Loss', in: Marysia Lwandowska & Lauren Ptak (Eds.) *Undoing Property*. Berlin: Sternberg Press, 2013, pp.183-94.

Drott, Eric, 'Music in the Work of Social Reproduction', *Cultural Politics* 15, no.2, 2019, pp.162-83.

Drott, Eric, 'Why the Next Song Matters: Streaming, Recommendation, Scarcity'. *Twentieth-Century Music* 15, no.3, 2018, pp.325-57.

Drott, Eric, 'Music as a Technology of Surveillance', *Journal for the Society of American Music* 12, no.3, 2018, pp.233-67.

DuBois, W.E.B., *Black Reconstruction in America*. New York: Free Press, 1998.

Duda, Mark & William C. Apgar, *Foreclosure Rates in Atlanta: Patterns and Policy Issues*. Washington, DC: Neighborworks America, 2005.

Dussel, Enrique, 'Eurocentrism and Modernity (Introduction to the Frankfurt Lectures)'. *Boundary 2* 20, no.3, 1993, pp.65-76.

Dyer-Witherford, Nick, *Cyber-Proletariat*. London: Pluto Press, 2015.

Eidsheim, Nina Sun, *Sensing Sound: Singing and Listening as Vibrational Practice*. Durham & London: Duke University Press, 2019.

Electronic Beat, 'Listen to 10 Recently Uncovered Japanese Ambient Masterpieces', *Electronic Beats*, 31 May 2017, www.electronicbeats.net/the-feed/listen-to-a-10-record-primer-of-japanese-minimal-masterpieces/ [accessed January 22, 2019].

Ellison, Ralph, *Shadow and Act*. New York: Vintage, 1995.

Endnotes, 'The Logic of Gender: On the Separation of Spheres and the Process of Abjection', *Endnotes* 3, September 2013, https://endnotes.org.uk/issues/3/en/endnotes-the-logic-of-gender.

Erlmann, Veit, 'The Politics and Aesthetics of Transnational Musics', *The World of Music* 35, no.2, 1993, pp.3-15.

Eshun, Kodwo, *More Brilliant Than the Sun: Adventures in Sonic Fiction*. London: Quartet Books, 1998.

Fanon, Frantz, *Black Skin, White Masks* (Charles Lam Markmann, Trans.). London: Pluto Press, 2008.

Fanon, Frantz, *Wretched of the Earth*. New York: Grove Press 1963.

Farber, David, *Crack: Rock Cocaine, Street Capitalism and the Decade of Greed.* Cambridge: Cambridge University Press, 2019.

Farrar, Justin F., 'Group Doueh', *Broward Palm Beach New Times*, 27 September 2007, www.browardpalmbeach.com/browardpalmbeach/Print?oid=6313024 [accessed 4 July 2022].

Federici, Silvia, *Caliban and the Witch: The Body and Primitive Accumulation.* New York: Autonomedia, 2004.

Feld, Steven, 'A Sweet Lullaby for World Music', *Public Culture* 12, no.1, 2000, pp.145–71.

Feld, Steven, 'Pygmy Pop: A Genealogy of Schizophonic Mimesis', *Yearbook for Traditional Music* 28, 1996, pp.1–35.

Fennessey, Sean, 'Let's Get It: Thug Motivation 101', Pitchfork, 14 August 2005, https://pitchfork.com/reviews/albums/8916-lets-get-it-thug-motivation-101/ [accessed 9 September 2023].

Fisher, Mark, *Ghosts of My Life: Writings on Depression, Hauntology, and Lost Futures.* Alresford: Zero Books, 2014.

Fisher, Mark, *K-Punk: The Collected and Unpublished Writings of Mark Fisher (2004–2016)*, Darren Ambrose (Ed.). London: Repeater Books, 2018.

Fisher, Mark, *Capitalist Realism: Is There No Alternative?* Hampshire: John Hunt Publishing, 2009.

Fisher, Samuel, 'Race and Real Abstraction'. Unpublished paper shared with the author.

Fitzpatrick, Rob, 'The 101 Strangest Records on Spotify: Francis Bebey – African Electronic Music 1976–1982', *The Guardian*, 30 January 2013, www.theguardian.com/music/musicblog/2013/jan/30/101-strangest-spotify-francis-bebey [accessed 29 June 2022].

Fleischer, Rasmus. 'If the Song Has No Price, Is It Still a Commodity? Rethinking the Commodification of Digital Music', *Culture Unbound*, 9, no.2, 2017, pp.146–62.

Font-Navarrete, David, '"File Under Import": Musical Distortion, Exoticism, and Authenticité in Congotronics', *Ethnomusicology Review* 16, 2011, pp.1–19.

Forced Exposure, 'Francis Bebey', www.forcedexposure.com/Artists/BEBEY.FRANCIS.html [accessed 31 October 2023].

Fortunati, Leopoldina, *The Arcane of Reproduction: Housework, Prostitution, Labor and Capital.* New York: Autonomedia, 1996.

Foster, Hal, 'The "Primitive" Unconscious of Modern Art', *October* 34, 1985, pp.45–70.

Foucault, Michel, *The Birth of Biopolitics: Lectures at the College de France, 1978–1979* (Graham Burchell, Trans.). Basingstoke: Palgrave MacMillan, 2007.

Foucault, Michel, *Discipline and Punish: The Birth of the Prison* (Alan Sheridan, Trans.). New York: Vintage Books, 1995.

Franklin, Seb, *The Digital Disposed: Racial Capitalism and the Informatics of Value.* Minneapolis: University of Minnesota Press, 2021.

Friedman, Devin, 'Make it Reign: How an Atlanta Strip Club Runs the Music Industry', *GQ*, 8 July 2015, www.gq.com/story/atlanta-strip-club-magic-city [accessed 31 October 2023].

Frith, Simon, 'The Discourse of World Music' in: Georgina Born & David Hesmondhalgh (Eds.) *Western Music and Its Others: Difference, Repetition and Appropriation in Music*. London: University of California Press, 2000, pp.305-22.

Frith, Simon, *Performing Rites: On the Value of Popular Music*. Cambridge: Harvard University Press, 1996.

Frith, Simon & Angela McRobbie, 'Rock and Sexuality', in: Simon Frith & Andrew Goodwin (Eds.), *On Record*. London: Routledge, 1990, pp.317-32.

Fuchs, Christian & Eran Fisher, *Reconsidering Value and Labor in the Digital Age*. London: Palgrave, 2015.

Gaerig, Andrew. 'Laurel Halo, Chance of Rain', *Pitchfork*, 20 October 2013, https://pitchfork.com/reviews/albums/18678-laurel-halo-chance-of-rain/ [accessed 19 January 2019].

Galloway, Alexander. *The Interface Effect*. Cambridge: Polity Press, 2012.

Gardner, Abigail & Gerard Moorey, 'Raiders of the Lost Archives', *Popular Communication* 14, no.3, 2016, pp.169-77.

Gates, Henry Louis Jr., *The Signifying Monkey: A Theory of African American Literary Criticism*. Oxford: Oxford University Press, 2014.

Gibb, Rory, A.M. Kanngieser, & Paul Rekret, 'In Sonic Defiance of Extinction', *Transmediale Magazine*, 2018, pp.26-30

Gilligan, Melanie & Marina Vishmidt. '"The Property-Less Sensorium": Following the Subject in Crisis Times', *South Atlantic Quarterly* 114, no.3, 2015, pp.611-30.

Gilroy, Paul, *There Ain't No Black in the Union Jack*. London: Routledge, 2013.

Gilroy, Paul, *The Black Atlantic: Modernity and Double Consciousness*. Cambridge: Harvard University Press, 1993.

Gioia, Ted, *Work Songs*. Durham & London: Duke University Press, 2006.

Gilmore, Ruth Wilson, *Golden Gulag: Prisons, Surplus, Crisis, and Opposition in Globalizing California*. Berkeley: University of California Press, 2007.

Glennon, Mike. 'Mixtapes v. Playlists: Medium, Message, Materiality', Sound Out!, 25 June 2018, https://soundstudiesblog.com/2018/06/25/mixtapes-v-playlists-medium-message-materiality/ [accessed 26 January 2019].

Gogarty, Larne Abse, *What We Do Is Secret: Contemporary Art and the Antinomies of Conspiracy*. London: Sternberg Press, 2023.

Goh, Annie, 'Sounding Situated Knowledges - Echo in Archaeoacoustics', *Parallax* 23, no.3, 2018.

Goodman, Steve, *Sonic Warfare: Sound, Affect, and the Ecology of Fear*. Cambridge: MIT Press, 2009.

Gordon, Lewis, 'Another Green World: How Japanese Ambient Music Found a New Audience', *Factmag*, 14 January 2017, www.factmag.com/2018/01/14/japanese-ambient-hiroshi-yoshimora-midori-takada/ [accessed 22 January 2019].

Graham, Kevin Fox, 'Creating Liquidity Out of Spatial Fixity' in: Manuel B. Aalbers (Ed.) *Subprime Cities: The Political Economy of Mortgage Markets*. London: Wiley Blackwell, 2012, pp.25-52.

Green, Archie, *Only a Miner: Studies in Recorded Coal-Mining Songs*. Urbana: University of Illinois Press, 1972.

Green, Archie (Ed.), *Songs about Work: Essays in Occupational Culture for Richard A. Reuss*. Bloomington: Indiana University Press 1993.

Greenfield, Lauren (Dir.), 'Magic City', *GQ.com*, 2015, www.gq.com/video/series/magic-city [accessed 31 October 2023].

Groom, Nick. 'The Condition of Muzak', *Popular Music and Society* 20, no.3, 1996, 1-17.

Grossberg, Lawrence, 'Another Boring Day in Paradise: Rock and Roll and the Empowerment of Everyday Life,' *Popular Music* 4, 1984, pp.225-58.

Gucci Mane & Neil Martinez-Belkin, *The Autobiography of Gucci Mane*. New York: Simon and Schuster, 2017.

Haider, Shuja, 'Dropping Acid', *Logic*, 1 January 2019, https://logicmag.io/play/dropping-acid/ [accessed 4 July 2022].

Hall, Stuart, 'Notes on Deconstructing the Popular' in: David Morley (Ed.) *Essential Essays, Volume 1*. Durham & London: Duke University Press, 2018, pp.347-61.

Hall, Stuart, et al., *Policing the Crisis, Mugging, the State and Law and Order*. London: Bloomsbury, 2017.

Hann, Michael, 'Is Poptimism Now as Blinkered as the Rockism it Replaced?', *The Quietus*, 11 May 2017, https://thequietus.com/articles/22389-rockism-poptimism [accessed 6 October 2020].

Haraway, Donna, *Simians, Cyborgs, and Women: The Reinvention of Nature*. London: Routledge, 1991.

Hardt, Michael & Antonio Negri, *Empire*. Cambridge: Harvard University Press, 2000.

Harney, Stefano, 'Logistics Genealogies: A Dialogue with Stefano Harney', *Social Text* 36, 2018, pp.95-110.

Harney, Stefano & Fred Moten, *Undercommons: Fugitive Planning and Black Study*. Wivenhoe: Minor Compositions, 2013.

Harper, Adam, 'Vaporwave and the Pop-Art of the Virtual Plaza', Dummy, 12 July 2012, www.dummymag.com/news/adam-harper-vaporwave/ [accessed 31 October 2023].

Harper, Adam, 'How Internet Music is Frying Your Brain', *Popular Music* 36, no.1, 2017, pp.86-97.

Harris, Laura, *Experiments in Exile: C. L. R. James, Hélio Oiticica, and the Aesthetic Sociality of Blackness*. New York: Fordham University Press, 2018.

Harvey, David, *Rebel Cities: From the Right to the City to the Urban Revolution*. London: Verso, 2012.

Harvey, David, *The Condition of Postmodernity: An Enquiry into the Origins of Cultural Change*. London: Wiley-Blackwell, 1991.

Harvey, Eric, *Who Got the Camera? A History of Rap and Reality*. Austin: University of Texas Press, 2021.

Harvey, Eric. 'How Smart Speakers are Changing the Way We Listen to Music', *Pitchfork*, 29 June 2018, https://pitchfork.com/features/article/how-smart-speakers-are-changing-the-way-we-listen-to-music/ [accessed 26 January 2019].

Hassan, Aisha & Dan Kopf, 'The Reason Why Your Favorite Pop Songs are Getting Shorter', QZ, 27 October 2018, https://qz.com/quartzy/1438412/the-reason-why-your-favorite-pop-songs-are-getting-shorter [accessed 29 October 2023].

Heidegger, Martin, 'The Age of the World Picture' in: *The Question Concerning Technology & Other Essays* (William Lovitt, Trans.). London: Garland 1977, pp.115–54.

Heidegger, Martin, 'Only a God Can Save Us: The Spiegel Interview (1966)' in: Thomas Sheehan (Ed.) *Heidegger. The Man and the Thinker*. Piscataway: Transaction Publishers, 1981, pp.45–67.

Herndon, Holly, 'Holly Herndon', *Red Bull Music Academy*, 2014, www.redbullmusicacademy.com/lectures/holly-herndon-tokyo-2014 [accessed 31 October 2023].

Hesmondhalgh, David, 'Streaming's Effects on Music Culture: Old Anxieties and New Simplifications', *Cultural Sociology* 16, no.1, 2022, pp.3–24.

Hesmondhalgh, David & Leslie M. Meier, 'What the Digitalisation of Music Tells Us About Capitalism, Culture and the Power of the Information Technology Sector', *Information, Communication & Society* 21, no.11, 2018, pp.1555–70.

Hester, Helen, *Xenofeminism*. London: Polity Press, 2018.

Hoard, Christian, 'Let's Get It: Thug Motivation 101', *Rolling Stone*, 7 August 2005, https://web.archive.org/web/20081227030514/http://www.rollingstone.com/artists/youngjeezy/albums/album/7490389/review/7504105/lets_get_it_thug_motivation_101 [accessed 9 September 2023].

hooks, bell, *We Real Cool: Black Men and Masculinity*. New York & London: Routledge, 2004.

Horkheimer, Max & Theodor Adorno, *Dialectic of Enlightenment* (G. Noeri, Trans.). Stanford: Stanford University Press, 2002.

Horning, Rob, 'Poptimism: The Death of Pop Criticism', *PopMatters*, 11 May 2006, www.popmatters.com/2413-poptimism_the_death_of_pop_criticism-2495679181.html [accessed 6 October 2020].

Hunter, Margaret & Kathleen Soto, 'Women of Color in Hip Hop: The Pornographic Gaze', *Race, Gender & Class*, 2009, pp.170–91.

Iles, Anthony & Mattin, 'Introduction', *Abolishing Capitalist Totality: What is To be Done Under Real Subsumption?* Berlin: Archive Books, 2024.

Irele, Abiola, 'Négritude: Literature and Ideology', *Journal of Modern African Studies* 3, no.4, 1965, pp.499–526.

Irele, F. Abiola, *The Negritude Moment: Explorations in Francophone African and Caribbean Literature and Thought*. Trenton: Africa World Press, 2011.

Iton, Richard, *In Search of the Black Fantastic: Politics and Popular Culture in the Post-Civil Rights Era*. Oxford: Oxford University Press, 2010.

Jack, Malcolm, 'Review: Omar Souleyman – Oran Mor Glasgow', *The Scotsman*, 10 December 2011, www.scotsman.com/arts-and-culture/review-omar-souleyman-oran-mor-glasgow-1651187 [accessed 30 June 2022].

Jackson, Bruce (Ed.), *Wake Up Dead Man: Afro-American Prison Worksongs From Texas Prisons*. Cambridge: Harvard University Press, 1972.

Jaji, Tsitsi Ella, *Africa in Stereo: Modernism, Music and Pan-African Solidarity*. Oxford: Oxford University Press, 2014.

Jakob, Doreen, 'Crafting Your Way Out of the Recession? New Craft Entrepreneurs and the Global Economic Downturn', *Cambridge Journal of Regions, Economy and Society* 6, no.1, 2013, pp. 127–40.

James, Robin, 'Neoliberal Noise: Attali, Foucault & the Biopolitics of Uncool', *Culture, Theory & Critique* 55, no.2, 2014, pp.138–58.

James, Robin. 'Toned Down for What? How "Chill" Turned Toxic', *The Guardian*, 2 July 2018, www.theguardian.com/music/2018/jul/02/toned-down-for-what-how-chill-turned-toxic [accessed 22 January 2019].

Jameson, Fredric, 'Cognitive Mapping' in: C. Nelson & L. Grossberg (Eds.) *Marxism and the Interpretation of Culture*. Chicago: University of Illinois Press, 1990, pp.347–58.

Jameson, Fredric, *Postmodernism, Or, the Cultural Logic of Late Capitalism*. Durham & London: Duke University Press, 1991.

Jameson, Fredric, 'The End of Temporality', *Critical Inquiry* 29, no.4, Summer 2003, pp.695–718.

Jameson, Fredric. *The Political Unconscious: Narrative as a Socially Symbolic Act*. London: Routledge, 2013.

Jansse, Volker, 'Sunbelt Lock-Up: Where the Suburbs Meet the Super-Max', in: Michelle Nickerson & Darren Dochuk (Eds.) *Sunbelt Rising: The Politics of Space, Place and Region*. Philadelphia: University of Pennsylvania Press, pp.217–39.

Jeffries, Michael P., *Thug Life: Race, Gender, and the Meaning of Hip-Hop*. Chicago: University of Chicago Press, 2011.

Jenkins, Craig. 'The Sound of Modern Pop Peaked This Year – and Now It Needs To Change', *Vulture*, 11 December 2017, www.vulture.com/2017/12/defining-the-decade-in-pop-music.html [accessed 19 January 2019].

Jennings, Keith, 'The Politics of Race, Class and Gentrification in the ATL', *Trotter Review* 23, no.1, 2016, pp.1–38.

Jeppesen, Travis, 'The New Gods in the Machine: Holly Herndon's Vehicularity', *Afterall* 41, Spring/Summer 2016, pp.80–89.

Johansson, Sofia, Ann Werner, Patrik Åker, & Greg Goldenzwaig, *Streaming Music: Practices, Media, Cultures*. London: Routledge, 2018.

Johnson, Joseph 'Chinaman' and Group, 'This Old Hammer Killed John Henry' in: Bruce Jackson (Ed.) *Wake Up Dead Man: Afro-American Prison Worksongs From Texas Prisons*. Cambridge: Harvard University Press, 1972, pp.238–39.

Jones, Mikey IQ, 'The Incredible Story of Ata Kak's *Obaa Sima*, the Original Awesome Tape From Africa', Fact, 3 October 2015, www.factmag.com/2015/03/10/the-incredible-story-of-ata-kaks-obaa-sima-the-original-awesome-tape-from-africa/ [accessed 4 July 2022].

Jones, Donna V., *The Racial Discourses of Life Philosophy: Négritude, Vitalism and Modernity*. New York: Columbia University Press, 2010.

Jones, Simon C., & Thomas G. Schumacher, 'Muzak: On Functional Music and Power', *Cultural Studies in Mass Communication* 9, 1992, pp.156–69.

Juan, Steve 'Flash', 'Gucci Mane: Trap House', *Rap Reviews.Com*, 31 May 2005, www.rapreviews.com/2005/05/gucci-mane-trap-house/ [accessed 9 September 2023].

Judy, R.A.T., 'On the Question of Nigga Authenticity', *Boundary 2*, 21, no. 3, 1994, pp.211–30.

Kane, Brian, *Sound Unseen: Acousmatic Sound in Theory and Practice*. Oxford: Oxford University Press, 2016.

Kane, Brian, 'Sound Studies Without Auditory Culture: A Critique of the Ontological Turn', *Sound Studies* 1, no.1, 2015, pp.2–21.

Kassabian, Annahid, *Ubiquitous Listening: Affect, Attention, and Distributed Subjectivities*. Berkeley/Los Angeles: University of California Press, 2013.

Katz, Mark. *Capturing Sound: How Technology Has Changed Music, Revised Edition*. Berkeley: University of California Press, 2010.

Kelley, Robin, D.G., *Race Rebels: Culture, Politics, and the Black Working Class*. New York: Simon and Schuster, 1996.

Kelley, Robin D.G., *Yo' Mama's Disfunktional!: Fighting the Culture Wars in Urban America*. Boston: Beacon Press, 1998.

Kelly, Lauren, 'Re-Politicising the Future of Work: Automation Anxieties, Universal Basic Income, and the End of Techno-Optimism', *Journal of Sociology* 59, no.4, 2022, pp.828–43.

Kemp, Sophie, 'Love in the Time of Lexapro EP', *Pitchfork*, 2018, https://pitchfork.com/reviews/albums/oneohtrix-point-never-love-in-the-time-of-lexapro-ep/ [accessed 31 October 2023].

Kennedy, Sean M., 'Trap Spaces, Trap Music: Harriet Jacobs, Fetty Wap, and Emancipation as Entrapment', *The Popular Culture Studies Journal* 8, no.2, 2020, pp.68–84.

Kheshti, Roshanak, *Modernity's Ear: Listening to Race and Gender in World Music*. New York: New York University Press, 2015.

Kim-Cohen, Seth. *Against Ambience*. London: Bloomsbury, 2013.

Kinkle, Jeff & Alberto Toscano, *Cartographies of the Absolute*. Winchester: Zero Books, 2015.

Kittler, Friedrich, *Gramophone, Film, Typewriter* (G. Winthrop-Young & M. Wutz, Trans.). Stanford: Stanford University Press, 1999.

Kitwana, Bakari, *Why White Kids Love Hip-Hop: Wankstas, Wiggers, Wannabes, and the New Reality of Race in America*. New York: Civitas Books, 2005.

Koc, Alican, 'Do You Want Vaporwave or Do You Want The Truth?' *Capacious* 1, no.1, 2017, pp.57–76.

Kojikawa, Lauren, *Sounding Race in Rap Songs*. Berkeley: University of California Press, 2015.

Korczynski, Marek, *Songs of the Factory: Pop Music, Culture, and Resistance*. Ithaca: Cornell University Press, 2015.

Korczynski, Marek, Michael Pickering, & Emma Robertson, *Rhythms of Labour: Music at Work in Britain*. Cambridge: Cambridge University Press, 2013.

Kramer, Lawrence. 'Caliban's Ear: A Short History of Ambient Music', in: Marta Garcia Quinoes, Anahid Kassabian, & Elena Boschi (Eds.) *Ubiquitous Musics: The Everyday Sounds That We Don't Always Notice*. London: Routledge 2013, pp.15–30.

Krims, Adam, *Music and Urban Geography*. London: Routledge, 2011.

Laboria Cuboniks, *Xenofeminism: A Politics for Alienation*, n.d., https://laboriacuboniks.net/manifesto/xenofeminism-a-politics-for-alienation/ [accessed 31 October 2023].

Land, Nick, 'Machinic Desire' in *Fanged Noumena: Collected Writings 1987–2007*. Falmouth: Urbanomic, 2011, pp.319–44.

Lanza, Joseph, *Elevator Music: A Surreal History of Muzak, Easy Listening and Other Moodsong*. Ann Arbor: University of Michigan Press, 2004.

Latour, Bruno, *We Have Never Been Modern*. Cambridge: Harvard University Press 1991.

Lazarus, Neil, *The Postcolonial Unconscious*. Cambridge: Cambridge University Press, 2012.

Leadbelly, 'Take This Hammer', in: Robert Hedin (Ed.) *The Great Machines: Poems and Songs of the American Railroad*. Iowa City: University of Iowa Press, 1996.

League of Revolutionary Black Workers (dir. Stewart Bird, Rene Lichtmann, & Peter Gessner), *Finally Got the News*, Icarus Films, 1970.

Lefebvre, Henri, *Critique of Everyday Life*. London: Verso, 2014.

Léon, Javier F., 'Music, Music Making and Neoliberalism', *Culture Theory and Critique* 55, no.2, April 2014, pp.129-37.

Leslie, Esther, 'Ruin and Rubble in the Arcades' in: Beatrice Hansen (Ed.), *Walter Benjamin and the Arcades Project*. London: Continuum, 2006, pp.87-112.

Leys, Ruth, 'The Turn to Affect: A Critique', *Critical Inquiry* 37, no.3, Spring 2011, pp.434-72.

Linhart, Robert, *Lénine, Taylor, les Paysans*. Paris: Seuil, 1976.

Lipsitz, George, *Time Passages: Collective Memory and American Popular Culture*. Minneapolis: University of Minnesota Press, 1997.

Lloyd, Richard, 'Urbanisation and the Southern United States', *Annual Review of Sociology* 38, May 2012, pp.483-506.

Locke, John, *Two Treatises on Government. Volume V, The Works of John Locke in Ten Volumes*. Darmstadt: Scientia Verlag Aalen, 1963.

Lopez, Francisco, 'Blind Listening' in: D. Rothenberg & M. Ulvaeus (Eds.) *The Book of Music and Nature: An Anthology of Sounds, Words, Thoughts*. Middletown: Wesleyan University Press, 2001, pp.163-68.

Luckman, Susan, 'The Aura of the Analogue in a Digital Age: Women's Crafts, Creative Markets and Home-Based Labour After Etsy', *Cultural Studies Review* 19, no.1, 2013, pp.249-70.

Mackay, Robin & Armen Avanessian (Eds.) *#Accelerate#: the Accelerationist Reader*. Falmouth: Urbanomic, 2014.

Mackey, Nathaniel. 'The Changing Same: Black Music in the Poetry of Amiri Baraka', *Boundary 2* 6, no.2, 1978, pp.355-86.

Maher, Geo, *A World Without Police: How Strong Communities Make Cops Obsolete*. London: Verso, 2021.

Malewitz, Raymond, *The Practice of Misuse: Rugged Consumerism in Contemporary American Culture*. Stanford: Stanford University Press, 2014.

Malm, Andreas, *Fossil Capital: The Rise of Steam Power and the Roots of Global Warming*. London: Verso, 2016.

Malm, Andreas, *The Progress of this Storm: On the Dialectics of Society and Nature in a Warming World*. London: Verso, 2018.

Manovich, Lev. *The Language of New Media*. Cambridge: MIT Press, 2001.

Manuel, Peter, 'Modernity and Musical Structure: Neo-Marxist Perspectives on Song Form and its Successors', in: Regula Burckhardt Qureshi (Ed.) *Music and Marx*. London: Routledge, 2002, pp.45-62.

Marcuse, Herbert. *One-Dimensional Man: Studies in the Ideology of Advanced Industrial Society*. Boston: Beacon Press, 1991.

Margasak, Peter, 'Konono No. 1', *Chicago Reader*, 10 November 2005, https://chicagoreader.com/music/konono-no-1-2/ [accessed 30 June 2022].

Markley, Scott & Makuri Sharma, 'Gentrification in the Revanchiste Suburb: the Politics of Removal in Roswell Georgia', *Southeastern Geographer* 56, no.1, 2016, pp.57-80.

Marshall, Lee, '"Let's Keep Music Special. F--- Spotify": On Demand Streaming and the Controversy Over Artist Royalties', *Creative Industries Journal* 8, no.2, 2015, pp.177-89.

Martineau, Jonathan, *Time, Capitalism and Alienation: A Socio-Historical Critique into the Making of Time*. Leiden: Brill, 2015.

Marx, Karl, *Economic and Philosophic Manuscript of 1844*. Progress Publishers, 1959, www.marxists.org/archive/marx/works/1844/manuscripts/preface.htm.

Marx, Karl, *Capital: A Critique of Political Economy, Volume I* (Ben Fowkes, Trans.). London: Penguin, 1976.

Marx, Karl, *Grundrisse: Foundations of the Critique of Political Economy* (Martin Nicolaus, Trans.). London: Penguin, 1993.

Massumi, Brian, 'The Autonomy of Affect', *Cultural Critique* 31, 1995, pp.83-109.

McCarthy, Jesse, 'Notes on Trap: A World Where Everything is Dripping', *N Plus One* 32, October 2018. nplusonemag.com/issue-32/essays/notes-on-Trap/ [accessed November 2018].

McCartney, Andra Shirley Jean, *Sounding Places: Situated Conversations Through the Soundscape Compositions of Hildergard Westerkamp*. PhD Dissertation, York University, 1999.

McClanahan, Annie, *Dead Pledges: Debt, Crisis, and Twenty-First Century Culture*. Stanford: Stanford University Press, 2018.

McClary, Susan, 'Living to Tell: Madonna's Resurrection of the Fleshly' in: *Feminine Endings: Music, Gender and Sexuality*. Minneapolis & London: University of Minnesota Press, 1991, pp.148-68.

McGraw, Andrew C. 'Radio Java' in: Michael E. Veal & E. Tammy Kim (Eds.), *Punk Ethnography: Artists and Scholars Listen to Sublime Frequencies*. Middletown: Wesleyan University Press, 2016, pp.323-39.

McLeod, Ken, 'Vaporwave: Politics, Protest, and Identity', *Journal of Popular Music Studies* 30, no.4, 2018, pp.123-41.

McNally, David, 'From Financial Crisis to World-Slump: Accumulation, Financialisation and the Global Slowdown', *Historical Materialism* 17, no.2, 2009, pp.35-83.

Mercer, Kobena, 'Black Art and the Burden of Representation', *Third Text* 4, no.10, 1990, pp.61–78.

Middleton, Richard, *Voicing the Popular: On the Subjects of Popular Music*. London and New York: Routledge, 2006.

Middleton, Richard, 'Musical Belongings: Western Music and Its Low-Other', in: *Western Music and Its Others: Difference, Representation, and Appropriation in Music*. Berkeley and Loss Angeles: University of California Press, pp.59–85.

Middleton, Richard, '"Play It Again Sam": Some Notes on the Productivity of Repetition in Popular Music', *Popular Music* 3, 1983, pp.235–70.

Mies, Maria, *Patriarchy and Accumulation on a World Scale: Women in the International Division of Labor*. London: Zed, 1999.

Mieville, China, 'The Limits of Utopia', Salvage, 1 August 2015, https://salvage.zone/the-limits-of-utopia/ [accessed 4 July 2022].

Miller, Matt, 'Dirty Decade: Rap Music and the U.S. South, 1997–2007', Southern Spaces, 10 June 2008, http://southernspaces.org/2008/dirty-decade-rap-music-and-us-south-1997%E2%80% [accessed 1 November 2021].

Mitropoulos, Angela, *Contract and Contagion: From Biopolitics to Oikonomia*. Wivenhoe, New York, Port Watson: Minor Composition, 2012.

Moody, Kim, *On New Terrain: How Capital is Reshaping the Battleground of Class War*. Chicago: Haymarket Books, 2017.

Moreno, Louis, 'The Sound of Detroit: Notes, Tones and Rhythms from Underground', in: Matthew Gandy & B.J. Wilson (Eds.) *The Acoustic City*. Berlin: Jovis, 2014, pp.98–109.

Moreno, Louis, 'The Urban Regeneration of the Plantation Age', in: K. Vermeir & R. Heiremans (Eds.) *A Modest Proposal*. London: Jubilee, 2018, pp.2–10.

Morton, Timothy, *Realist Magic: Objects, Ontology, Causality*. London: Open Humanities Press, 2013.

Morton, Timothy, *Hyperobjects: Philosophy and Ecology After the End of the World*. Minneapolis: University of Minnesota Press, 2013.

Moten, Fred, *In the Break: The Aesthetics of the Black Radical Tradition*. Minneapolis: University of Minnesota Press, 2003.

Moten, Fred, *Stolen Life, Consent Not to Be a Single Being, Vol.2*. Durham & London: Duke University Press, 2018.

Moten, Fred, 'The Subprime and the Beautiful'. *African Identities* 11, no.2, 2013, pp.237–45.

Mullen, Patrick B. *The Main Who Adores the Negro: Race and American Folklore*. Chicago: University of Illinois University Press, 2008.

Munro, Kirstin & Chris O'Kane, 'Autonomy and Creativity in the Artisan Economy and the New Spirit of Capitalism', *Review of Radical Politics Economics* 49, no.4, 2017, pp.582–90.

Nathan, Fernand. *Francis Bebey: Ecrivain et Musicien Camerounais*. Paris: Editions Fernand Nathan, 1979.

Needham, Jack, 'How Japan's Landscape Inspired a New Kind of Electronic Music', Bandcamp Daily, 23 June 2017, https://daily.bandcamp.com/2017/06/23/japanese-landscape-inspired-electronic/ [accessed 22 January 2019].

Neel, Phil A., *Hinterland: America's New Landscape of Class and Conflict*. London: Reaktion Books, 2018.

Negri, Antonio, *The Politics of Subversion: A Manifesto for the Twenty-First Century* (J. Newell, Trans.). London: Polity Press, 2005.

Nelson, Scott Reynolds, *Steel Drivin' Man: John Henry, the Untold Story of an American Legend*. Oxford: Oxford University Press, 2006.

Novak, David, 'The Sublime Frequencies of New Old Media', *Public Culture* 23, no.3, 2011, pp.601–34.

Noys, Benjamin, *Malign Velocities: Acceleration and Capitalism*. Alresford: Zero Books, 2014

O'Loughlin, Colm, 'On Our Radar: The Music You Must Hear', DJ Mag, 8 June 2008, https://djmag.com/node/1228 [accessed 4 July 2022].

Okiji, Fumi, *Jazz as Critique: Adorno and Black Expression Revisited*. Stanford: Stanford University Press, 2018.

Osborne, Peter, *The Politics of Time: Modernity and Avant-Garde*. London: Verso, 1995.

Osborne, Peter, *Anywhere or Not At All: Philosophy of Contemporary Art*. London: Verso, 2013.

Osborne, Peter, *Crisis as Form*. London: Verso, 2022.

Parker, James, 'Internet Club', *Tiny Mix Tapes*, 2012, www.tinymixtapes.com/music-review/internet-club-vanishing-vision [accessed 31 October 2023].

Pearce, David. 'The Secret Hit-Making Power of the Spotify Playlist', Wired, 5 March 2017, www.wired.com/2017/05/secret-hit-making-power-spotify-playlist/ [accessed 23 January 2019].

Pelly, Liz. 'The Problem With Muzak', *The Baffler*, December 2017, https://thebaffler.com/salvos/the-problem-with-muzak-pelly [accessed 19 January 2019].

Petridis, Alex, 'Assume Crash Position', *The Guardian*, 4 April 2006, www.theguardian.com/music/2006/apr/04/popandrock1 [accessed 4 July 2022].

Perry, Imani, *Prophets of the Hood: Politics and Poetics in Hip Hop*. Durham & London: Duke University Press, 2004.

Postone, Moishe, *Time, Labor and Social Domination: A Reinterpretation of Marx's Critical Theory*. Cambridge: Cambridge University Press, 1993.

Pratt, Mary Louise, *Imperial Eyes: Travel Writing and Transculturation*. London: Routledge, 1992.

Quinn, Eithne, *Nuthin' but a 'G' Thang: The Culture and Commerce of Gangsta Rap*. New York: Columbia University Press, 2004.

Redmond, Shana L., *Anthem: Social Movements and the Sound of Solidarity in the African Diaspora*. New York: New York University Press, 2014.

Rekret, Paul, 'Seeing Like a Cyborg? The Innocence of Posthuman Knowledge', in: David Chandler & Christian Fuchs (Eds.). *Digital Objects, Digital Subjects: Interdisciplinary Perspectives on Capitalism, Labour and Politics in the Age of Big Data*. London: University of Westminster Press, 2019, pp.81–94.

Rekret, Paul, 'The Head, the Hand and Matter: New Materialism and the Politics of Knowledge', *Theory, Culture & Society* 35, no.7–8, 2018/2019, pp.49–72.

Rekret, Paul, *Down With Childhood: Pop Music and the Crisis of Innocence*. London: Repeater, 2018.

Reynolds, Simon. 'Maximal Nation', *Pitchfork*, 6 December 2011, https://pitchfork.com/features/article/8721-maximal-nation/ [accessed 19 January 2019].

Reynolds, Simon, 'Xenomania: Nothing is Foreign in an Internet Age', *MTV*, December 2011, www.mtviggy.com/articles/xenomania-nothing-is-foreign-in-an-internet-age/ [accessed 20 December 2011].

Reynolds, Simon. *Energy Flash: A Journey Through Rave Music and Dance Culture*. London: Picador, 1998.

Richards, Chris 'Do You Want Poptimism? Or do you Want the Truth?' *The Washington Post*, 16 April 2015.

Richards, Chris. 'Soft, Smooth and Steady: How Xanax Turned American Music Pill-Pop', *The Washington Post*, 20 April 2017, www.washingtonpost.com/lifestyle/style/soft-smooth-and-steady-how-xanax-turned-american-music-into-pill-pop/2017/04/19/535a44de-1955-11e7-bcc2- [accessed 22 January 2019].

Richardson, Mark. 'Oneohtrix Point Never, R Plus Seven', *Pitchfork*, 4 October 2013, https://pitchfork.com/reviews/albums/18537-oneohtrix-point-never-r-plus-seven/ [accessed 19 January 2019].

Riva, Chris Dalla. 'The Death of the Key Change', *Tedium*, 9 November 2022, https://tedium.co/2022/11/09/the-death-of-the-key-change/ [accessed 29 October 2023].

Roberts, John W., *From Trickster to Badman: The Black Folk Hero in Slavery and Freedom*. Philadelphia: University of Pennsylvania Press, 1989.

Roberts, John. *Philosophizing the Everyday: Revolutionary Praxis and the Fate of Cultural Theory*. London: Pluto Press, 2006.

Roberts, Randall, 'In Rotation: Francis Bebey's "African Electronic Music, 1975–1982"', *Los Angeles Times*, 21 June 2012, https://latimesblogs.latimes.com/music_blog/2012/06/in-rotation-francis-bebeys-african-electronic-music-1975-1982.html [accessed 26 May 2022].

Robinson, Cedric, *Black Marxism: The Making of the Black Radical Tradition*. Chapel Hill & London: University of North Carolina Press, 2000.

Roedinger, David, *The Wages of Whiteness: Race and the Making of the American Working Class*. London: Verso, 1991.

Rose, Tricia, *Black Noise: Rap Music and Black Culture in Contemporary America*. Middletown: Wesleyan University Press, 1994.

Rothenberg, David, 'Nature's Greatest Hit: The Old and New Songs of the Humpback Whale', *The Wire*, September 2014, www.thewire.co.uk/in-writing/essays/nature_s-greatest-hit_the-old-and-new-songs-of-the-humpback-whale.

RwdFwd, 'Francis Bebey', https://rwdfwd.com/products/francis-bebey-psychedelic-sanza-1982-1984.

Sanchez, Daniel, 'Hip-Hop Has Replaced Rock as Music's Most Consumed Genre', *Digital Music News*, 4 January 2018, www.digitalmusicnews.com/2018/01/04/hip-hop-rock-2017-biggest-genre/ [accessed 28 October 2021].

Sanneh, Kelefa 'The Rap Against Rockism', *The New York Times*, 31 October 2004.

Sarig, Ronny, *Third Coast: Outkast, Timbaland, and How Hip-Hop Became A Southern Thing*. New York: Da Capo Press, 2007.

Sartre, Jean-Paul, 'Black Orpheus' in: *'What Is Literature?' And Other Essays*. Cambridge: Harvard University Press, 1988.

Schaeffer, Pierre, *Treaty on Musical Objects: An Essay Across Disciplines* (Christine North & John Dack, Trans.). Berkeley: University of California Press, 2017.

Schafer, R. Murray. *The Soundscape: Our Sonic Environment and the Tuning of the World*. Rochester: Destiny Books, 1977.

Scherzinger, Martin. 'The Political Economy of Streaming', in: Nicholas Cook, Monique M. Ingalls, & David Trippett (Eds.) *Music in Digital Culture*. Cambridge: Cambridge University Press, 2019, pp.282–83.

Schiller, Dan, *Digital Depression: Information Technology and Economic Crisis*. Chicago: University of Illinois Press, 2014.

Schmidt, Alfred, *The Concept of Nature in Marx*. London: NLB, 1971.

Schmidt, Eric J., 'Arid Fidelity, Reluctant Capitalists: Salvage, Curation, and the Circulation of Tuareg Music on Independent Record Labels', *Ethnomusicology Forum* 28, no.3, 2019, pp.260–82.

Seccombe, Wally, *Weathering the Storm: Working-Class Families from the Industrial Revolution to the Fertility Decline*. London: Verso, 1995.

Senghor, Léopold Sédar, 'African-Negro Aesthetics' (Elaine P. Halperin, Trans.) *Diogenes* 16, no.4, 1956, pp.23–38.

Senghor, Léopold Sédar, 'Negritude: A Humanism of the Twentieth Century', in: W. Carty & M. Kilson (Eds.) *The African Reader: Independent Africa*. New York: Vintage, 1970, pp.179–92.

Senghor, Léopold Sédar, 'What the Black Man Contributes', in: Robert Bernasconi (Ed.) *Race and Racism in Continental Philosophy*. Bloomington: Indiana University Press, 2003, pp.287–301.

Shalloup, Maya, *BMF: The Rise and Fall of Big Meech and Black Mafia Family*. New York: St. Martin's Press, 2010.

Sharma, Ashwani, 'Sounds Oriental: The (Im)possibility of Theorizing Asian Musical Cultures' in: Sanjay Sharma, John Hutnyk, & Ashwani Sharma (Eds.) *Dis-Orienting Rhythms: The Politics of the New Asian Dance Music*. London & New Jersey: Zed Books, 1996, pp.15–31.

Sharma, Sanjay, John Hutnyk, & Ashwani Sharma (Eds.) *Dis-Orienting Rhythms: The Politics of the New Asian Dance Music*. London & New Jersey: Zed Books, 1996.

Shaviro, Steven, *No Speed Limit: Three Essays on Accelerationism*. Minneapolis: University of Minnesota Press, 2015.

Simondon, Gilbert, *On the Mode of Existence of Technical Objects* (Cecile Malaspina & John Rogove, Trans.). Minneapolis: University of Minnesota Press, 2016.

Smith, Jason, *Smart Machines and Service Work: Automation in an Age of Stagnation*. New York: Reaktion Books, 2020.

Smith, Neil, *The New Urban Frontier: Gentrification and the Revanchist City*. London: Routledge, 1996.

Snead, James, 'On Repetition in Black Culture', *Black American Literature Forum* 15 no.4, 1981, pp.146–54.

Snickers, Pelle. 'More of the Same: On Spotify Radio', *Culture Unbound* 9, no.2, 2017, pp.184–211.

Sohn-Rethel, Alfred, *Intellectual and Manual Labour: A Critique of Epistemology*. New Jersey: Humanities Press, 1978.

Solomos, Makis, 'A Phenomenological Experience of Sound: Notes on Francisco López', *Contemporary Music Review* 38, no.1–2, 2019, pp.94–106.

Spence, Lester K., *Stare in the Darkness: The Limits of Hip-Hop and Black Politics*. Minneapolis: University of Minnesota Press, 2011.

Spillers, Hortense, 'Mama's Baby, Papa's Maybe: An American Grammar Book', *Diacritics* 17, no.2, Summer 1987, pp.64–81.

Spivak, Gayatry Chakravorty, *A Critique of Postcolonial Reason: Toward a History of the Vanishing Present*. Cambridge: Harvard University Press, 1999.

Spotify for Brands, *Understanding People Through Music: Millenium Edition*, https://spotifyforbrands.com/en-GB/insights/millennial-guide [accessed 26 April 2019].

Stahl, Matt, *Unfree Masters: Popular Music and the Politics of Work*. Durham & London: Duke University Press, 2012.

Stallings, L.H., *Funk the Erotic: Transaesthetics and Black Sexual Cultures*. Chicago: University of Illinois Press, 2015.

Sterne, Jonathan, 'Soundscape, Landscape, Escape' in: Karin Bijsterveld (Ed.) *Soundscapes of the Urban Past: Staged Sound as Mediated Cultural Heritage*. Bielefeld: Transcript Verlag, 2013, pp.181-94.

Stevens, Dennis, 'Validity is in the Eye of the Beholder: Mapping Craft Communities of Practice' in: Maria Elena Buszek (Ed.) *Extra/Ordinary: Craft and Contemporary Art*. Durham & London: Duke University Press, 2011, pp.43-58.

Straw, Will, 'Music as Commodity and Material Culture', *Repercussions* 7-8, Spring-Fall, 1999-2000, pp.147-72.

Suisman, David, 'Sound, Knowledge and the "Immanence of Human Failure": Rethinking Musical Mechanization Through the Phonograph, Player-Piano, and the Piano', *Social Text* 28, no.1, 2010, pp.13-34.

Suisman, David, *Selling Sounds: The Commercial Revolution in American Music*. Cambridge: Harvard University Press, 2012.

Szabo, Victor. 'Unsettling Brian Eno's *Music for Airports*', *Twentieth-Century Music*, 14, no.2, 2017, pp.305-33.

Tagg, Phillip. 'Understanding Musical Time Sense: Concepts, Sketches, Consequences', 1997, http://tagg.org/articles/xpdfs/timesens.pdf [accessed 27 April 2019].

Tagne, David Ndachi, *Francis Bebey*. Paris: L'Harmattan, 1993.

Taussig, Michael, *Mimesis and Alterity: A Particular History of the Senses*. London: Routledge, 1993.

Taylor, Timothy D., *Beyond Exoticism: Western Music and the World*. Durham & London: Duke University Press, 2007.

Taylor, Timothy D., *Music and Capitalism: A History of the Present*. Chicago: Chicago University Press, 2015.

Terranova, Tiziana. *Network Culture: Politics for the Information Age*. London: Pluto Press, 2004.

Thompson, E.P., 'Time, Work-Discipline and Industrial Capitalism', *Past and Present* 38, 1967, pp.56-97.

Thompson, Marie, *Beyond Unwanted Sound: Noise, Affect, and Aesthetic Moralism*. London: Bloomsbury, 2017.

Thompson, Marie, 'Whiteness and the Ontological Turn in Sound Studies', *Parallax*, 23, no.3, 2018, pp.266-82.

Thoburn, Nicholas, *Deleuze, Marx and Politics*. London: Routledge, 2003.

Thrift, Nigel, 'Intensities of Feeling: Towards a Spatial Politics of Affect', *Geografiska Annaler: Series B, Human Geography* 86, no.1, 2004, pp.57-78.

Toop, David, *Haunted Weather: Music, Silence and Memory*. London: Serpent's Tail, 2004.

Toop, David, *Ocean of Sound: Ambient Sound and Radical Listening in the Age of Communication*. London: Serpent's Tail, 2018.

Toscano, Alberto, 'Lineaments of the Logistical State', *Viewpoint Magazine*, 28 September 2014, https://viewpointmag.com/2014/09/28/lineaments-of-the-logistical-state/ [accessed 31 October 2023].

Tronti, Mario, *Workers and Capital* (David Broder, Trans.). London: Verso, 2019.

Tucker, Boima, 'The Scramble for Vinyl', *Africa is a Country*, 14 September 2010, https://africasacountry.com/2010/09/the-scramble-for-vinyl [accessed 3 July 2022].

Turner, Luke, 'Chris Watson on Recording the Music of the Natural World', *The Quietus*, 24 January 2013, https://thequietus.com/articles/11222-chris-watson-interview [accessed 31 October 2023].

Urry, John, & Jonas Larsen, *The Tourist Gaze 3.0*. London: Sage 2011.

Veal, Michael E., 'Dry Spell Blues: Sublime Frequencies Across the West African Sahel', in: Micheal E. Veal & E. Tammy Kim (Eds.) *Punk Ethnography: Artists & Scholars Listen to Sublime Frequencies*. Middletown: Wesleyan University Press, 2016, pp.210–36.

Veal, Michael E., & E. Tammy Kim (Eds.), *Punk Ethnography: Artists & Scholars Listen to Sublime Frequencies*. Middletown: Wesleyan University Press, 2016.

Virno, Paolo, *A Grammar of the Multitude* (Isabella Bertoletti et al., Trans.). New York: Semiotexte, 2004.

Vishmidt, Marina, *Speculation as a Mode of Production: Forms of Value Subjectivity in Art and Capital*. Leiden: Brill, 2018.

Vishmidt, Marina, 'Bodies in Space: On the Ends of Vulnerability', *Radical Philosophy* 2, no. 8, Autumn 2020, pp.33–46.

Voegelin, Salome, *The Political Possibility of Sound: Fragments of Listening*. London: Bloomsbury, 2019.

Vonderau, Patrick, 'The Spotify Effect: Digital Distribution and Financial Growth', *Television & New Media* 20, no. 4, 2017.

Wagner, Bryan. *Disturbing the Peace: Black Culture and the Police After Slavery*. Cambridge: Harvard University Press, 2010.

Waugh, Michael, '"Every Time I Dress Myself, it Go Motherfuckin' Viral": Post-Verbal Flows and Memetic Hype in Young Thug's Mumble Rap', *Popular Music* 39, no.2, 2020, pp.208–32.

Weeks, Kathi, 'Marxism, Productivisim, and the Refusal of Work' in: *The Problem with Work*. Durham & London: Duke University Press, 2011, pp.79–112.

Weheliye, Alexander, 'Feenin: Posthuman Voices in Contemporary Black Popular Music,' *Social Text* 20, no.2, 2002, pp.21–47.

Weheliye, Alexander, *Phonographies: Grooves in Sonic Afro-Modernity*. Durham & London: Duke University Press, 2005.

Welsh, April Clare, 'Bird Sound Power: How Björk, Equinoxx and more Embraced Field Recording in 2017', *Factmag*, 14 December 2017, www.factmag.com/2017/12/14/field-recording-music-2017-bjork-equiknoxx/ [accessed 31 October 2023].

Whiteley, Sheila (Ed.), *Sexing the Groove: Popular Music and Gender*. Abingdon & New York: Routledge, 1997.

Wilder, Gary, *Freedom Time: Negritude, Decolonization and the Future of the World*. Durham & London: Duke University Press, 2015.

Williams, Alex, & Nick Srnicek, '#Accelerate: Manifesto for an Accelerationist Politics' in: Robin Mackay & Armen Avanessian (Eds.) *#Accelerate#: The Accelerationist Reader*. Falmouth: Urbanomic, 2014.

Williams, Evan Calder, *Combined and Uneven Apocalypse*. London: Zero, 2011.

Williams, Raymond, *Problems in Materialism and Culture*. London: Verso, 1980.

Williams, Raymond. *Television: Technology and Cultural Form*. London: Routledge, 2003.

Wilson, Carl. '2017 Saw Empowering Pop Replaced By Mumbling Men', *Slate.com*, 25 December 2017, https://slate.com/culture/2017/12/2017-saw-empowering-pop-replaced-by-mumbling-men.html?via=gdpr-consent [accessed 22 January 2019].

Wright, Chris, 'Its Own Peculiar Décor: Capital, Urbanism, and the Crisis of Class Politics in the US', *Endnotes*, 4 October 2015, https://endnotes.org.uk/translations/chris-wright-its-own-peculiar-decor

Wright, Steve, '*Quaderni Rossi* and the Workers' Enquiry' in: *Storming Heaven: Class Composition and Struggle in Italian Autonomist Marxism*. London: Pluto Press, 2002, pp.29-57.

Wynter, Sylvia, *We Must Learn to Sit Down Together and Talk About a Little Culture: Decolonising Essays, 1967–1984*. Leeds: Peepal Tree Press, 2022.

Wynter, Sylvia, 'Novel and History, Plot and Plantation', *Savacou* 5, June 1971, pp.95-102.

Young, Rob, 'Konono No.1', *The Wire* 253, March 2005, p.52.

Zelizer, Viviana, *Pricing the Priceless Child: The Changing Social Value of Children*. Princeton: Princeton University Press, 1994.

Discography

2 Chainz, *Based on a T.R.U. Story*. Def Jam, 2012.

Aphex Twin, *Selected Ambient Works 1985-1992*. Apollo, 1992.

Artificial Intelligence. Warp Records, 1992.

Ashikawa, Satoshi, *Still Way*. Sound Process, 1982.

Autechre, *Incumabula*. Warp Records, 1993.

Ata Kak, *Obaa Sima*. Awesome Tapes From Africa, 2015.

Bebey, Francis, *African Electronic Music 1975-1982*. Born Bad Records, 2011.

Bebey, Francis, *Psychedelic Sanza 1982-1984*. Born Bad Records, 2014.

Buena Vista Social Club, *Buena Vista Social Club*. World Circuit, 1997.

Chief Keef, *Finally Rich*. UMGRI Interscope, 2012.

Child, Anthony, *Electronic Recordings from Maui Jungle*. Editions Mego, 2015.

Chuck Person's Eccojams Vol.1. The Curatorial Club, 2011.

Crampton, Elysia, *Moth/Lake*. Boomkat, 2015.

Cusack, Peter, *Sounds from Dangerous Places*. ReR Megacorp, 2012.

Desiigner, 'Panda'. Def Jam, 2015.

DJ Shadow, *Entroducing*. Mo Wax, 1996.

Eno, Brian, *Ambient 1: Music for Airports*. Polydor, 1981.

Egyptrixx, *Pure, Beyond Reproach*. Halocline Trance, 2017.

Ferraro, James, *Far Side Virtual*. Hippos in Tanks, 2011.

Future, *Pluto*. Epic, 2012.

Future, *DS2*. Epic, 2015.

Grande, Arianna, *Sweetener*. Republic Records, 2018.

Group Doueh, *Guitar Music From the Western Sahara*. Sublime Frequencies, 2007.

Group Inerane, *Guitars From Agadez (Music of Niger)*. Sublime Frequencies, 2008.

Group Inerane, *Guitars From Agadez Volume 3*. Sublime Frequencies, 2010.

Group Inerane, *Guitars From Agadez Volume 4*. Sublime Frequencies, 2011.

Gucci Mane, *Trap House*. Big Cat Records, 2005.

Halo, Laurel, *Chance of Rain*. Hyperdub, 2013.

Hassell, Jon, & Eno, Brian, *Fourth World: Possible Musics*. Polydor, 1980.

Hassell, Jon, *Dream Theory in Malaya*. Editions EG, 1981.

Haxan Cloak, *Excavation*. Tri Angle, 2013.

Herndon, Holly, *Platform*. 4AD, 2015.

Herndon, Holly, *Movement*. RVNG. Intl., 2012.

Hopkins, Al, and His Buckle Busters, *The Nine Pound Hammer/C. & O. No.558*. Brunswick, 1927.

Hurt, John, 'Spike Driver Blues', *The Greatest Songsters 1927–1929*. Document Records, 1990.

I Am the Center: Private Issue New Age Music in America 1950–1990. Light in the Attic, 2013.

Konono No.1, *Congotronics*. Crammed Discs, 2005.

KMRU, *Logue*. Injazero, 2021.

Lana Del Rey, *Honeymoon*. Interscope, 2015.

Leadbelly, 'Take This Hammer'. RCA Victor Group, 2003.

Levi, Mica, *Delete Beach*. DDS, 2017.

López, Francisco, *La Selva*. V2_Archief, 1998.

López, Francisco, *Untitled # 104*. Alien8 Recordings, 2000.

López, Francisco, *Buildings [New York]*. V2_Archief, 2001.

López, Francisco, *Wind [Patagonia]*. And/OAR, 2007.

Lorde, *Melodrama*. Lava Records, 2017.

Lykke Li, *So Sad So Sexy*. RCA Records, 2018.

Migos, *Yung Rich Nation*. Atlantic, 2015.

Migos, *Culture*. Quality Control Music, 2017.

Music From Saharan Cellphones, Vol.1. Sahel Sounds, 2011.

Oneohtrix Point Never, *R Plus Seven*. Warp Records, 2013.

Onyeabor, William, *Who Is William Onyeabor?* Luaka Bop, 2013.

Rae Sremmurd, 'Black Beatles' (featuring Gucci Mane), *Sremmlife 2*. Interscope Records, 2016.

Ross, Rick, 'B.M.F. (Blowin' Money Fast)', *Teflon Don*. Maybach Music, 2010.

Schaffer, Pierre, *Cinq Études De Bruits: Étude Aux Objects*. INA-GRM, 1948.

Simon, Paul, *Graceland*. Warner Bros., 1986.

Singh, Charanjit, *Synthesizing: Ten Ragas to a Disco Beat*. Bombay Connection, 2010.

Souleyman, Omar, *Highway to Hassake (Folk and Pop Sounds of Syria)*. Sublime Frequencies, 2007.

Takada, Midori, *Through the Looking Glass*. RCA Red Seal, 1983.

T.I., *Trap Muzik*. Atlantic, 2003.

Travis, Merle, 'Nine Pound Hammer', *Folk Songs of the Hills*. Capitol Records, 1947.

Triple Six Mafia, *Underground Vol.1 (1991–1994)*. Smoked Out Music, 1999.

UGK, *Too Hard to Swallow*. Jive, 1992.

Waka Flocka Flame, 'Hard in Da Paint', *Flockaveli*. Warner Bros., 2010.

Watson, Chris, *Outside the Circle of Fire*. Touch, 1998.

Watson, Chris, *Weather Report*. Touch, 2003.

Watson, Chris, 'Ant-Steps', *Interpreting the Soundscape*. Leonardo Music Journal, 2006.

Westerkamp, Hildergard, 'Beneath the Forest Floor', *Transformations*. Empreintes Digitales, 1996.

Yoshimura, Horishi, *Music for Nine Postcards*. Sound Process, 1982.

Yoshimura, Horishi, *Green*. Sona Gaia Productions, 1986.

Yoshimura, Hiroshi, *Surround*. Misawa Home, 1986.

Young Jeezy, *Let's Get It: Thug Motivation 101*. Def Jam Recordings, 2005.

Young Thug, *1017 Thug*. RBC Records, 2013.

Young Thug, *Barter 6*. Atlantic, 2015.

Acknowledgements

I am grateful to all the people who have read or discussed this book in part or whole: Noah Angell, David Arditi, Nicholas Beuret, Dhanveer Singh Brar, Gabriel Bristow, Christina Chalmers, Saskia Fischer, Samuel Fisher, Edward George, Rory Gibb, Annie Goh, Francis Gooding, Larne Abse Gogarty, David Grundy, Stefano Harney, Adam Harper, Gabriel Humberstone, Anneke Kampman, AM Kanngieser, Louis Moreno, Fred Moten, Fumi Okiji, Ronald Rose-Antoinette, Ash Sharma, and Marie Thompson. I am obliged to the generosity of three enormously astute and discerning anonymous reviewers of the manuscript. A special thank you to Roisin O'Cearnaigh for her hospitality in Kalyvia, Greece, where so much of this book was written. Thanks also to Atau Tanaka, Angela Thompson, and everyone at Goldsmiths Press for outstanding support and editorial guidance executed with care and attention. I'm thankful to have had the support through difficult times of Philip Rekret and Teresa Rekret. I owe an infinite debt of gratitude to Yung Kha, without who's unbending encouragement and kindness this book would never have been written. An earlier version of chapter 2 was published as 'Melodies Wander Around as Ghosts: On Playlist as Cultural Form' in *Critical Quarterly* 61(2) 2019. Parts of chapter 1 were published as 'Beneath the Opulent Surface: Adorno and Popular Music Reconsidered', *Journal of Popular Music Studies* 31(2) 2019. An early version of chapter 3 was published as 'Labour and Leisure in Trap' in *Cesura/Acceso*, volume 2, 2017. Early versions of chapter 1 were presented to Sonic Cyberfeminisms conference, University of Lincoln, May 2017; Cultural Studies Association Annual Conference, Carnegie Mellon University, Pittsburgh, June 1, 2018; and Marxism in Culture Seminar at the Institute of Advanced Studies, University College London, 24 May 2019. Parts of chapter 2 were presented to London Conference in Critical Thought, June 29, 2018; Alien Sound Symposium, Tate Liverpool, 9 February 2019; CTM Festival/Transmediale, Berlin, 31 January 2019; Goldsmiths University of London, 31 October 2019; Basis Voor Actuele Kunst, Utretch, 13-14 November 2021; and University of Oslo, 19 October 2020. Parts of chapter 3 were presented to Gentrifying the Political conference, University of Kent, June 2016 and

London Conference in Critical Thought, 2017. An early version of chapter 4 was presented to Regenerative Feedback Conference, WORM Institute for Avantgardiste Recreation, Rotterdam, 25–26 May 2019. Parts of chapter 5 were first developed for 'Amplification//Annihilation', *Unsound Festival*, Krakow, October 2018 with AM Kanngieser and Rory Gibb. I am grateful to all the editors, organisers, and participants for their feedback. I am grateful to the family of Francis Bebey for permissions to quote from his lyrics and to Bruce Jackson for permission to quote from his transcription of Joseph 'Chinaman' Johnson and Group's version of 'This Old Hammer Killed John Henry' in: Bruce Jackson (Ed.) *Wake Up Dead Man: Afro-American Prison Worksongs From Texas Prisons.* Cambridge: Harvard University Press, 1972.

This book is for my friends.

Index

#Accelerate#, 140, 155n
(Untitled # 104) (Francisco López), 132
2 Chainz, 14, 76, 98n
2Pac, 80
50-Cent, 83
1017 Thug (Yung Thug), 76, 98n

Aaltonen, Lari, 126n
Abel, Mark, 25-26, 46n
accelerationism, 15, 130, 140-2, 144, 146-50
Achebe, Chinua, 103
Adorno, Theodor, 13, 17n, 25-6, 32, 37, 46n, 47n, 68-69, 74n, 115, 125n, 155n
Adkins, Lisa, 100n
aesthetic, 8, 10, 11, 37, 38, 129, 132, 136-7
    autonomy of, 8, 19, 20, 26, 27, 32, 34, 36
    critique, 121-2
    and nature, 128
affect, 22, 61, 62, 152
Africa, African, 103, 112, 113, 114, 115, 116
African Electronic Music: 1975-1985 (Francis Bebey), 104
African Music: A People's Art (Francis Bebey), 103, 112, 114, 124
Against Ambience (Seth Kim-Cohen), 61
Agatha Mudio's Sons (Francis Bebey), 103
Agawu, Kofi, 125n
AirBnB, 120-1
Akiyama, Mitchell, 130, 153n, 155n
algorithm, 50, 65, 66, 145
alterity, 36, 107 (*see also* otherness)
amapiano (music), 152
Amaro, Ramon, 145, 156
Amazon (retailer), 58
ambient, 61, 62, 65-7
    ambient house (music sub-genre), 55
    music, 50, 51-3, 55, 56, 65-6, 148
Atanasoski, Neda, 156n
Anderson, Paul Allen, 72n
Andrejevic, Mark, 73n, 74n
Angell, Noah, 100n
Ant-Steps (Chris Watson), 133, 139, 154n
Anthropocene, 135-6
anthropocentrism, 22, 135, 136
Apache Indian, 106

Apgar, William C., 101
Aphex Twin, 54, 71n
Apple (retailer), 58, 61
Arca, 143
Arditi, David, 18n, 73n
Arthur, Christopher J., 46n
Artificial Intelligence (Warp), 54, 71n
artist, sovereignty of, 10, 15, 130, 143, 149
Ashanti Doll, The (Francis Bebey), 113, 124n
'Asheville Junction' (song), 2
Ashikawa, Satoshi, 51, 70n
DJ Assault, 153
Atlanta, 76, 77, 81, 92, 94, 95-6
Autechre, 54, 71n
authenticity, 26, 32-3, 36-7, 48n, 93, 95
    crisis of, 10, 12, 20-1, 22, 23, 148
    and hip-hop, 80-1, 82-3, 85, 93, 94-5
    as metaphysics of presence, 12, 80
    performance of, 8, 19-20, 31, 80-1
    and world music, 106-8, 119, 120, 121
Awesome Tapes From Africa, 14, 105
Axelrod, David, 52
Azerbaijan, 133

BaBenzele music, 112, 114
Balaji, Murali, 99n
Balbaud, René, 122n
Balibar, Étienne, 107, 123n
Banaji, Jairus, 16n
Baraka, Amiri (Leroi Jones), 13, 32, 34, 47, 48, 68, 69, 74n, 119, 126n
Barclay, Leah, 134, 154n
Barrett, Michele, 47n
Barter 6 (Young Thug), 98n
Barthes, Roland, 143, 156n
Bartók, Béla, 32
Based on a T.R.U. Story (2 Chainz), 98n
Bastani, Aaron, 140, 155n
Bebey, Francis, 14, 103-4, 108, 109, 110, 112-17, 122n, 123n, 124n, 125n, 126n
    musical philosophy, 113-14, 115, 116
    work as novelist, 113, 116-17
Bebey, Kidi, 122n, 125-6n
Beech, Dave, 74n, 146, 156n

Bell, Taylor, 102n
Beller, Jonathan, 68, 73n, 74n
Benanav, Aaron, 49n
'Beneath The Forest Floor' (Hildergard Westerkamp), 131, 153n
Benjamin, Walter, 88, 96, 100n, 102n, 119, 126n
Bennett, Jane, 62n
Bensaïd, Daniel, 25, 46n
Bergson, Henri, 115
Berlant, Lauren, 88, 100n
Beta, Andy, 52, 70n, 124n
Beti, Mongo, 103
Beyoncé, 152
Bhaba, Homi, 106-7, 123n
Billboard (periodical), 14, 76, 96
Billic, Pasko, 74n
Bishop, Alan, 109
'Bissau' (Francis Bebey), 116
Bjornson, Richard, 125n
'Black Beatles' (Rae Sremmurd), 76, 98n
Black Skin, White Masks (Frantz Fanon), 115, 125n
Blair, Elizabeth, 101n
blues (music), 1, 7, 32, 34, 46n, 67, 87
Blues People (Amiri Baraka), 32, 48n
'B.M.F. (Blowin' Money Fast)' (Rick Ross), 76, 98n
body, 43, 57, 67, 96, 122, 133, 143, 146, 152
Boggs, James, 43, 49n
Boltanski, Luc, 121-2, 127n
Boon, Marcus, 45n
Born Bad Records, 104
Boyle, Michael Shane, 18n
Bradley, Regina, 98n
Braidotti, Rosi, 62, 73n
Brar, Dhanveer Singh, 17n, 37, 47n, 48n
Brassier, Ray, 140, 155n
Braverman, Harry, 24, 46n
Brazier, Lottie, 153n
Brenner, Robert, 17n, 49n
Bronson, Zack, 126n
Bronx, 76
Brooks, Siobhan, 102n
Brouillette, Sarah, 17n, 18n
Brown, James, 69, 75, 153
Brown, Nathan, 42, 49n
Brunner, Anja, 125n
Bruyninckx, Joeri, 153n
Buena Vista Social Club (album), 106, 123n

Buildings [New York] (Francisco López), 132, 154n
Bull, Michael, 58, 72n
Burckhardt, Patrick, 73n
Burdon, George, 72n
Burton, Justin Adams, 98n, 99n

Cabaret Voltaire, 128
Cabral, Amilcar, 125n
Caffentzis, George, 4, 16n, 94, 101n
Cairo, 76
Camatte, Jacques, 145, 156
Cameroon, 116, 125
Capital, Vol. 1 (Karl Max), 144-5
capitalism, 3, 7, 26, 38-39, 60-3, 107
  crisis of, 7-9, 12, 39-44, 63, 84, 91-92, 118, 121, 141-2, 146-7
  exchange value, 40, 59, 62, 63, 64-5, 68, 83, 87, 105, 119-20, 145
  and finance, 42, 83
  and internet platforms, 62-4, 66, 87
  and processes of abstraction, 4, 7, 24, 25, 28, 46n, 63-65, 66, 73n, 81-2, 87, 97, 137, 139, 146
  and race, 32-4
  and recording industry, (*see* recording)
  and subsumption, 15, 20, 39, 144-7, 149-51 (*see also* labour)
  uneven development of, 12, 32, 40, 42, 68, 108, 117-19
Caraway, Brett, 74n
Caribbean, 33, 46n, 76, 111, 116
Carroll, Lewis, 50
Cartesian, (*see* Descartes, René)
Cauty, Jimmy, 54
Chakrabarty, Dipesh, 154n
Chance of Rain (Laurel Halo), 61, 73n
Chandler, Nahum, 36, 48n
Chernobyl, 133
Chiapello, Eve, 120-1, 127n
Chief Keef, 76, 98n
child, 29, 30, 47n
Child, Anthony, 128, 153n
Chuck Person's Ecojams Vol.1, (Daniel Lopatin) 148, 157n
Cinq Études de Bruits (Pierre Schaeffer), 131n
The Chronic (Dr. Dre), 79, 101n
Clarke, David, 67, 74n
class, 2, 3, 29, 33-4, 67, 79, 85, 151
  lumpen, 33

Cleveland, 56
Cockrel, Ken, 38
'Coffee Cola Song, The' (Francis Bebey), 114, 116, 124n
Cohen, Norm, 15n, 16n
Coleman, Ornette, 34
Collins, Patricia Hill, 102n
colonialism, 28-9, 107, 111, 125n, 137, 138-9
    decolonisation, 115-6
Coltrane, John, 34
Congotronics (Konono No. 1), 104, 123n
Connolly, William, 62, 73n
Cooder, Ry, 106
Cooper, Melinda, 8, 17n, 29, 44, 47n, 49n, 100n
Cox, Christoph, 45n, 154n
craft, 2, 6, 24, 119-22
Crammed Discs, 104
Crampton, Elysia, 128, 153n
Crary, Jonathan, 8, 17n, 74n
criminality, 33, 41, 93
    representation of, 77-80, 82-3, 84-5, 86, 95
Culture (Migos), 76, 98n
Cunningham, David, 156n
Cusack, Peter, 15, 129, 133-4, 139, 154n, 155n
Cybernetic Culture Research Unit, 141-2

Dalla Riva, Chris, 71n
Dart, Chris, 101n
Darville, Jordan, 156n
Davis, Angela Y., 16n
Dayal, Geeta, 71n
Dean, Jodi, 74n
Debord, Guy, 92, 93, 101n
Del Rey, Lana, 14, 77, 98n
Delete Beach (Mica Levi), 128, 153n
Denning, Michael, 28, 47n
DeNora, Tia, 57, 58, 59, 72n
Denselow, Robin, 123n
D'Eramo, Marco, 126n
Descartes, René, 135, 146
    Cartesian rationalism, 115
Desiigner, 76, 98n
Devine, Kyle, 47n
Dinerstein, Joel, 16n, 71n
Dibango, Manu, 110-11
disco (music), 6, 105
Discogs (web site), 51
DivX, 109

DJ Mag (periodical), 104
DJ Screw, 76
DJ Shadow, 52, 70n
Dockray, Sean, 73n
Doggystyle (Snoop Dogg), 79
Douala, 103
Dre, Dr., 79, 89, 101n
Dream Theory in Malaya (Jon Hassell), 52, 70n
Drott, Eric, 58-59, 72n, 74n
drum n' Bass (music), 119
Dryhurst, Mat, 144
DS2 (Future), 98n
DuBois, W.E.B., 94, 101n
dubstep (music), 21
Duda, Mark, 100n
Dussel, Enrique, 111, 124n
Dyer-Witherford, Nick, 74n, 157n

ecological crisis, 40, 135-7
Eidsheim, Nina Sun, 45n
Egyptrixx, 128, 153n
Ek, Daniel, 63
Electronic Recordings from Maui Jungle (album), 128, 153n
Elliott, Missy, 143
Ellison, Ralph, 16n
employment (*see* labour)
Endnotes, 47n
Endtroducing (DJ Shadow), 52, 71n
Eno, Brian, 51, 55, 70n, 74n, 114
entanglement, 15, 62, 130, 136, 138, 139, 142, 152
environment
    crisis of, 40, 132, 134, 135-7
    as object, 129, 132, 136, 137
    see also nature
Erlmann, Veit, 123n
Eshum, Kodwo, 89, 100n
Europe, European, 51, 112, 113, 115, 116
Exorcist, The (film), 89
Eyidi, Marcel Bebey, 126n

family, 43, 93, 96, 100, 144
Fanon, Frantz, 115, 116, 125n
Far Side Virtual (James Ferraro), 148, 157n
Farber, David, 100n
Farrar, Justin F., 123n
Federici, Silvia, 146, 155n, 156n
Feld, Steven, 114, 125n
Fennessey, Sean, 98n

Ferraro, James, 15, 130, 148–9, 151, 157n
Fever Ray, 143
field recording, 11, 12, 15, 128–9, 130–4, 136, 139
Finally Got the News (film), 38
Finally Rich (Chief Keef), 76, 98n
Fisher, Eran, 73n
Fisher, Mark, 21, 23, 26, 39, 45n, 48n, 118, 147, 156n
Fisher, Samuel, 47n
Fitzpatrick, Rob, 122n
Fleischer, Rasmus, 72n, 73n
Flenory Jr., Demetrius 'Big Meech', 96
folk culture, 1, 7, 32, 33, 34, 36, 86, 108, 109, 111
    badman tales, 79–80, 81–2
folklorism, 2, 139
Font-Navarrete, David, 109, 124n
footwork (music), 21
Fordism, 13, 24, 27, 28, 29, 30, 31, 43, 122, 147, 151
Fortunati, Leopoldina, 16n, 30, 47n, 96, 102n
Foster, Hal, 111, 124n
Foucault, Michel, 20, 45n, 157n
Fourth World Vol. 1 (Eno & Hassell), 51, 70n
France, 116
Franklin, Seb, 156n
Friedman, Devin, 101n
Frith, Simon, 17, 47n, 123n
Fuchs, Christian, 73n
Fuck Buttons, 61
'Fuck that Police' (N.W.A.), 79
funk (music), 6, 75, 110
Funkadelic, 105
Future (artist), 76, 98n

Gaerig, Andrew, 73n
Galloway, Alexander, 74n
Gardner, Abigail, 126n
Gates Jr., Henry Louis, 79, 99n
gender, 30, 31, 138, 149
    feminist, 4, 141
Ghana, 116
ghetto, 33, 41, 82–3
Gibb, Rory, 153n
Gilligan, Melanie, 17n
Gilmore, Ruth Wilson, 41, 49n, 100n
Gilroy, Paul, 13, 35, 48n
Gioia, Ted, 16n, 17n

Glennon, Mike, 72n
globalisation, 39–41, 117
Gogarty, Larne Abse, 151, 157n
Goh, Annie, 22, 45n
Goodman, Steve, 45n
Google, 58
Gordon, Lewis, 71n
gqom (music), 152
Graceland (Paul Simon), 106, 123n
Graham, Kevin Fox, 100n
Grande, Arianna, 14, 77, 98n
'Great Recession', 9, 12, 42
Green, Archie, 16n
Greenfield, Lauren, 101n
Groom, Nick, 72n
Grossberg, Lawrence, 8, 17n, 44n
Group Doueh, 104, 108, 123n, 124n
Group Inerane, 104, 108, 123n, 124n
Guardian, The (newspaper), 103, 104
Gucci Mane, 14, 75, 80, 86–8, 89, 91, 92, 93, 98n, 99n, 100n

Hall, Stuart, 7, 17n, 33, 48n, 95, 101n
Halloween (film), 89
Halo, Laurel, 61, 73n
Hann, Michael, 44n
Haraway, Donna, 135, 154n
'Hard in Da Paint' (Wacka Flocka Flame), 76, 98n
Hardt, Michael, 155n
Harney, Stefano, 17n, 48n, 93, 101n
Harper, Adam, 143, 156n, 157n
Harris, Laura, 92, 93, 101n
Harvey, David, 49n, 100n
Harvey, Eric, 71n, 95, 99n, 101n
Hassan, Aisha, 72n
Hassell, Jon, 51–2, 61, 70n, 114
Haxan Cloak, The, 61, 73n
Hecker, Tim, 61
Heidegger, Martin, 135, 155n
Herndon, Holly, 15, 130, 142–4, 149, 151, 156n
Hesmondhalgh, David, 72n, 73n, 123n
hip-hop, 8, 11, 12, 14, 35, 41, 53, 68, 75–97, 106, 110, 119
    bounce, 85, 86, 100
    chopped and screwed, 85, 86
    crunk, 85, 86, 89
    and drug dealing, 77–8, 80, 87, 91, 97, 98
    gangsta, 78–81, 89

and gender, 96–7
interpretations of, 78–80, 81–2
popularity of, 76
and representation of reality, 77–82
Southern, 12, 84, 85–6, 91
trap, 75–8, 80–2, 86, 89–90, 97, 98, 100
history, 3, 9, 10, 12, 26, 32, 40, 109, 136, 138, 140
and consciousness, 25
and crisis, 13, 21, 39–41, 42–3
as linear, 12, 23, 25, 26–7, 31, 37, 39–41, 43, 88, 111, 118, 147
Hoard, Christian, 98n
Holden, James, 61
'Holly+' (Holly Herndon), 144
home, subprime market for, 8, 91–3
(*see also* private and public)
Honeymoon (Lana Del Rey), 76, 98n
hooks, bell, 54, 71n
Hopkins, Al and His Buckle Busters, 2, 16n
Horning, Rob, 45n
house (music), 6, 8, 21, 53, 119
Horkheimer, Max, 17, 46n
Human League, The, 20
Hunter, Margaret, 102n
Hurt, John, 1, 16n
'Hustle' (Gucci Mane), 99
hybridity, 106–7, 108, 111, 117

I Am the Center (Numero Group), 51, 61, 70n
Iceland, 136
ideology, 7, 68, 134
Iles, Anthony, 157n
Incumabula (Autechre), 54, 71n
Independent, The (newspaper), 104
International Monetary Fund, 117
Irele, F. Abiola, 125n
Iton, Richard, 36, 48n
iTunes, 61, 63

Jack, Malcolm, 124n
Jackson, Bruce, 15n
Jackson, Michael, 111
Jaji, Tsitsi Ella, 125n
Jakarta, 28
Jakob, Doreen, 126n, 127n
Jamaica, 76
James, C.L.R., 92n
James, Robin, 20, 23, 26, 45n, 56, 71n

Jameson, Fredric, 7, 17n, 37–40, 48n, 49n, 147, 156n
Janáček, Leoš, 32
Japan, 50, 51
Jay-Z, 83
jazz (music), 28, 32, 34, 46n, 75, 110, 199
Jeffries, Michael P., 99n, 102n
Jenkins, Craig, 53, 71n
Jennings, Keith, 101n
Jodeci, 143
Johansson, Sofia, 72n
John Henry, 1–2, 4, 5–6
Johnson, Joseph 'Chinaman' and Group, 15n, 16n
Jones, Donna V., 125n
Jones, Mikey IQ, 123n, 124n
Jones, Simon C., 72n
Juan, Steve 'Flash', 98n
Judy, R.A., 81, 82, 99n
jungle (music), 21

Kak, Ata, 105, 108, 123n
Kane, Brian, 45n, 154n
Kanngieser, A.M., 153n
Katz, Mark, 72n, 73n
Kassabian, Anahid, 21, 45n, 71n
Kelley, Robin D.G., 49n, 71, 87, 99n, 100n
Kelly, Lauren, 156n
Kemp, Sophie, 157n
Kennedy, Sean M., 98n
Kheshti, Roshanak, 47n, 153n, 154n
Kim-Cohen, Seth, 61, 73n
King Albert (Francis Bebey), 113, 116, 124n, 126n
Kittler, Friedrich, 140, 155n
Kitwana, Bakari, 99n
KMRU, 128, 153n
Kojikawa, Lauren, 99n
Koc, Alican, 157n
Konings, Martin, 100n
Konono No.1, 104, 108, 109, 123n
Kopf, Dan, 72n
Korczynski, Marek, 16n, 17n, 46n
Kramer, Lawrence, 68, 74n
Krims, Adam, 82, 99n, 100n
kuduro (music), 152

'La Condition Masculine' (Francis Bebey), 113
La Selva (Francisco López), 132, 154n

Index

labour, 2, 3, 4, 5, 6, 10, 11, 12, 24, 29, 37, 65, 83, 87
   abolition of, 3, 4
   contract, 12, 29, 43, 119
   and creativity, 121–2
   domestic, 4, 29–30, 137
   exploitation, 25
   factory, 28, 141
   as figure, 12, 87
   and flexibility, 5, 39, 43, 106, 122
   forced, 7, 33, 34, 94, 137
   and gender, 29–32, 151
   industrial, 4, 6, 43, 57
   and leisure, 11, 31, 43, 57, 69, 87, 97, 139
   as music, 5, 10, 65, 86–88, 100
   precarity of, 8, 9, 12, 13, 42–4, 87, 90, 97, 119, 122
   racialised experience of, 12, 29
   refusal of, 3, 4, 5, 24, 37
   sex work, 11, 95–7
   subsumption of, 4, 24, 27, 122, 144–7
   and time, 30, 43, 88 (*see also* time)
   and unemployment, 33, 44, 54, 87
   and value, 120
   wage, 5, 8, 9, 12, 24, 27, 30, 42
   wage relation, 3, 4, 11, 32, 33, 152
   wagelessness, 12, 33, 43, 94
Land, Nick, 141, 156n
Lanza, Joseph, 71n, 72n
Larsen, Jonas, 126n
Latour, Bruno, 135, 154n
Lazarus, Neil, 123n
League of Revolutionary Black Workers, 38, 48
Ledbetter, Huddie Leadbelly, 1, 16n
Lefebvre, Henri, 28, 46n
Léon, Javier F., 45n
Leslie, Esther, 102n
Let's Get It: Thug Motivation 101 (Young Jeezy), 14, 75, 77, 81, 85, 86, 94, 98n, 99n
Levi, Mica, 128, 153n
Leys, Ruth, 45n
Light in the Attic, 52
Lil Wayne, 76, 105
Linhart, Robert, 145, 156n
Lipsitz, George, 16n, 17n, 47n
listening, 22, 58–9, 135
Lloyd, Richard, 99n
Locke, John, 138–9, 155n
Lockwood, Annea, 153n

Logue (KMRU), 128, 153n
Lomax, John, 139
'Lonely At The Top' (Holly Herndon), 143
Lopatin, Daniel, 15, 61, 130, 148–9, 151, 157
López, Francisco, 15, 11, 129, 132–3, 153n, 154n
Lorde, 14, 77, 98n
Li, Lykke, 77, 98n
Los Angeles Times (newspaper), 103, 122n
Luaka Bop, 105
Luckman, Susan, 126n
Luger, Lex, 14, 76

Mackey, Nathaniel, 70, 74n
Mad Max (film), 117
Madonna, 114
Maher, Geo, 94, 101n
Malewitz, Raymond, 126n
Malm, Andreas, 17n, 40, 49n
Mancuso, David, 110
Manovich, Lev, 66, 74n
Manuel, Peter, 124n
Marcuse, Herbert, 10, 18n
Margasak, Peter, 124n
Markley, Scott, 100n
Marshall, Lee, 73n
Martineau, Jonathan, 46n
Marx, Karl, 24, 43, 46, 49n, 155n, 156n
   'Fragment on Machines', 141, 149
Massumi, Brian, 22, 45n
Mattin, 157n
McCarthy, Jesse, 100n
McClanahan, Annie, 49n, 92, 101n
McClary, Susan, 17n
McGraw, Andrew C., 126n
McIntosh, Mary, 47n
McLeod, Ken, 157n
McNally, David, 49n
McRobbie, Angela, 47n
Mediafire, 109
Megaupload, 109
Meier, Leslie I., 72, 73n
Melodrama (Lorde), 98n
Memphis, 76, 85, 90
Mercer, Kobena, 79, 99n
Miami, 76
Middleton, Richard, 23, 45n, 124n
Mieville, China, 117, 126n
Mies, Maria, 47n
Migos, 14, 76, 98n
Mike-Will-Made-It, 14

Miller, Matt, 100n
mimesis, 25-6
Mitropoulos, Angela, 8, 17n, 29, 47n
Mixmaster Morris, 54
Mo' Wax, 55
Moctar, Mdou, 105
modernism, 8, 26, 29, 32, 34, 35, 37, 147
  popular, 21, 23, 39, 44
  and pre-modern, 35, 39
modernity, 39, 42, 111
Monk, Thelonius, 34
Moody, Kim, 49n
Moorey, Gerard, 126n
Moreno, Louis, 17n, 47n
Morton, Timothy, 62, 73n, 155n
Moth/Lake (Elysia Crampton), 128, 153n
Moten, Fred, 13, 17n, 37-40, 48n, 92, 93, 100n, 101n
Movement (Holly Herndon), 142, 156n
Mullen, Patrick B., 155n
Munro, Kirstin, 121-2, 127n
music industry, 54, 60-5, 85, 106, 117-18
music, as mobile, 57-58
music playlist, 53-54, 55-6, 58, 61, 66-8
music streaming platform, 11, 13, 14, 41, 53, 55-6, 58-61, 63-4, 66, 109, 140, 149
Music and Urban Geography (Adam Krims), 82
Music for Airports (Brian Eno), 51
Music for Nine Postcards (Hiroshi Yoshimura), 51
Music From Memory, 52
Music From Saharan Cellphones (Sahel Sounds), 105, 108, 123
Muzak, 56-7, 148
'My Hood' (Gucci Mane), 99n

Nathan, Fernand, 122n
National Security Agency (NSA), 142
nature, 12, 15, 40, 129
  and human, 135, 137-8, 140-1, 152
  sonic representation of, 128-9, 131-5, 140
  see also environment
Needham, Jack, 71n
Neel, Phil A., 84, 99n, 100n
Negarestani, Reza, 142
negativity, 4
Negri, Antonio, 3, 141, 149-50, 155n, 157n
Negritude, 114-16

Nelson, Scott Reynolds, 15-16n
neoliberal, neoliberalism, 5, 8, 20, 45, 53, 78, 150
Neptunes, The, 143
new age (music), 50, 51, 61
new materialism, 62
New Orleans, 28, 76, 85
New Spirit of Capitalism, The (Luc Boltanski & Eve Chiapello), 121, 127n
'New Track' (Francis Bebey), 113, 116
New York, 103
'Nine Pound Hammer' (song), 2
Ninja Tune, 55
Nkrumah, Kwame, 113
noise, 28
Notorious B.I.G., the, 83, 89
Nowak, David, 124n
Noys, Benjamin, 147, 156n
N.W.A., 79, 89, 101n

Oakenfold, Paul, 54
Obaa Simba (Ata Kak), 105, 123n
O'Kane, Chris, 121-2, 127n
OK Computer (Radiohead), 51
Okeh Records, 1
Okiji, Fumi, 37, 46n, 48n, 74n
Oliveros, Pauline, 153n
O'Loughlin, Colm, 123n
Oneohtrix Point Never, 61, 73
Onyeabor, William, 105, 123n
Optimo, 52
Osborne, Peter, 17n, 40-1, 42, 49n
otherness, 14, 103-5, 109, 111-12
  folk-other, 7, 105, 36, 121
Oticia, Hélio, 92
Outside the Circle of Fire (Chris Watson), 133, 154n
Ozileka Records, 104

Panzieri, Raniero, 3
Palto Flats Records, 50
'Panda' (Desiigner), 76, 98n
Paris, 103
Parker, James, 157n
patriarchy, 23, 29, 30, 31
Patterson, Alex, 54
Pearce, David, 72n, 74n
Pelly, Liz, 56, 71n, 72n
Perry, Imani, 99n
Petridis, Alex, 123n
Pickering, Michael, 16n, 17n, 46n

Planet Earth (television programme), 129
plantation, 33, 34, 46n
Platform (Holly Herndon), 142, 144, 156n
Pluto (Future), 76, 98n
Policing the Crisis (Stuart Hall *et al*), 33
police, 81, 94
Polli, Andrea, 129, 134, 154n
poptimism, 19, 23
Port Arthur, 76
post-Fordism (see also Fordism), 8, 12, 42, 57, 84, 100, 122
posthuman, 62, 135
postmodern, 12, 35, 37, 39, 40
postmodern, postmodernity, 12, 35, 37, 39, 40
Postone, Moishe, 24, 45n, 46n
Pratt, Mary Louise, 126n
Presley, Elvis, 31
Pretty Girls Like Trap Music (Future), 76, 98n
primitive accumulation, 137, 138-9
primitivism, 52, 111–112, 114 135
private and public spheres, 30, 31, 43, 58
   domesticity, 31, 57, 68, 92–3, 97, 137
   see also domestic labour
prison, 2, 41, 82, 84–85
   carceral power, 93-6
   see also incarceration, police
production, 2, 5–6, 7–8, 12, 13, 25
   industrial, 2, 5–6, 7–8, 12, 28, 29, 30, 43, 82, 144, 145, 146, 151
   see also craft
productivity, 25, 30–1, 147
progressive rock, 6
property, 93, 94, 96, 97, 138 (see also private and public spheres)
   intellectual property, 109, 138, 143, 144
   piracy, 61, 63
Proto (Holly Herndon), 144
Psychedelic Sanza 1982–1984 (Francis Bebey), 104, 113, 123
Pure, Beyond Reproach (Egyptrixx), 128
'Pygmy Love Song' (Francis Bebey), 114, 125
'Pyrex Pot' (Gucci Mane), 77

Quaderni Rossi (periodical), 3
Quinn, Eithne, 79, 99n

R Plus Seven (Oneohtrix Point Never), 61, 73n
radio, 60, 68
Radiobroadcasting in Black Africa (Francis Bebey), 103

Radiohead, 51
Rae Sremmurd, 76, 98n
ragga, 106
rap (*see* hip-hop)
Rap-A-Lot Records, 80
Reagan, Ronald, 21
RCA Victor, 1
Ready to Die (the Notorious B.I.G.), 83
recording, 129, 133, 139, 142–5, 148–9;
   album, 13, 60
   industry, 2, 10, 18n, 31, 41, 61, 63–4, 85, 106, 117–18, 138, 144
   phonograph, 27, 28, 46n, 57, 129
   studio, 107–8, 130, 131
Red Dog Unit, 81, 101n
Redd, Shawty, 89
Redmond, Shana L., 16n
refusal of work, 3, 4, 11, 68
Reich, Steve, 50
repetition, 20, 21, 23, 25, 26–7, 29, 37–8, 86, 88–9
Reynolds, Simon, 53, 55, 56, 71n, 124n
rhythm, 26, 27, 29
Richards, Chris, 44n, 71n
Richardson, Mark, 73n
Rio de Janeiro, 28
RnB, 8, 57, 106, 143, 152
Robinson, Cedric, 36, 48n
Roberts, John, 17n
Roberts, John W., 99n
Roberts, Randall, 122n
Robertson, Emma, 16n, 17n, 46n
Roc-A-Fella Records, 80
rock n' roll, 6, 8, 31, 76, 106
Roedinger, David, 47n
Roland TR-808, 75
'Roll on Buddy' (song), 2
Rollins, Sonny, 34
Rose, Tricia, 49n, 99n
Ross, Rick, 76, 98n
Rothenberg, David, 155n
Russell, Arthur, 52
Ruthless Records, 80
RVNG International, 52

Sahel Sounds, 14, 105
Salvagepunk, 118–19
samba (music), 28
Sanchez, Daniel, 98n
Sanneh, Kelefa, 44n
Sarig, Ronnie, 98n

Sartre, Jean-Paul, 115, 125n
Satie, Eric, 55
Schaeffer, Pierre, 131, 153n
Scherzinger, Martin, 72n
Schiller, Dan, 72n, 73n
Schmidt, Alfred, 137, 155n
Schmidt, Eric J., 124n
Schumacher, Thomas G., 72n
Seccombe, Wally, 47n
Selected Ambient Works 1985–1992 (Aphex Twin), 55
Senghor, Léopold Sédar, 114–15, 116, 125n
sha'bi (music), 104
Schafer, R. Murray, 131, 153n
Shalloup, Mara, 99n, 101n
Sharma, Ashwani, 107, 117, 123n, 126n
Sharma, Makuri, 101n
Shaviro, Steven, 149–51, 157n
Shirelles, The, 31
Simon Fraser University, 131
Simon, Paul, 106, 123n
Simondon, Gilbert, 140, 155n
Singh, Charanjit, 105, 123n
slavery, 3, 7, 29, 35, 36, 81, 85, 94, 95
Smith, Jason, 49n
Smith, Neil, 99n
Snead, James, 23, 45n
Snickers, Pelle, 74n
Snoop Dogg, 79, 80
Snowden, Edward, 142
So Sad, So Sexy (Lykke Li), 98
'Sober 2' (Lorde), 77
Sohn-Rethel, Alfred, 24, 46n, 73n, 146, 156n
son (music), 28
song, 4, 5, 6, 7, 13
  as form, 4, 5, 6, 13, 53, 59, 65, 66–8, 90
  as refusal of work, 5–7, 13, 23, 27, 28, 37, 68–9, 90
  and time (*see* time)
  work song, 2–3, 14, 32, 57, 77, 86
Songs of the Humpback Whale (recording), 139
SOPHIE, 143
Soto, Kathleen, 102n
soul (music), 6, 75, 79, 108, 110
'Soul Makossa' (Manu Dibango), 110–11
sound, 130–4
  art, 61–2
  ontology of, 10, 21–3, 44, 135
Sounds from Dangerous Places (Peter Cusack), 133, 154n

Sound Process (music label), 51
Souleyman, Omar, 104, 108, 123n
space, 12
  and economic crisis, 12, 14, 39–41, 63, 82–3, 84–5, 90, 91, 120–1
  and gentrification, 82–3, 84, 85
  'spatial fix', 39–40, 90–1, 117
Spandau Ballet, 20
Speculative Turn, The, 62
speculative realism, 62
Spence, Lester K., 99n
'Spike Driver Blues' (song), 1
Spillers, Hortense, 96, 102n
Spivak, Gayatri Chakravorty, 107, 123n
Spotify, 53, 54, 56, 58, 59, 63, 64, 66, 68, 71
Srnicek, Nick, 140, 142, 144, 147, 155n
Stahl, Matt, 5, 16n
Stallings, L.H., 97, 102n
'Standing Ovation' (Young Jeezy), 94
Stellar Om Source, 61
Sterne, Jonathan, 154n
Stevens, Dennis, 127n
Still Way (Satoshi Ashikawa), 51
Straight Outta Compton (N.W.A.), 79
Straw, Will, 119, 126n
Structural Adjustment Programs, 117
Sublime Frequencies, 14, 104, 109, 123
Suisman, David, 47n
surplus population, 43, 82–3, 95
Surround (Hiroshi Yoshimura), 51
'Swannanoa Tunnel' (song), 2
Sweetener (Arianna Grande), 77
Swift, Taylor, 152
syncopation, 35, 37
Synthesizing: Ten Ragas to a Disco Beat (Charanjit Singh), 105
Szabo, Victor, 71n

Tagg, Phillip, 71n
Tagne, David Ndachi, 122n
Takada, Midori, 50, 70
tarab (music), 28
Taussig, Michael, 124n
Taylor, Cecil, 34
Taylorism, 145
Taylor, Timothy D., 18n, 124n
'Tear Da Club Up' (Three 6 Mafia), 90

Index

technology, 3, 6, 7, 12, 140–1, 144–7
  automation, 15, 59, 60, 61, 130, 141–2, 145, 149
  and development, 12, 23, 24, 48n
  mediation, 129–30, 133
  'smart' speakers, 56
  and technique, 15, 143, 152
techno (music), 6, 8, 21, 119
Teflon Don (Rick Ross), 98
television, 60
'Ten Pound Hammer' (song), 1
Terranova, Tiziana, 73n
Thatcher, Margaret, 20
The State Vs. Radric Davis (Gucci Mane), 94
'This Old Hammer Killed John Henry' (song), 1
Thoburn, Nicholas, 16n
Thompson, E.P., 23, 45n
Thompson, Marie, 22, 45n, 154n
Three 6 Mafia, 76, 90
Thrift, Nigel, 45n
Through the Looking Glass (Hidori Takada), 50, 52
'Thug Motivation 101' (Young Jeezy), 77, 89, 94, 98, 100
T.I., 76, 98n
time, 3, 4, 5–7, 8, 10, 11, 12, 13, 24–7, 28, 32, 34, 37, 39, 42, 43, 68, 88
  as abstraction, 7, 13, 24, 28, 42, 44
  chronology, 13
  and music, 3, 4–5, 21, 27–8, 34, 35, 43, 44, 50, 53, 68, 86, 88, 100
  as site of struggle, 25, 28, 35, 40
  temporal fix, 42–3
  temporality, 4, 10, 11, 28, 35, 40
  time-discipline, 13, 24, 25, 30, 32, 35
Too Hard to Swallow (UGK), 76, 98n
Toop, David, 55, 56, 71n, 131, 153n
Toscano, Alberto, 156n
tourism, 12, 105, 119
trap (*see* hip-hop)
Trap House (Gucci Mane), 14, 75, 76, 77, 80, 81, 86, 91, 93, 94, 98n, 99n
'Trap House' (Gucci Mane), 77, 86, 89, 90, 92, 93, 98n, 99n, 100n
Trap Muzik (T.I.), 76, 98n
'Trap or Die' (Young Jeezy), 99n
Trap Or Die 3 (Young Jeezy), 94
Travis, Merle, 2, 16n
Triple Six Mafia, 98
Tronti, Mario, 3, 16n

Truax, Barry, 131
Tuareg, 104–5
Tucker, Boima, 126n
Turner, Luke, 154n

UGK, 76, 98n
'Un Petit Ivorien' (Francis Bebey), 114
UNESCO, 103, 104
Urry, John, 126n
uTorrent, 63

vaporwave (music), 147–9
Vatnajökull, 136
Veal, Michael E., 123n
Velvet Underground, 104
Vibrant Matter (Jane Bennett), 62
Virno, Paolo, 141, 149, 155n
Vishmidt, Marina, 16n, 18n, 49n
Voegelin, Salomé, 154n
voice, 143
Vondereau, Patrick, 73n, 74n
Vora, Kalindra, 156n

Wacka Flocka Flame, 76, 98n
wage (*see* labour)
Wagner, Bryan, 101n
'Wanna Be Startin' Something' (Michael Jackson), 111
Warp Records, 54
Watson, Chris, 14, 128, 133–4, 135, 138, 139, 154n, 155n
Waugh, Michael, 98n
Weather Report (Chris Watson), 133, 154n
Weeks, Kathi, 16n
Weheliye, Alexander, 17n, 48n, 143
welfare, 24, 42
Welsh, April Clare, 153n
Westerkamp, Hildergard, 131, 133, 153n
White Skin, Black Masks (Frantz Fanon), 115
whiteness, 2, 8, 13, 22, 29, 31, 34, 36, 41, 43, 82, 85, 93, 94, 99n
Whiteley, Sheila, 47n
Wilder, Gary, 116, 125n, 126n
Williams, Alex, 140, 142, 144, 147, 155n
Williams, Evan Calder, 118, 126n
Williams, Raymond, 58, 60, 72n, 137, 155n
Wilson, Carl, 71n
Wind (Francisco López), 132, 154n
Winderen, Jana, 129
Wire, The (periodical), 104
work (*see also* labour), 3, 5–6, 11, 24, 28

and non-work, 8, 9, 31, 43
social wage, 8
world music, 11, 12, 14, 41, 105-10, 118, 120
and collection, 110-11, 119-20
and exoticism, 14, 103, 104-6, 108-10, 111, 116, 119
and global popular forms, 110
and world beat, 106
World Soundscape Project (WSP), 131, 132
Wretched of the Earth (Frantz Fanon), 115, 125n
Wright, Chris, 101n
Wright, Steve, 16n

WRWTFWW Records, 51
Wynette, Tammy, 31
Wynter, Sylvia, 5, 13, 17n, 33, 47n

Yoshimura, Hiroshi, 51, 71n
Young Jeezy, 14, 80-2, 86-8, 93-4, 96, 98n, 99n
Young, Rob, 123n
Young Thug, 76, 98, 105
YouTube, 50, 53, 68

Zap Mama, 106
Zelizer, Viviana, 47n